Concept of Cow in the Rigveda

CONCEPT OF COW IN THE RIGVEDA

DORIS SRINIVASAN

MOTILAL BANARSIDASS PUBLISHERS
PRIVATE LIMITED • DELHI

Reprint : Delhi, 2017
First Edition : Delhi, 1979

ISBN: 978-81-208-3983-0 (Cloth)
ISBN: 978-81-208-4118-5 (Paper)

Also available at
MOTILAL BANARSIDASS
41 U.A., Bungalow Road, Jawahar Nagar, Delhi 110 007
8 Mahalaxmi Chamber, 22 Bhulabhai Desai Road, Mumbai 400 026
203 Royapettah High Road, Mylapore, Chennai 600 004
236, 9th Main III Block, Jayanagar, Bengaluru 560 011
8 Camac Street, Kolkata 700 017
Ashok Rajpath, Patna 800 004
Chowk, Varanasi 221 001

MLBD Cataloging-in-Publication Data
Concept of Cow in the Rigveda
DORIS SRINIVASAN
ISBN: 978-81-208-3983-0 (HB)
ISBN: 978-81-208-4118-5 (PB)
Includes Bibliography, Index of
Rigvedic Passages,and Word
I. Hinduism II. Rigveda III. Cow
IV. Srinivasa, Doris

Printed in India
by RP Jain at NAB Printing Unit,
A-44, Naraina Industrial Area, Phase I, New Delhi–110028
and published by JP Jain for Motilal Banarsidass Publishers (P) Ltd.,
41 U.A. Bungalow Road, Jawahar Nagar, Delhi-110007

To the memory

of my Teacher

W. Norman Brown

PREFACE

I remember, with fondness, how as a graduate student, I walked into the study of W. Norman Brown and told him that I wished to do research on a topic which could give me a good understanding of the Vedic age. It was in 1963 and he had at that time been engaged in tracing the developments leading up to the sanctity of the cow in Hinduism. He suggested that a paper treating the concept of the cow in the Vedas would penetrate into different areas of Vedic culture. Although the subject eventually came to be narrowed down so as to be a suitable dissertation topic, Professor Brown's acumen regarding the centrality of the cow in the Vedic period proved to be totally correct. In this way I benefitted not only from his guidance, valuable discussions and encouragements, but also from his wisdom to introduce me to a subject capable of yielding further insights into aspects of Vedic religion and Indian art.

The present work is a much revised version of the original study completed in 1967 and written as partial fulfillment of the Ph.D. requirements at the University of Pennsylvania.

I wish to thank the George Mason University Foundation for making available funds to type the final manuscript.

One section of Chapter IV has been previously published under the title "The Myth of the Panis in the Rig Veda", *JAOS* 93 (1973) 44-57.

The manuscript was partially seen through press during my stay in India as Senior Research Fellow of the American Institute of Indian Studies.

New Delhi
August 1979.

DORIS SRINIVASAN

CONTENTS

Preface vii
Abbreviations xi

Chapter I : Introduction 1

Chapter II : The Cow in Vedic Economic Life ... 12
A. Introduction 12
B. Summary 13
C. Exegesis on Selected Passages, arranged according to context 17
1. Cow as Economic Wealth ... 17
2. The Economic Uses of Cattle ... 18
3. Cattle as the Desired Object of a Fight or Contest 26
4. The Sacrificer Gains the Protection of his Cows 35
5. Divine Protection Sought for Cows 36
D. Similes 37
1. Introduction 37
2. Formulaic Similes 39
3. Deities compared to *Gó*, *Dhenú*, *Usrá*, *Vāśrá* 47
4. The Cow's Milk is Compared to Light 49
5. Milk Cows are compared to Water 52
6. Similes comparing the Milk Cow to Religious Thought ... 54

Chapter III : The Cow in the Vedic Ritual 56
A. Introduction 56
B. Contexts 58
1. The Cow as the Sacrificed Animal : *Vaśá* 58
2. *Gó* as 'Ox' in the Ritual ... 60
3. *Gó* as Metonymy for the Milk Oblation 61
4. *Gó* etc. in the Soma Preparation 62
5. *Gó* in other Śrauta Sacrifices ... 72
6. *Gó* in Household Ceremonies ... 73
7. *Gó* etc. as Dákṣiṇā ... 73

8. *Gó* as the Cow Desired by the Sacrificer 78
9. *Gó* and *Starí* Figuratively used to connote Ritual Implements ... 80

Chapter IV : 'Cow' in Vedic Mythology ... 82
A. 'Cow' in the Indra-Vṛtra Myth ... 82
B. 'Cow' in the Myth of the Paṇis ... 89
C. 'Cow' in other Mythological Contexts 130

Chapter V : Epithets 141
Bibliography 147
Index of Rigvedic Passages 155
Word Index 162

ABBREVIATIONS

AB	Aitareya Brāhmaṇa
AG	Āśvalāyana Gṛhya Sūtra
AiG	Wackernagel, J. and A. Debrunner, *Altindische Grammatik*
AOS	American Oriental Society
Auswahl	Geldner, K. F., *Der Rigveda in Auswahl*
AV	Atharva Veda
Bṛh-D.	Bṛhad-Devatā
EVP	Renou, L., *Études Vediques et Pāṇinéennes*
Gr. *RV*	Griffith, R.T.H., *Hymns of the Ṛgveda*
GRV	Grassmann, H., *Rig-Veda*
G *Wö*	Grassmann, H., *Wörterbuch zum Rig-Veda*
HOS	Harvard Oriental Series
I-E	Indo-European
IIJ	*Indo-Iranian Journal*
JA	*Journal Asiatique*
JAOS	*Journal of the American Oriental Society*
KEWA	*Kurzgefasstes etymologisches Wörterbuch des Altindischen* by M. Mayrhofer
KSA	Kāṭhaka-Saṃhitā Aśvamedhagrantha
LRV	Ludwig, A., *Der Rigveda*
Mayrhofer	*Mayrhofer*, M., *Kurzgefasstes etymologisches Wörterbuch des Altindischen*
M-W *Dict*	Monier-Williams, M., *A Sanskrit-English Dictionary*
N	Nirukta
Noten	Oldenberg, H., *Ṛgveda, Textkritische und exegetische Noten*
P myth	Myth of the Paṇis
PW	Böhtlingk, O. and Roth, R., *Sanskrit-Wörterbuch*
RV	Rig Veda or Rig Vedic
RV Rep	Bloomfield, M., *Rig-Veda Repetitions*
Sāy.	Sāyaṇa
SBE	Sacred Books of the East

SV	Sāma Veda Saṃhitā
s.v.	under the world or the heading
ŚŚ	Śāṅkhāyana Śrauta Sūtra
TS	Taittirīya Saṃhitā
v. cit.	verse or verses cited
Ved. Stud.	Pischel, R., and Geldner, K. F. *Vedische Studien*
VS	Vājasaneyi Saṃhitā
V.V.R.I.	Viśva-Bandhu Śāstrī, *Vaidika-Padānukrama-Koṣaḥ*
ZDMG	*Zeitschrift der deutschen morgenländischen Gesellschaft*

CHAPTER I

INTRODUCTION

The purpose of this study is to isolate and define the concepts associated with the cow in the RV so as to aid in the overall comprehension of passages wherein terms for 'cow' appear. The usual terms for 'cow' are *aghnyā́* (*ághnyā*), *usrā́, usríyā, dhenú, gó, vaśā́,* and *starī́.* Together, they occur nearly 700 times in the RV, that is, more frequently than any other animal, and about as frequently as references to Indra, the most popular god in the RV. The significant feature of this vast amount of material on the cow is that 'cow' terms appear in every major subject treated in the Rigveda. This text considers the economic, ritual, and mythological aspects of Rigvedic life, though not with equal emphasis. Being a collection of hymns to be recited by the Hotar priest at the sacrifice, the hymns present a fairly good idea of the earliest Aryan ritual practices, especially those associated with the Soma rite. Since mythology is incorporated into hymnology, the RV is a very rich source of the mythopoeic thought current in this period. Economic considerations are least well represented, being but incidental to the actual intent of the text. The contextual usages of 'cow' terms demonstrate this unequal emphasis. *Gó,* for example, is mentioned twice as often in ritual and mythological contexts as in economic contexts. In addition, about one third of *gó* verses in the economic contexts occur in similes, where some characteristic or daily habit of the cow, ox, or bull is compared to a ritual or mythological phenomenon.

A study of the unit of 'cow' verses in the Rig Veda, important for a progressively better understanding of both the RV and the culture it reflects, has not been previously undertaken. The present work attempts to provide insight into both these areas through a philological analysis of the 'cow' terms cited above. As such, the study grows out of and builds upon previous works exploring some facets of the role of the cow in ancient Hinduism.[1]

1. For the interested reader, some recent works on the role of the sacred cow in modern Indian life are cited: T. Margul, "Present-day worship of the Cow in India", *Numen* XV (1968), 63-80; K. N. Raj, "India's Sacred Cattle",

Works dealing with Vedic religion and mythology have concentrated on concepts associated with the cow in the Vedas as part of some larger theme.[2] It is customary therein to present a particular view about 'cow' arising from exegetical analyses of Rigvedic passages relevant to the larger contextual framework. These views are reviewed in this book under the discussion of the appropriate RV verse. An overall picture of the close interrelationship between man and beast in ancient India has been well presented by Gonda.[3] The cow, however, according to evidence from Vedic and post-Vedic literature, seems never to have been considered solely as a 'beast' in the economic sense. The wealth of associative meanings applied to the cow from the earliest Brāhmaṇic literature through the Epic and Purāṇic texts indicates as W. Norman Brown has shown,[4] that this animal was placed on a special plane from the outset. In tracing the historical developments leading up to the doctrine of the sanctity of the cow in Hinduism, Brown isolates five elements, each in its own right signaling the cow's exalted position among animals, and together contributing to the cow's sanctity and inviolability from the Christian era onwards. These elements are : "importance of the cow and its products for the performance of the Vedic sacrificial ritual; the figurative uses of words for the cow in Vedic literature and the later understanding of these figurative expressions as indicating literal truth; the prohibitions against violation of the Brahman's cow; the inclusion of the cow under the general doctrine of Ahiṃsā; and the association of the cow with the mother-goddess cult".[5] It will be seen that in the RV, the cow already figures importantly in the first three of the above cate-

Economic and Political Weekly Vol. 6 (Jan-March, 1971), 717-722; A. Heston, "Approach to the Sacred Cow of India", *Current Anthropology* (April 1971), 191-209. H. D. Sankalia, *Aspects of Indian History and archaeology* (Delhi, 1977), Chap. 17 : "The Cow in History." Each of these papers contains ample further bibliography.

2. It is perhaps not necessary to cite here in detail the well-known works by Hillebrandt, Bergaigne, Oldenberg, Keith, Macdonell, and Bloomfield in this area; they are cited in the Bibliography.

3. J. Gonda, "Mensch und Tier im alten Indien", *Studium Generale* Vol. 20 (1967), 105-116.

4. W. Norman Brown, "The Sanctity of the Cow in Hinduism", *Journal of the Madras University*, Vol. 28, No. 2 (Jan. 1957), 29-49.

5. Brown, *ibid.* 39.

gories. In this way, the present work offers a close look at the concepts associated with the cow in three contexts destined to raise her to a sanctified position. Inquiry in this direction has already been attempted by M. A. Muusses, whose dissertation on the cow cult of the Hindus considers the position of the cow in the Brahmanical period.[6] The author's discussion of the cow's role in the Saṃhitās is brief, and touches upon some of the cow's economic and ritual uses as well as a few of the figurative occurrences of 'cow' terms. However, this work neither analyzes a particular 'cow' term, nor treats in detail the information contained in 'cow' similes and metaphors; thus the account of the cow's role in the RV is very general and the question of concepts is left unresolved:

The present study analyzes the concepts associated with 'cow' mainly through a comprehensive analysis of *gó*, the most inclusive term for 'cow' in the RV. Material from verses mentioning *gó* compounds as well as *aghnyā́* (*ághnyā*), *usrā́, usríyā, dhenú, vaśā́* and *starī́* are used if they offer information not contained in *gó* verses. The list of passages containing *gó* etc. was obtained from Grassmann's *Wörterbuch zum Rig-Veda* and the text from the *Rigveda-Saṃhitā* edition of the Tilak Maharashtra University's Vaidic Samshodhan Mandal and from T. Aufrecht's, *Die Hymnen des Rigveda*. The concepts associated with *gó* etc. have been established by means of a twofold classification process wherein:

1) each verse containing *gó* etc. has been placed into one (or more) of four possible contexts (i.e. economic, ritual, mythological, epithetical), depending upon,

2) the usage of *gó* etc. according to: literal or figurative application; number; gender; adjectives and verbs associated with *gó;* words in a series occurring with *gó;* meaning of *gó* when it occurs with other 'cow' terms in a passage.

The evidence thus brought to bear upon each *gó* passage has been treated in some order of preference. Greatest weight is given to testimony obtained through internal evidence, that is recurrent words, phrases, grammatical forms and contextual sequences appearing in the RV. Evidence from etymological analyses,

6. M. A. Muusses, *Koecultus bij de Hindoes*, Thesis (Utrecht, 1920).

word studies, Vedic parallel passages, exegetical material and commentaries follow roughly in that order of priority.

All concepts associated with the cow in the RV may be reduced to one image and its corresponding cultural attitude. That image is of the cow pouring out a flood of milk. Analogies of a strikingly singular nature are based upon this image : rays of light stream like milk; Cosmic Waters are like lowing cows which flow with milk; rain is shed as milk from cows; poetic vision is like a cow flowing with a thousand streams of milk; the breasts of a goddess are like the cow's udder. How can all these situations be compared to an ordinary milk cow ? Like the cow and her milk, light is thought of as a bright substance which sustains life; the Cosmic Waters are considered to be a feminine creative principle; rain fructifies; poetic vision translated into hymns yields wealth and well-being. The major concepts associated with the cow are demonstrated in these comparisons. Being conceived of as a creative and sustaining principle, the cow symbolizes motherhood, fertility, and liberality. The concepts reveal a particular cultural attitude towards the cow which may be summarized by stating that in the RV, the cow is emblematic of maternal vital energy.

As outlined below, these concepts develop from the cow's usefulness in the economic and ritual life; they occur figuratively in the epithetical and mythological contexts.

Factors rooted in experiences and observations of secular and religious life show that the actual cow is regarded as the provider of all good things munificently bestowed upon Vedic man. As supplier of enjoyable food and drink for men and gods, of hide and flesh for essential articles of daily and ritual use, the cow is considered as a creature who gives of herself continuously and unstintingly in the most vital areas of Rigvedic life. Being thus of intrinsic value, she confers wealth and prestige upon her owner who comes to regard her as symptomatic of a state of well-being and prosperity. The Vedic reaction to these bounties causes a specific set of virtues to be attributed to the ordinary milk cow. The mother cow's flow of milk becomes expressive of maternity and liberality. The cow beside her calf, licking it, feeding it, nuzzling it, exemplifies human love and pious devotion. Priests, for example, are said to call to god Indra as mother cows to the calf.

Descriptions of the preparation of a particular type of soma oblation reveal that the cow is also regarded as a fertility symbol. The oblation, called *gávāśir,* is a blend of soma juices and cow's milk. A characteristic analogy for the mixing of these two ingredients is the copulation of the bull (i.e., soma) with the cows (i.e., milk). Soma is the cows' beloved lord; as he draws near the mixing vessel, he bellows to them and they, lowing, answer him "as would a maid her lover". These mating calls having been performed, the bull approaches the cows "like a youth meeting a maiden for the tryst". When they unite, Soma stands among the cows as a conquering warrior.

The concepts which the cow expresses are very desirable Rigvedic attributes and contribute to her becoming a major epithet of gods and goddesses. 'Cow' as an epithet of a goddess is used to emphasize aspects in the deity's nature which coincide with those typified by a cow. When Pṛśni, Aditi, and Uṣas are called 'cow', their maternal character is stressed. Motherhood, in the case of Uṣas, the goddess of dawn, is a dominant theme in her mythology. Dawn and her rays are conceived as a herd of cows and their mother; the mother, moreover, also streams forth milk, only her 'milk' represents the light she emits. The goddess Dakṣiṇā is the personification of the ritual gift. The giving of *dakṣiṇā* to the priest is an esteemed act of generosity. Dakṣiṇā is no doubt called 'cow' to affirm the concept of liberality associated with her. Similarly Indra, when his liberality is described, is said to be a milk cow. Sacred Speech is likewise associated with liberality; the words enounced by the priests at the rites cause the gods to provide for man. Vāc, the personification of sacred speech, is also a creative principle. These qualities make her a 'cow'. The night, personified by Rātrī, is thought to be bright. Perhaps Rātrī is a 'cow' since brightness is likewise associated with a milk cow. Heaven and Earth are called two milk cows as a way of insisting upon their bountiful, generative qualities.

The figurative uses of 'cow' in the mythology grow out of the concepts associated with the actual cow. The most important metaphorical uses for 'cow' in the RV appear in two separate myths.

In the Indra-Vṛtra myth, 'cows' represent the Cosmic Waters. The Cosmic Waters are essential to the creation of the Vedic universe since they contain elements needed for life to begin and to flourish. They bring not only moisture into the world but also light and heat, for, these Waters (*áp* fem.) are pregnant and their embryo is the sun. Therefore they are called 'mothers' and 'cows'. Since the Waters represent a maternal, creative force in the myth, the metaphorical use of 'cow' is perfectly appropriate.

In the myth of the Paṇis 'cows' represent three different concepts. One of these is 'light', in particular, dawn's light. It is suggested that the relation between 'light' and 'cows' ought to be reduced to the analogy existing between 'light' and 'cow's milk'. Both are characterized by 'brightness' and 'radiance' (see RV 1.66.2b). With respect to the cow's milk, it is herein postulated that 'brightness' is attributed to milk due to the warmth of the extracted milk; 'brightness' may also be said of milk since it is believed that the power of heat has 'cooked' or prepared the milk inside the unprepared or 'raw' cow. The other concepts which 'cows' represent in the myth of the Paṇis are 'the oblation-giving cow' and the '*dákṣiṇā* cow'.

This myth, which has here been given a new interpretation is an allegory concerning the preservation of the Vedic world order. It tells the story of a group of demons, the Paṇis, who, representing anti-sacerdotal forces, withhold a treasure mainly from mythical priests. The treasure consists of cows and horses offered as the priests' honorarium (*dákṣiṇā*), the oblation-giving cows, rays of dawn, dawn itself, the ritual fire, the sun, the path of light and the day. What the Paṇis are in fact doing is to withhold items essential to the performance of the sacrifice. The rite may not begin in darkness,[7] nor can it proceed smoothly

7. The RV clearly indicates that the sacrifice, at the time of the RV, was contingent upon the appearance of dawn. RV 7.78.3 states that the dawns brought forth Sūrya, the sacrifice and Agni. The same idea is expressed in RV 7.80.2.

with neither the oblation nor the honorarium. However, should the sacrifice not be performed, disorder and chaos would engulf the world of men and gods, for the performance of the sacrifice promotes the *ṛtá,* a force which causes order to prevail throughout the organized universe. Therefore, for an ordered world structure to exist, a force is needed to release the Paṇis' treasure. Mere physical force, such as Indra used against Vṛtra, will not work against the Paṇis; the Paṇis are nearly indomitable due to the nature of the treasure they withhold. However, their great vulnerability stems from the fact that they have no magic power, or as the Veda says, their "words are no weapons" (10.108.6). The priests, on the contrary, have the most potent magical power at their command. Their chantings evoke that power, the *bráhman*. With their hymns and songs, the priests and their divine allies triumph over the Paṇis and cause the treasure to be released. As it streams forth, daylight commences. So, too, items necessary for the ritual appear : the ritual fire, the milk oblation and the most esteemed *dákṣiṇā*. Conditions are now such that the sacrifice may begin.

This myth treats a major problem in the RV, namely, how may the world function well; how may men live securely and gods receive praise when evil forces not only exist in the universe but actively work against the order established in it. The answer which the myth of the Paṇis provides is that the sacrifice (which maintains the order in the world) is safeguarded by the power inherent in the Vedic chants. In this way disorder and chaos are suppressed and an ordered existence is upheld in the world of men and gods.

We may conclude that the cow was an extremely appropriate figure to express some of the main interests of the Rigvedic age. This period, if it can be adequately understood from the hymns alone, is deeply concerned with personal security and knowledge about natural and supra-natural phenomena. Aspects of all of these concerns are expressed by the cow. That she represents material well-being is a well accepted fact. But it should also be noted that the cow seems to be an ideal figure to further man's knowledge of the unknown. Through similes and metaphors the cow, known so well through daily observation, is able to clarify and then identify cosmic phenomena as well as gods and goddesses. Even so, there is no evidence in the text that cows are regarded as sacred, or, that a taboo against cow-killing exists. A type of cow called *vaśā́*, possibly the cow relegated to the Brahman as his *dákṣiṇā* or as the offering animal, is one of the usual sacrificial animals; also, priests ate of the offered meat. Moreover, in daily life cows were slaughtered for food.[8] When a cow is referred to in the RV as *aghnyā* ('she who is not to be slain'), the usefulness of the cow is emphasized, not the doctrine of the cow's inviolability.[9] *Aghnyā, aghnya* are specialized terms in the RV for the precious cattle in a herd;[10] as such, *aghnyā* designates the mother, or milk cow in the RV.[11] Although the sanctity of the cow is not indicated in the RV, the cow undoubtedly occupied an extremely important position in the economic, ritual and mythopoeic activities of the age. Thus, to understand the concepts associated with the cow in the RV is, I believe, to gain better insight into the cultural dynamics of that period.

The meaning of Sanskrit *gó* as 'cow, ox, bull' is well established by the following IE cognates: "Avestan *gāuš, gə̄uš* Rind, Stier, Kuh, Old Persian *Gau–(baruya–*New Persian), Armenian *kov* Kuh, Greek *βοῦς*, Latin ("Sabellian") *bōs* Rind, Old Irish *bō*, Old Icelandic *kyr*, Old High German *chuo* Kuh, Tocharian A *ko* Rind; cf. Lettish *gùovs* Kuh, Bulgarian *govédo* Rindvieh".[12] It remains to summarize the way *gó* is used in RV.

In the RV, *gó* is used both in the fem. and mas.; however *gó* fem. 'cow', seems to be the more usual usage. The mas. only occurs under special conditions : when *gó* is used figuratively (e.g., when it is the epithet of a god); or, due to the exigency of a

8. E.g. see Chap. II, summary. Cf. also Laxmanshastri Joshi, "Was the Cow killed in Ancient India", *Quest* 75 (March-April, 1972), 83-87.

9. See W. Norman Brown, *op. cit.*, 32-34. See also pp. 663-664 of the same article transl. in French in *Annales* 4 (1964) wherein is contained a rejoinder to pp. 4-5 of H.P. Schmidt's article "*aghnya*", *Zeitschrift für vergleichende Sprachforschung auf dem Gebiet der Indogermanischen Sprachen*, 78 (1963), pp. 1-46.

10. See Johanna Narten, "Vedisch *aghnyā*-und die Wasser", *Acta Orientalia Neerlandica*, ed. P. W. Pestman (Leiden, 1971), 120-134.

11. Narten, *ibid.*

12. Mayrhofer I, p. 351.

comparison (e.g., 5.56.3; 6.45.22, etc.) or, a particular theme (e.g., 'plowing' 5.27.1; 10.27.20 etc.).

Applied literally *gó* is the most general term for bovines in the RV; it denotes cow, ox, and bull in the singular, dual, and plural.[13] The singular of *gó* occurs predominantly when used

1) as an epithet
2) in the collective sense (Economic context, e.g. 1.43.2, 6; 4.57.1; 8.5.20; 8.14.3; 8.30.4; 8.68.13; 9.11.3, 7; 9.61.15; 9.62.3; Mythological context, e.g. 7.44.3; 1.121.2, 7; 4.28.5; 4.58.4 [?]; 3.30.10; 5.45.6; 8.32.5).
3) literally in the sense of the 'oblation-giving cow' (Ritual context : 1.173.8; 3.55.8; 9.91.3).
4) in certain myths (e.g., Śayu's cow; Ṛbhus' cow).
5) in literal sense as the cow desired by the priest and yajamāna (8.52.5; 9.94.5; 9.9.9; 10.97.4; 6.46.2).

Gó 'cow' may assume a more restricted meaning through the use of appositional modifiers : *gó dhenú* (9.68.1; 9.66.12; 10.95.6); *starí gó* (7.23.4; 1.116.22); *gó sudúghā* (7.18.1).

Gó, 'cow' in the literal sense, used alone, may also convey a more restricted meaning. *Gó* is capable of having a calf (10.145.6, 9.12.2; 7.103.2). *Gó* is 'milk cow' in the ritual context (e.g. 1.135.8) though in the majority of cases the idea of 'milk' is specifically posited in the accompanying verb and/or noun. The evidence for *gó* as 'barren cow' is scant and inconclusive.[14]

Gó (sg. and pl.) is used as a metonymy in the economic and ritual contexts. As such, the term signifies 'leather straps' (6.75.11; 6.47.26); 'bowstring(s)' (10.27.22; 6.67.11); 'rein(s) of leather' (4.22.8; 6.46.14); 'leather strap' (of a sling ?) (1.121.9); 'ghee' or 'milk' (1.151.8); both the 'hide' (10.94.9; 10.116.4) which catches the soma drops and the 'leather' of which it is

13. Fem. s. 'cow' (e.g. 8.94.1); Mas. s. 'bull' (e.g.8 .1.2; 8.81.3); 'ox' (10.155.5; 10.165.5). Fem. pl. 'cows' (e.g. 9.62.5; 9.84.5). Mas. pl. 'bulls' (e.g. 3.45.3); 'oxen' (e.g. 1.23.15; 8.20.19). Fem. dual 'cows' (3.33.1); mas. dual ('oxen' e.g. 3.53.17; 10.85,11).

14. The goddess Night is compared to a *starí* (i.e., a barren cow) 1.122.2 and *gó* in 4.3.9. Probably *gó* in 5.41.18 does not designate the cow killed at the sacrifice. This sort of cow normally called *vaśá*, is considered to be a sterile cow by some scholars (see discussion in Chap. III).

made (e.g. 9.66.29; 9.79.4); 'omentum' to cover a corpse (10.16.7); and 'milk' (e.g. 1.134.2; 3.50.3). Bergaigne does not favor the metonymic translation[15] for *gó*. Conceding that *gó* may be used to signify products coming from a cow, ox or bull, he believes that where *gó* is so used, it is employed as a mythic and liturgical metaphor and not as a common figure of speech; thus he wishes to keep the metaphor and translate *gó* as 'cow(s)' throughout. However I do not find that the usages of *gó*, as listed above, possess mythological or magical significance. The metonymic usages are not here seen as an attempt to establish, for magical purposes, an esoteric correspondence between concepts. As such they function differently from the metaphorical usages of *gó*.

When *gó* is used metaphorically it connotes the 'Cosmic Waters', the 'rays' of dawn, possibly the 'soma juice' (5.30.7); 'stones which press soma' (9.99.3) and 'stars' or 'clouds'(see 1.154.6.).

As an epithet, *gó* fem. 'cow' describes Uṣas, Rātrī, Aditi, Pṛśni, Dakṣiṇā, Vāc. *Gó* mas. 'bull' is an epithet for Indra, Agni, Soma, Sūrya, and the priests.

Most of the literal and figurative meanings cited for *gó* have been noted in lexicographical works listed in the bibliography. New however are the following: *gó* as 'Cosmic Waters'; 'press-stones'; 'soma juice'. Some meanings offered in lexicons are clearly debatable as definitions for *gó* in the RV. These are:

G*Wö* No. 6: 'stars' in 7.36.1; 1.164.3 (?). The meaning of *gó* in 7.36.1 and 1.164.3 is problematic and has been variously explained (see Verse Index). *Gó* in 1.154.6 is equally obscure; numerous scholars have defined it as 'stars', thus making this the only occurrence for this meaning. Likewise, Macdonell's suggestion 'clouds' has also not been found elsewhere in the RV to be a meaning for *gó*.

G*Wö* No. 8: 'rays of the Sun' or 'flames of Agni' (Grassmann: 7.9.4; 2.19.3: 6.60.2). In 5.47.4 *gó* could possibly be the 'rays of Sūrya', or 'the three dawns'. *Gó* in 5.2.5. is defined by Ludwig (*RV*) and Geldner (*HOS* 34) as 'flames of Agni'; in this case Grassmann, (*Wö*) understands *gó* as 'oxen', used literally.

15. "Quelques Observations sur Les Figures de Rhétorique dans le Ṛig-Veda", *Mém. de la Société de Linguistique de Paris*, T. 4 (1881), 96-137.

G*Wö* No. 9 'earth' (Grassmann: 10.31.6; 4.41.5; 10.101.9; 10.133.7; 10.67.5; 8.101.15, 16). This meaning is not upheld for these verses in the present study.

G*Wö* No. 18 'fat' (Grassmann 10.16.7). *Gó* in this verse is understood as a metonymy for 'omentum'; Geldner (*HOS* 35): cf. AG 4.3.20 *vapā*.

Listed below are the numbers of the definitions given for *gó* in the *PW* which do not apply to *gó* in the RV: Nos. 2, 4, 6, 8, 10, 11, 14, 15, 16, 18, 21, 22, 23.

CHAPTER II

THE COW IN VEDIC ECONOMIC LIFE

A. INTRODUCTION

This chapter, dealing with the cow's position in the economy, aims to bring into focus not only the cow's uses, but also the attitudes and modes of thinking her uses aroused. Thus, this chapter has a twofold purpose: to present a complete picture of the cow's functions, and, to determine whether these functions inspired any patterns of conceptualization which could elucidate the metaphorical applications of 'cow' in Vedic mythology.

The following terms for 'cow' occur in this chapter: *aghnyā*, *usrā́*, *usríyā*, *gó*, *dhenú*, *vāśrā́*, *sudúghā*, *starī́*. All of these terms, except *gó*, are applied only in the literal sense. *Gó* is also used as a metonymy to denote an article made of cow or ox hide.

The analysis offered below, presents detailed evidence for the well-known fact that the cow played a vital role in the economy of the Aryan settlers.[1] A summary of the cow's practical uses is given in section B; those verses requiring further exegetical comments are contained in section C.

The importance of the cow is seen not only in the many references to her practical uses. Another indicator is the frequency with which the activity of the cow is compared to the gods, and to events which describe natural, ritual and cosmic phenomena. Those expressions which employ *gó*, etc. as one member of a simile construction bring out most clearly the thought patterns associated with the cow's usefulness. The similes discussed in section D demonstrate that attitudes towards the cow's usefulness were expressed as ideations and images which contributed to the development of the cow's many and often obscure meta-

1. For example this subject has been mentioned in: W. Norman Brown, "Sanctity", 30ff. V. R. Ramachandra Dikshitar, "A Note on Cow Veneration in Ancient India", *Vol. of Eastern and Indian Studies* (1939) 75-77. A. A. Macdonell and A. B. Keith, *Vedic Index* (London, 1912), s.v. *gó*.

phorical uses. Such uses, evident in mythological and epithetical references to the cow, often result from some concrete image associated with the cow's function in the daily life of the Vedic people.

B. SUMMARY

The Aryans at the time of the Rig Veda followed a rural type of existence which was based upon a pastoral and agricultural economy. The tribal community was composed of the chief, essentially a war leader, the priests, stockbreeders, farmers, artisans and serfs. They had domesticated the horse, sheep, cattle, goat, ass, dog and buffalo; of these, cattle represented a principal unit and the general expression for wealth[2] (1.33.1; 1.90.8; 1.191.4; 2.25.2; 5.20.4; 6.28.1; 7.103.10c; 7.41.3; 7.18.1; 7.54.2; 8.4.18; 8.14.3 [*gó*][3]; 8.47.12; 8.70.6; 9.64.3; 9.112.3; 10.34.13; 10.166.1).

The high value placed upon the cow resulted from the many uses she served. Cows were slaughtered (cf. 10.79.6; 10.89.14) and provided the people with nourishment (6.28.6). Their meat was eaten by the priests who partook of the ritual offering and those of the community who could afford it.[4] Their milk was drunk (cf. 1.120.9) for enjoyment (cf. 3.30.14).[5]

2. Note that eminence could be achieved among the people through the possession of cattle (cf. 10.64.11).

3. Used in the collective sense; cf. Geldner, *HOS* 35, p. 345, fn. lb.

4. See Brown, "Sanctity," 31; Macdonell and Keith, *Ved. Index*, 145 (*māṃsa*). For the positions taken on meat eating in the post-Vedic period see L. Alsdorf, "Beiträge zur Geschichte von Vegetarismus und Rinderverehrung in Indien" No. 6 (1961), 557-625 in *Abhandlungen der Geistes und sozialwissenschaftlichen Klasse* published by Akademie der Wissenschaften und der Literatur, Mainz.

Cf. A. Chattopadhyay, "A note on beef-eating in Mauryan times", *Indo-Asian Culture* 17, (1968), 49-51, for textual references to support the following conclusion: "The wide prevalence of the killing of horned cattle like cows, bulls, buffaloes etc. at sacrifices is noticed in the Digha Nikāya and its corroboration is noticed in the Dharma-sūtras. ... So beef-eating prevailed throughout the land and Aśoka could not take a drastic step by stopping it by legislation" (p. 50).

5. It should be noted that the mention of the daily use of the cow's milk and flesh is extremely rare in the Rig Veda. Of the verses cited by O. Prakash, *Food and Drinks in Ancient India*, (Delhi, 1961), on p. 12, footnotes 6 and 7, 9.67.32 and 10.87.16 could refer to milk in a daily context; the others refer to the oblation milk. But, *gā́ḥ* in 1.33.10 is 'cows' in the figurative sense; *gó* in 1.181.8 is taken as 'bull'. 6.63.8 gives evidence that nourishment (*íṣ*) was obtained from the milk cow (*dhenú*).

Oxen were used as draught animals (see 5.27.1 for other examples). Spurred by the plougher's song (8.20.19) oxen pulled the plow (cf. 1.23.15). They were harnessed to ceremonial cars as well; in 10.85.11 two oxen pull Sūryā's bridal car; this probably reflects actual custom.

A variety of products, leather and otherwise, were made from the hide of cattle. A leather strap was bound around the arrow, securing the point to the shaft (6.75.11). The bowstring was made of some part of the cow, probably either gut or sinew (6.67.11; 10.27.22); perhaps even Indra's *vájra* is hurled with the aid of a leather sling (1.121.9). The parts of a chariot were tied together with leather straps (6.47.26; 8.48.5). The horse's reins consisted of leather (4.22.8; 6.46.14; 6.67.11). Leather strings were used to make snares (10.28.10,11) as well as some kind of musical string instrument called a *godhá* (8.69.9). The goad which the herder used to drive his animals was fashioned from the cow's hide or tail (*góopaśa*, 6.53.9).

Because of their great economic value, men prayed to be lords of cattle (10.166.1); priests asked for *dákṣiṇā* in cattle; warriors sought to fight for cattle (9.87.7; *gá gavyánn abhí śúro ná sátvā*) in order to become winners of cattle (*gojít* 3.31.20). Cattle are *pradhanyà*, that is, they constitute the prize of war (10.99.4).

The Rig Veda describes cattle wars (*gáviṣṭi, góṣāti*) in such vivid detail that one can readily imagine these contests: a group of warriors (2.25.4) seeking cattle (*gavíṣ, gaviṣá*) riding horses,[6] using chariots (cf. 5.63.5), waving banners (cf. 4.13.2), are ready to contend for "offspring, cattle, progeny, waters, and fertile lands" (6.25.4). The scene of the clash is tumultuous. Warriors with bows and arrows (6.75.2; 10.38.1) keep the adversary at bay; horses are used to stampede the cattle (cf. 5.6.7; 4.38.4) and flaming torches drive the herd together (6.6.5: 8.75.7; 10.156.2). To assure success in gaining booty, the gods' assistance and protection is implored (6.59.7; 6.66.8; 8.5.26). The favorite god for such requests is Indra (1.33.3; 2.30.5; 3.30.20, 21; 3.50.3; 6.19.12; 6.26.2;[7] 6.35.2 (?);

6. See S. D. Singh, *Ancient Indian Warfare with Special Reference to the Vedic Period*, (Leiden, 1965) p. 58.

7. *Gáve..yúdhyan* 5.33.4 in the sense of *góṣu yúdhyan* 6.26.2.

7.32.16). His cosmic feats establish him as releaser and lord of cows par excellence (see Chap. IV); also he gives herds of cattle at the times when he drinks soma (1.81.7). The descriptions of cattle fights could refer to secular skirmishes or formal ritualized combats.

Cattle fighters (*goṣuyudh-*)[8] rode out against non-Aryan tribes (3.53.14),[9] hostile strangers (*arí*:[10] 1.121.15; 1.33.3) and the type of miser (*paṇí*) who stinted with regard to the sacrificial offerings (8.75.7). However, on whatever pasture they might go[11] (8.4.18) cattle belonging to the Aryans were regarded as Aryan property. It is hard to believe that their herds were free from attack; but for the Vedic sacrificer there was a very real distinction between his herd and that of an outsider. That distinction rested in the belief that the power of the sacrifice benefited the worshipper and his possessions (cf. 8.68.13). It protected the worshipper's herd from theft and slaughter, and secured the grazing areas (6.28.4). Further, it was thought that Pūṣan would follow the cattle of the yajamāna and of the singers (6.54.6), and that the milk cows would flow to him who had sacrificed in the past and would do so again in the future (1.125.4). On the contrary, as seen above, the cattle of strangers[12] and those who abused or neglected the sacrifice were attacked by Aryan fighters.

Concomitant with faith in the power of the sacrifice, is the idea that a state of well-being indicates divine favor bestowed upon the pious: Indra imparts most wealth in horses and milk cows (*gó sudúghā*) to the one who sacrifices (cf. 7.18.1); the god does not give away the cattle of the soma-presser (10.160.3).

8. 6.6.5; 10.30.10. Note the regularity of the loc. pl. of *gó* in the context of a cattle fight (cf. 6.26.2 *góṣu yudhyan*). See also 1.151.1; 10.99.4 and pp. 26-35.

9. See C. J. Blair, *Heat in the Rig Veda and Atharva Veda*, in AOS 45 (New Haven, 1961), p. 24.

10. P. Thieme, *Der Fremdling im Ṛgveda*, in *Abhandlungen für die Kunde des Morgenlandes*, XXIII/2 (1938) 61. Thieme defends this meaning for *arí* against the objections of Lommels and Dumézil in *ZDMG* 107 (1957), 96-104. The latest dissatisfaction comes from Reinhold G. F. Müller, "Zu dem 'Fremdling im Ṛgveda", *Wiener Zeitschrift für die Kunde Süd- und Ostasiens* 10 (1966), 1-5. He understands "den Ausdruck *arí* usw.... Einschätzung" (p. 5).

11. Insertion of 'go' follows Sāyaṇa who supplies *gacchanti*; *párā* from v. 18; $\sqrt{vī}$ from v. 17.

12. Cf. 9.49.2: *táyā pavasva dhárayā yáyā gā́va ihā́gaman/jányāsa úpa no gṛhám*: Renou (*EVP* 8, p. 27): "Clarifie toi grâce à cette coulée (même) par laquelle les vaches de l'étranger/accèderont à notre maison."

To guard against a condition of want, the gods are asked to give special consideration to man's cattle. General well-being (*śám* 9.11.3,7; 9.61.15) for the herd is requested of Soma,[13] the Aśvins (8.5.20), Rudra (1.43.6), the Lords of Righteousness (7.35.12). Should the cow's milk come into the sorcerer's possession (e.g. 10.87,16, 17) the worshippers implore that it turn into poison for these evil doers (10.87.18; see Renou's translation *EVP* 14).

Entrusted to the appropriate gods are the pleas for the cows' fertility and for the protection of their milk. Parjanya, in his capacity as a god of fecundity, prepares the womb of the cows for productivity (7.102.2). The Aśvins, renowned for making a cow fertile, are asked to make the cows flow with milk (see 1.118.2; 10.106.11). The guardians of the world, Mitra-Varuṇa, are said to guard the beloved nectar in the cows (1.71.9).

The sacrificers seek to shield the cattle from natural, human and divine disaster. They ask that the Maruts' deadly weapon, the lightning, which kills cattle and men, be kept afar (7.56.17). A request to Agni says: "Whoever O Agni tries to injure the sap of our drink, or of our horses, cows, selves, may he, our enemy, a thief and a sorcerer fail; may he be put down [in the darkness], himself and his offspring" (7.104.10)[14]. It is hoped that Rudra, capable of killing cattle (*goghná* : 1.114.10) with his weapon (cf. 6.28.7), brings no harm to the herd; may only the blessings of Rudra be granted to the cattle (1.43.2).[15]

To keep the cows content and secure Pūṣan is asked to follow the cows (6.54.5), Varuṇa to watch over herds of cattle[16] (8.41.1), Agni to protect them (1.31.12)[17] and Vāta to blow upon the cows (*usrá* 10.169.1); Parjanya is requested to provide a good water supply for the cows (*aghnyá* 5.83.8), Uṣas to banish their evil

13. For a similar idea associated with the soma drops, cf. 9.62.3.

14. W. Norman Brown, "The Rigvedic Equivalent for Hell", *JAOS* 61 (1941), 77.

15. *Śám* to be understood with $\sqrt{kr}$. Cf. verse 6. *áditi*: adj. modifying Rudra (Hillebrandt, *Ueber die Göttin Aditi* (Breslau, 1876), p. 6.

16. On *paśvó gâḥ* see Renou (*EVP*, 7, p. 28).

17. Agni protects the cows by encircling them (see 10.80.5).

dreams far off (8.47.14),[18] and the Viśvedevas to grant the cows[19] full protection (8.30.4).

C. EXEGESIS ON SELECTED PASSAGES, ARRANGED ACCORDING TO CONTEXT

1. *The Cow as Economic Wealth*

6.28.1 (In praise of Cows)

á gávo agmann utá bhadrám akrant sīdantu goṣṭhé raṇáyantv asmé

prajávatīḥ pururūpa ihá syur índrāya pūrvīr uṣáse dúhānāḥ

The cows have come and brought luck; let them rest in the pen and feel glad among us.

May the variegated ones be fertile here, yielding milk for Indra many mornings.

Pāda a: cf. 8.47.12c.

goṣṭha: Also in 1.191.4 (*ní gávo goṣṭhé asadan*) *goṣṭhá* designates a place where cattle rest for the night. Cf. Avestan *gaostānō* mas. 'cowstall' (Mayrhofer).[20] This verse sums up the prevailing attitude towards the cow. She is considered an auspicious creature. She brings good fortune to the owner by providing, in large measure, for his economic and ritual needs.

1.90.8c (To the All-Gods)

mádhvīr gávo bhavantu naḥ

Let our cows be [full of] sweetness.

The request is that cows be full of milk; see 10.106.11 where *mádhu* means milk.

1.33.1 cd (To Indra)

anāmṛṇáḥ kuvíd ád asyá rāyó gávāṃ kétam páram āvárjate naḥ

Perhaps the Indestructible One would bestow on us [our] chief desire for cattle, for this wealth ?

18. Pāda a: The dream which foretells hardship for the cattle—Sāy. Pādas cd: *tritáya..āptyáya:* sending something to Trita is, in effect, to send it off as far as possible (A. Bergaigne, *La Religion Védique*, II (Paris, 1883), p. 328.

19. *Gáve* used in the collective sense, as also *gám* 4.57.1 (Geldner, *HOS* 35, 345).

20. Mayrhofer I, s.v. *goṣṭhánaḥ*, p. 350.

The worshippers who desire cattle (*gavyát* — pāda a) ask Indra to help them fulfill their wish. Verse 1 is the introduction to a plea for divine assistance in a cattle raid (cf. v. 3). Indra's heroic exploits are retold in the remainder of the hymn (vss. 4-15) as if to incite the god to influence the battle.

9.64.3 (To Soma)

áśvo ná cakrado vŕṣā sáṃ gā́ indo sám árvataḥ
ví no rāyé dúro vṛdhi

As a horse, you, the Bull, neigh together cows and horses O Indu. Open us the doors to wealth.

The language of this verse is reminiscent of the myth of the Paṇis. *Gā́ḥ* and *árvataḥ* could be the *dákṣiṇā*; however in the following verse cows, horses and heroes represent the desires of the yajamāna.

1.10.7cd (To Indra)

gávām ápa vrajáṃ vṛdhi kṛṇuṣvá rā́dho adrivaḥ

Open the stall of the cattle, bring riches O Possessor of the Press-Stones.

ápa √*vṛ vrajám* and the genitive of *gó* is an expression used to indicate the giving of cattle as wealth. The usage of *gó* in this and the following verse is probably literal and refers to cattle as the prize of war (see verse 10 *vā́ja*), or as the priest's *dákṣiṇā* (so Geldner *HOS* 33, p. 11 and H.-P. Schmidt, *Bṛhaspati und Indra*, Wiesbaden, 1968, p. 154). Schmidt's suggestion that *gó* in vss. 7 and 8 could be taken both in the literal and figurative sense (i.e. *gó* as Cosmic Waters, or, Dawns) is less likely here. The hymn dwells more on Indra's renown liberality than his mythic feats. *Ápa* √*vṛ vrajá* reoccurs in the context of Indra's liberality in 4.20.8, where likewise *gó* signifies actual cattle wealth.

Closely allied is the phrase *vrajá gómat*. In the following instances it is used in the same literal sense as above: 1.86.3; 5.34.5; 7.27.1; 7.32.10; 8.51.5; 8.46.9; 8.70.6.

2. *The Economic Uses of Cattle*

10.79.6cd (To Agni)

ákrīḷan krī́ḷan hárir áttave 'dán ví parvaśáś cakarta gā́m ivāsíḥ

Not playing, playing, the golden one [having] to eat without teeth, cut through [the wood] piece by piece, as a knife through the cow.

hári: Agni

Is *gā́m ivāsíḥ* an allusion to killing for the ritual offering or for daily food ? It might very well be the latter. The Rig Veda indicates that on special occasions, such as a marriage (10.85.13) or elaborate banquets,[21] cattle (*gó*) were slain, presumably for food. Cows were also used as the sacrificial offering,[22] but rarely if ever in the RV is such a cow specifically designated as *gó*. Therefore *gó* here seems to show that cows were slaughtered for economic purposes, the comparison is obviously based on the equally facile power of fire and knife to consume.

a) *gó* — 'ox' : 5.27.1ab (To Agni)

ánasvantā sátpatir māmahe me gā́vā cétiṣṭho ásuro maghónaḥ

The righteous lord gave me two oxen yoked to a cart, (he who is) godlike, of liberal, the most outstanding.

ánasvantā....gā́vā are received as *dákṣiṇā*

In this verse as in 10.85.11; 6.27.7; 3.53.17; 10.27.20 the dual mas. of *gó* designates the ox as draught animal. A synonym, *anaḍvā́ḥ*, occurs only in the mas. in the RV (3.53.18; 10.85.10). *Gā́m* (mas.) *anaḍvā́ham* occurring in 10.59.10 is the ox which pulls a wagon. Cows were not used to draw loads; the RV contains no examples. The sing. mas. of *gó* also designates 'ox' (e.g. *gā́m ná dhurí*, 'as an ox to the yoke' 1.151.4).

b) *gó* — the strap binding the shaft of an arrow: 6.75.11 (Consecration of Weapons)

suparṇáṃ vaste mṛgó asyā dánto góbhiḥ sáṃnaddhā patati prásūtā yátrā náraḥ sáṃ ca ví ca drávanti tátrāsmábhyam íṣavaḥ śárma yaṅsan

Her tooth [is] a deer, [she is] clothed in feather; bound with straps, she soars when released.

21. Bloomfield, in "American Oriental Society's Proceedings, March 1894", *JAOS* 16, (1896) cxxiv: the name Atithigvá means 'he who has or offers a cow for the guest...At the *arghya*-ceremony, performed at the arrival of an honored guest, the preparation of a cow is the central feature". This ceremony is called *go-argha* in the TS.

22. Cf. 10.169.3. The sacrificed cow is commonly called *vaśā́* in the RV.

Where men run to and fro, there may arrows provide us shelter.

Nirukta 2.5 cites 6.75.11 as an example where *gó* means "tendon and phlegm"[23] which are used to bind an arrow. See also Nirukta 9.19 for commentary on 6.75.11.

c) *gó* — bowstring : 10.27.22ab (To Indra)

vṛkṣé-vṛkṣe níyatā mīmayad gaús táto váyaḥ prá patān pūruṣā́daḥ
The cow lows, tied to each tree; from there let man-devouring birds fly.

Bṛhad-devatā 7.27 says that 10.27.22 praises Indra's bow. Sāyaṇa understands the 'cow' to be the 'bowstring', the 'tree' to be the 'bow', and the 'birds' to be the 'arrows'. Thus the three metaphors are based upon what the object resembles or is made of. Gut or sinew of a cow should have been used for the string of a bow. Other interpretations for 'cow' are: Nirukta 2.6 — a form of light; L*RV*, V. — vāk ?; G*RV* — the cow of death, cf. v. 20.

gó — bowstrings: 6.67.11 (To Mitra and Varuṇa)

avór itthā́ vāṃ chardíṣo abhíṣṭau yuvór mitrāvaruṇāv áskṛdhoyu ánu yád gā́vaḥ sphurā́n ṛjípyáṃ dhṛṣṇúṃ yád ráṇe vṛ́ṣaṇaṃ yunájan

Thus in your protection of the home, [let] your [help be] unstinting O Mitra-Varuṇa.
When bowstrings discharge the upward moving [arrow], when they would harness a courageous stallion in battle.

The meaning of *gó* is problematic; *gó* is the subject of *ánu* √*sphur*. *Ánu* √*sphur* is a hapax legomenon in the RV. Three adjectival derivatives of √*sphur* occur in the RV. *Ánapasphurat* modifies *dhenú* in 4.42.10; *ánapasphura* modifies *dhenú* in 6.48.11; in 8.69.10 *ánapasphur* describes *sudúghā*. These occurrences, all with the privative *an*, indicate that *ápa* √*sphur* is an undesirable characteristic for a milk cow. This evidence implies that in 6.67.11 *gó* is not to be taken in the literal sense. The figurative use for *gó* is also supported by AV 1.2.3 where *ánu* √*sphur* de-

23. L. Sarup, *The Nighaṇṭu and the Nirukta*, (Delhi, 1962), p. 25.

scribes the whizzing action of an arrow on a bowstring (*gó*). In vs. 11c *ṛjipyá* refers to the arrow (so Geldner *HOS* 34 p. 171; also Oldenberg, *Noten* Vol. 11, p. 413).
L*RV* takes *gó* literally: "wenn heran springen die kühe". For Renou (*EVP* 7, p. 54) padas cd are primarily a soma image.

d) *gó* — leather strap (of a sling ?) from which Indra's *vájra* is hurled:

1.121.9 (To Indra)

tvám āyasáṃ práti vartayo gór divé áśmānam úpanītam ṛbhvā
kútsāya yátra puruhūta vanváñ chúṣṇam anantaíḥ pariyā́si vadhaíḥ

From [the sling's] leather strap you hurled the metal bolt, brought by the skillful from the sky.

When assisting Kutsa, O Much-invoked One, you surrounded Śuṣṇa with never-ending deadly weapons.

The verse speaks of Indra's slaying Śuṣṇa. He accomplishes this feat with his *vájra* (1.33.12; 5.32.4) which in pāda ab is described as *āyasá áśman* (both common terms for the *vájra*, see A. A. Macdonell, *Ved. Myth.*, p. 55). With *gó* taken as a leather strap, the image is one of Indra using a sling to thrust his *vájra* from the sky and into the demon Śuṣṇa. This interpretation of *gó* is the prevailing one (L*RV*, G*Wö*, Gr. *RV* and Keith and Macdonell, *Ved. Ind.*). Geldner's translation (*HOS* 33) indicates a different approach: Indra turned around the metal (lance ?) of the cow into the thunderbolt. He is of the opinion that this verse hints at the mystery of the *vájra* in the battle with Śuṣṇa. Geldner suggests that perhaps, as in the Namuci legend, Indra could not use the genuine *vájra* and cunningly obtained a substitute.

e) *gó* — leather strap binding a chariot: 6.47.26 (v. 26, to the Lord of the Wood)

vánaspate vīḍvàṅgo hí bhūyā́ asmátsakhā pratáraṇaḥ suvī́raḥ
góbhiḥ sáṃnaddho asi vīḷáyasvāsthātā́ te jayatu jétvāni

O Lord of the Wood, may you be strong of limbs, our helpful friend, an excellent hero.

You are tied together with leather straps; be strong; let your rider conquer wealth.

The chariot is addressed as the Lord of the Wood (cf. 3.53.20). This passage also occurs in AV 6.125.1 forming part of a hymn invoked to the War Chariot. Nirukta 2.5 mentions 6.47.26 as an example where *gó* means "skin and phlegm" of a chariot (Sarup, *Nighaṇṭu and Nirukta*).
Góbhiḥ sáṃnaddhaḥ is comparable to *varatráyā náhyanti* (10.60.8).

f) *gó* — leather straps binding a car: 8.48.5ab (To Soma)
imé mā pītā́ yaśása uruṣyávo rátham ná gā́vaḥ sám anāha párvasu
These honored [draughts of soma] have been drunk, my protectors; as leather straps [bind] a wagon, it [i.e. soma] holds my limbs together.
The verb *sám anāha* is problematic; Oldenberg (*Noten*, Vol. 13) takes it as a third person singular from the root $\sqrt{}$*nah*. *Sám* $\sqrt{}$*nah gó* meaning 'tied together with leather straps' occurs in 6.75.11 and 6.47.26.

g) *gó* — either milk used as the oblation, or, leather straps binding a chariot: 6.47.27cd (v. 27 To the Chariot)
apā́m ojmā́naṃ pári góbhir ā́vṛtam índrasya vájraṃ havíṣā rátham yaja
The power of the waters,[24] bound with leather, Indra's *vájra*, honor the chariot[25] with oblation.

Two meanings are possible for *góbhiḥ*. It could refer to the milk offering (*LRV*) as in 9.86.27 (the only other *RV* occurrence of *góbhiḥ pári ā́* $\sqrt{}$*vṛ*). In that case, the phrase would read 'covered with milk'. It is more probable that *gó* stands for the leather straps binding a chariot. Pāda c reoccurs in other contexts dealing with the chariot (e.g. AV 6.125.2c; for variant reading *ā́bhṛtam* see Whitney, *Atharva Veda* in *HOS* 7, p. 375).

h) *raśmí gó* — rein of leather: 4.22.8 cd (To Indra)
asmadryàk śuśucānásya yamyā āśúr ná raśmíṃ tuvyójasaṃ góḥ

24. The *vájra* rests in the sea: 8.100.9.
25. Indra's *vájra* may be identified with the chariot — A. Hillebrandt, *Vedische Mythologie* III (Breslau, 1902), 172, fn. 1.

Of the bright one, may you give heed to us, as a horse to the very strong rein of leather.

śuśucānásya refers to Indra; perhaps what is meant is: 'having drunk of the bright soma juice'; cf. *śuci-pā́* (G*Wö*) which refers to Soma, as do *śúci* and *śukrá*. Oldenberg (*Noten* 11, p. 287) takes *suśucāna* to refer to Agni. *Góḥ*: Oldenberg (*ibid.*) and Grassmann (*Wö*; under *gó*) translate *góḥ* as 'bull'. Oldenberg identifies the bull as Indra. He interprets pādas cd to mean that Agni (the horse) leads Indra to the sacrifice. Also he states that it is difficult to determine whether an actual situation is depicted (i.e. a horse guiding the movements of a cow) or whether the close association between Agni and Indra is depicted through their animal counterparts. Geldner (*HOS* 33 p. 449) supports the first idea, namely that a bridled horse leads the cow to which it is yoked. I believe that the simile is taken from the daily context (cf. 6.46.14 below) and is to be understood literally, thus: As a horse responds quickly to the reins, so Indra is asked to respond to the requests of the sacrificers. These requests are enumerated in the next three verses.

i) *gó* — rein of a horse: 6.46.14cd (To Indra)

ā́ yé váyo ná várvṛtaty ā́miṣi gṛbhītā́ bahvór gávi

Those who like birds draw near to the bait, held fast with the rein in both arms.

The general plea of this hymn is for victory in battle through Indra's help. The subject of verse 14 is *árvat* - in verse 13, the horses that Indra is to impel into the fray. It is they who are drawn 'to the bait' and are held in check by the rein.

Different interpretations for *gávi* are given by Bergaigne[26] and Geldner (*HOS* 34, p. 143). Bergaigne compares this passage to 10.27.22 and considers *gávi* to be the bowstring on which the arms hold arrows (i.e. the birds). He believes that this image is compared to the speedy advance of the horses. In 10.27.22 *gó*, *ví* and *vṛkṣá* must all be taken figuratively. However, in this case, *váyo ná....*, in the primary sense, acts as a very suitable comparison to the chargers. As such, the simile continues the

26. *La Religion Védique* II, 182.

style set in verse 13 where the horses are compared to falcons, and verse 14 where they are said to be like rushing waters. Geldner's translation, which uses too many insertions, takes *gávi* as war booty. The present study has not found any occurrence of the loc. sing. of *gó*, and only one sing. (*gáve* 5.33.4) to denote 'cattle as the prize of war'. By far the more usual form of *gó* with this meaning, as Geldner also recognizes, is *góṣu*.

j) *godhā́* — a musical instrument : 8.69.9 (To Indra)

áva svarāti gárgaro godhā́ pári saniṣvaṇat
píṅgā pári caniṣkadad índrāya bráhmódyatam

Let the *gárgara* sound; let the *godhā́* richly play.
Let the *píṅgā* surge; a hymn is offered to Indra.

Indra is praised with both music and song (v. 8). Hillebrandt (*Ved. Myth.* I, 143-144) considers verses 8-10 of this hymn to reflect a more popular and festive musical tradition than is usually found in the RV. The terms *gárgara-*, *godhā́*, and *píṅgā* are usually taken as referring to musical instruments; their precise meaning is however problematic. As regards *godhā́*, Lüders, in his study of this term ("Von indischen Tieren," *ZDMG*, 96 [1942] 23-81) shows that from the period of the Yajurveda Saṃhitā, *godhā́* designates a type of lizard. Evidence from later works shows that objects made from its hide may also be called *godhā́*. Lüders therefore understands the earliest appearance of this term to mean 'lizard' (RV 10.28.10) and 'a musical instrument whose sound box is covered with the hide of lizard' (8.69.9).

The contexts of the RV passages in themselves do not require the specific meaning 'lizard'. However, Lüders is of the opinion that even from the earliest period *godhā́* designated this type of animal. He accepts the *PW* analysis of *godhā́* as *gó dhā*, but not the meaning "das was man vom Rinde erhält". This meaning, based on taking *dhā* from √*dhā* 'to put' is rejected in favor of √*dhā* 'to suck'. Thus Lüders' considers the original meaning of *godhā́* to be "Kuhsaugerin". He shows that the literature throughout the world signals out snakes and toads in particular as animals who draw the milk of the cow. However this special characteristic, as Lüders concedes, cannot be associated with the *godhā́* in either

Sanskrit literature or Indian folklore. Turner suggests that *godhá* is probably a loanword from the Dravidian and changed by popular etymology to 'cow-sucker' (*Comp. Dict. of Indo-Aryan Languages*, p. 230). *Godhá* occurs three times in the RV. In 8.69.9 it appears in a musical context. As Lüders has pointed out (p. 41-42), *godhá* is likely to be an abbreviation for *godhā-vīṇākā*, a string instrument having a resonating chamber which has leather stretched over it.

Godhá in 10.28.10,11 is not in a musical context. Ludwig (*RV*, II, 618) translates: "ihm zerrt der riemen den einen fuss" (v. 10), "denen möge zerren der strick den fuss" (v. 11). Here *godhá* is another type of object consisting of leather, perhaps a snare, as *paripád* in 10 b. Other translators (aside from Lüders, and Geldner [*HOS* 35, v. cit] 'Krokodil') have proposed similar ideas: *PW* and G*Wö*: 'Sehne' G*RV*: 'Riemen'.

k) *áṣṭrā góopaśā* — a goad of leather strands, or, a cow-tail goad: 6.53.9 (To Pūṣan)

yá te áṣṭrā góopaśághṛṇe paśusádhanī
tásyās te sumnám īmahe

Your goad of leather strands which urges animals on, O Glowing One,[27]
From her[28] do we desire your favor.

Góopaśā is a hapax legomenon; *opaśá* occurs in four passages in the RV (10.85.8; 9.71.1; 8.14.5; 1.173.6;) with the general meaning of 'head-dress, head decoration' assigned to it by Geldner (*HOS* 34, p. 157). G*Wö* translates *opaśá* as 'tuft of hair, braid, tail'.

The compound *góopaśā*, describing as it does a goad (*áṣṭrā*) used to drive a herd, may signify a tuft of leather strands attached to the *áṣṭrā*. It could also be, as pointed out by L*RV*, a goad made of a cow-tail. In either case, *áṣṭrā góopaśā* is a sort of whip used to move animals. Cf. 7.33.6. Atkins[29] who discusses fully this term, defines it here as 'leather-bound' or 'equipped with

27. Pūṣan.
28. The goad.
29. S. D. Atkins, *Pūṣan in the Rig-Veda*, Ph. D. diss. (Princeton, 1941) p. 60.

leather thongs'. The *áṣṭrā* according to Renou's suggestion (*EVP* 15, p. 148) seems more like a spur: "Ton aiguillon qui a pour ornement-frontal (l' image d') une vache..".

l) *gó* — a hide: 10.106.10ab (To the Aśvins)
ārañgaréva mádhv érayethe sāraghéva gávi nīcīnabāre
Like two bees you produce honey, like two bees in a hide which opens downward.

Gávi nīcīnabāre has been discussed by H. Lüders.[30] He has demonstrated that *gó* probably represents a container made of leather since *nīcīnabāra*, in its only other two occurrences, is used with *kávandha* (5.85.3) and *avatá* (8.72.10). *Avatá* in 1.116.9 is described as *jihmábāra* 'having an opening on one side'. Cf. Hillebrandt, *Ved. Myth.* I, 478; Renou, *EVP* 16, p. 75.

3. *Cattle as the Desired Object of a Fight or Contest*

2.25.4b (To Brahmaṇaspati)
sá sátvabhiḥ prathamó góṣu gacchati
He[31] goes as first with warriors for cattle.
2b may be compared to 1.83.1a
√gam góṣu also in 4.38.4; 8.71.5: *góṣu gántā*

6.66.8 (To the Maruts)
nā́sya vartā́ ná tarutā́ nv àsti máruto yám ávatha vā́jasātau
toké vā góṣu tánaye yám apsú sá vrajáṃ dártā pā́rye ádha dyóḥ
There is certainly neither obstructor nor conqueror for him O Maruts whom you protect in battle,
Or when [it is] for offspring and cattle, for progeny, for waters.
He is moreover, the splitter of the cow-pen at the decisive day.

6.66.8c = 6.25.4c (except 8c has '*yám*' where 4c has '*yád*'); also cf. 6.19.12d.
In 6.31.1 *gó* is replaced by *sū́ra* in the series: *toká, áp, tánaya, sū́ra*.

30. *Varuṇa* II, (Göttingen, 1959), 342, fn. 6.
31. The mortal whom Brahmaṇaspati protects.

Vrajá: Geldner, in his study of this term (*Ved. Stud.* II, 282) defines this occurrence of *vrajá* as 'herd' following Sāyaṇa's interpretation (p. 283). In his translation (*HOS* 34. p. 169) Geldner renders the term as 'pen', which does seem to be better in this verse. Cf. 8.32.5 where *gó vrajá*, obj. of *ví* √*dṝ* is compared to *púr*; see 4.20.6 where *vrajá* obj. of *ádatṛ* is modified by *sthávira*, thus indicating a structure. Further, 6.66.8 as well as 3.30.21 (see below) evoke, probably for magical intent, the language and imagery associated with the myth of cows withheld by the Paṇis. In that myth, *vrajá* also signifies an enclosure (see p. 102 cf. Geldner, *Ved. Stud.* II, 283ff).
Párye....dyóḥ — according to Grassmann 'on the decisive day', like *párye diví*; so also Ludwig (*RV* V, p. 257); cf. Renou (*EVP* 10, p. 99). The 'decisive day' could be 'the day of the contest' and/or 'the day of the New Year, celebrated by a potlatch festival' (see F. B. J. Kuiper, "Rigvedic *párye diví*" *IIJ* 5, p. 171).

5.34.8 (To Indra)

sáṃ yáj jánau sudhánau viśváśardhasāv áved índro maghávā góṣu śubhríṣu
yújaṃ hy ànyám ákṛta pravepany úd īṃ gávyaṃ sṛjate sátvabhir dhúniḥ

When Indra Maghavan came to know[32] that two rich groups with [their] full array [were fighting][33] for splendid cattle,

The Shaker[34] made one of them [his] friend; the Thunderer[34] with [his] followers sets free the herd for him.

The meaning of *gó* is 'cattle as the prize of war'. In keeping with the tenor of the rest of the hymn, verse 8 speaks of the decisive nature of Indra's support; in this case, the favored side wins the herd (*gávya*). The particular interest of this verse lies in its use of the verb *úd* √*sṛj* with *gávya*. Here the verb describes an actual situation. *Úd* √*sṛj* is frequently employed in the myth of the Paṇis. See Geldner (*HOS* 34, p. 35, fn. 8d) for *ud* √*sṛj* passages in this myth.

32. *Ávet*: Sāy. √*vid* (so also L*RV*); Geldner (*HOS* 34, p. 34) √*av* also possible. Oldenberg (*Noten* 11, p. 332) rejects √*av* in favor of √*vid*, possibly √*vi*.
33. Sāy. — *janau* : *parasparapratidvandvinau*.
34. Indra.

6.35.2cd (To Indra)

tridhā́tu gā́ ádhi jayāsi góṣv índra dyumnáṃ svàrvad dhehy asmé

Threefold may you gain cattle in addition to cattle,
O Indra give us lustrous splendour.

It is in combat (pāda b) that Indra is to help his worshippers capture cattle. Yet it is difficult to determine whether the reference here is to an actual cattle raid or to the struggle to free the cows from the Paṇis' hold. *Tridhā́tu* and *dyumná svàrvat* suggest the myth of the Paṇis (cf. 10.67.4); on the other hand, the general tone of 6.35 points to a real request for cattle as the prize of war. Note that *svar*-sustains the ambiguity, implying as it does both material and immaterial gains.

7.32.16cd (To Indra)

satrā́ víśvasya paramásya rājasi nákiṣ ṭvā góṣu vṛṇvate

You always rule over all of the highest; none can restrain you among the cattle.

Pāda d signifies: none can restrain you in a fight for cattle. Geldner (*HOS* 34, p. 209) compares pāda d to 8.45.21 where *yudhí* replaces *góṣu.*

3.30.21ab (To Indra)

ā́ no gotrā́ dardṛhi gopate gā́ḥ sám asmábhyaṃ sanáyo yantu vā́jāḥ

O Lord of the Kine, split open the cow-stalls for us; [let us have] cattle that rewards come to us, the gains of war.

Again ambiguity of context; probably a plea for successfully capturing actual cattle, couched in the language of the myth. *Gotra*[35] *ā́√dṛ* is reminiscent of Indra's release of the Paṇis' cows.[36] Also, as pointed out by Geldner (*HOS* 33, p. 366) pāda 21a may be compared with 8.34.14 wherein *gávya sahásra ā́√dṛ* seems to be used literally. The use of equivocal terminology should be considered intentional. The whole point of the hymn is to secure

35. See Geldner, *Ved. Stud.* II, 275ff for a complete discussion on *gotrá*; he favors the meaning 'here' and not 'cow-stall'. However, 'stall' seems to be intended here; cf. 6.66.8 *vrajáṃ dártā.*

36. See Chap. IV ff. Cf. phrase with 4.16.8; 8.32.5. Both these verses describe the myth of the Paṇis.

Indra's aid and protection in battle (vss. 15, 22). Among the rewards for the victor are cattle (v. 21). The worshippers address their pleas for wealth and victory specifically to Indra because his great cosmic deeds involve, in part, the piercing of the cow-stall and the freeing of cows (cf. v. 10). For assurance of similar success on earth, the language of v. 21 is evocative of mythic parallels attributed to Indra.

3.31.21 (To Indra)

ádediṣṭa vṛtrahā́ gópatir gā́ antáḥ kṛṣṇā́m̐ aruṣaír dhā́mabhir gāt
prá sūnṛ́tā diśámāna ṛténa dúraś ca víśvā avṛṇod ápa svā́ḥ

a) The Vṛtra-killer, the lord of cows, has granted cattle. He removed the black ones (i.e. the enemies of the Vedic peoples[37]) [from the booty] by the instrumentality of the "seat" of power[38] (residing) in the reddish-colored (gods).
Exhibiting liberality in accordance with the *ṛtá*, he opened all his doors.

b) The Vṛtra-killer, lord of the cows, has granted cattle. He scattered the darkness by means of the phenomena (in which reside the power) of the reddish-colored (gods).
Exhibiting liberality in accordance with the *ṛtá*, he opened all his [i.e. Vala's] doors.

These two translations try to demonstrate that verse 21 can be read and interpreted as belonging to two domains of action: the actual (a) and the mythological (b). The first meaning centers on Indra's known liberality, especially in granting cattle to his worshippers (pāda a; see p. 14 above). He favors his followers and takes the spoils of war from their enemies (pāda b) by marshalling the *dhāman* - of the gods of light (i.e. Agni [cf. 4.28.3; 7.5.6], Sūrya, Uṣas etc). Imparting wealth to the sacrificers (i.e. pāda d), Indra's liberality[39] works to support Cosmic Law (pāda c).

37. The meaning of *kṛṣṇá* here follows Gonda (*The Meaning of the Sanskrit term dhāman-*, in *Verhandelingen der Koninklijke Nederlandse Akademie van Wetenschappen, Afd. Letterkunde* N. S. 73, No. 2,1967, p. 41) and Renou (*EVP* 17, p. 73 "indigènes").

38. On *dhāman* — see Gonda, ibid. especially 40-41.

39. On *sūnṛta* see Renou, *Études sur le Vocabulaire du Ṛgveda,* No. 5 in Publications de l'Institut Français d'Indologie (Pondichéry, 1958), 8ff. Cf. Kuiper, "Verbal Contest", p. 236, 232: "vital strength".

This meaning underscores the main concern of verse 21, namely achieving success and booty in battle (see v. 20). The mythological meaning strengthens the actual objective since it refers to that mythic exploit of Indra wherein he released cows from the enemies of the Vedic sacrifice and gave them to its upholders; thus verse 21 can be read as a reference to the myth of the Paṇis. Pāda b then alludes to the dispersal of darkness (on *kṛṣṇá* as Night cf. 10. 61.4) by the light of the dawns which are released by Indra (e.g. 10.120.8; cf. Gonda, "dhāman-" p. 41). This release, also done in accordance with *ṛtá*, constitutes Indra's *sūnṛ́ta*; it was effected when the doors of Vala were opened (see under 6.17.6 and also Geldner, *HOS* 34, ad 6.35.5). Note that pāda d = 10.120.8d, a verse dealing with the myth of the Paṇis.

Verse 21 demonstrates how well suited are pleas to Indra regarding the winning of cows in battle since he won them from the Paṇis as well as from Vṛtra (*vṛtrahā́* in 'a').

See also Geldner's discussion on 3.31.21 in *Der Rigveda in Auswahl,* II, 53.

5.6.7. (To Agni)

táva tyé agne arcáyo máhi vrādhanta vājínaḥ
yé pátvabhiḥ śaphā́nāṃ vrajā́ bhuránta gónām íṣaṃ stotṛ́bhya ā́ bhara

These flames of yours, O Agni, rise up mightily, [as] spirited [steeds].
Who, with blows of their hoofs, shake the stalls of cattle; bring food to the praisers.

Double imagery is sustained in this verse. Agni's flames are metaphorically called charging, or spirited steeds (cf. Geldner, *HOS* 33: 2.5.1). This metaphor allows pādas cd to be understood in two ways, namely from the point of view of the flames or the horses. Correspondingly, *gó* has two connotations:

a) the milk oblation which the flames agitate
b) the enclosed cattle which the horses try to stir up during battle.

Vrajā́ m.; case for *ā* ending ? M-W *Dict.* and G*Wö* consider this example as the only neuter occurrence. Geldner's proposal (*HOS* 34, p. 9) has greater possibility: *vrajā́* - dual, acc. m., as *dárvī* in verse 9. *Vrajā́*, from the standpoint of the flames, could be the containers or implements in contact with the milk oblation. For *bhur*-and fire see Renou *EVP* 13, p. 109.

4.38.4ab (To Dadhikrā)

yáḥ smārundhānó gádhyā samátsu sánutaraś cárati góṣu gácchan

He who always besieges booty in battles, furtive [or 'winning more' *sánutara-*] he roams about, setting out for cattle.

The subject is the horse Dadhikrā, believed by some scholars to be an actual charger, and by others to be a symbolic reference to the sun or lightning.[40] Dadhikrā excels in capturing booty, especially cattle; the reference seems to reflect an actual method employed in cattle wars, where the horse is used to drive off the herd (cf. 6.28.4).
G*Wö*: *góṣu* = milk or butter (especially as oblation for Agni). This meaning is unlikely; compare 2.25.4 where √*gam góṣu* also denotes 'going for cattle' in battle.
Renou (*EVP* 15, p. 162): "*gádhya* est ailleurs ép. de *vā́ja*, *EVP* 13, p. 131: ici en emploi absolu ou elliptique." See also p. 162 for *sánutara-*. Mayrhofer (Leiferung 23, p. 427) under *sanutáḥ*: "Fraglich bleibt, ob RV 4.38.4 sánutara - als etwa 'verstohlen, heimlich' hierhergehört; besser als 'mehr gewinnend' aufzufassen (:sanóti) ? S. Wach. II/2, 596, 608, 698."

8.75.7 (To Agni)

kám u ṣvid asya sénayāgnér ápākacakṣasaḥ
paṇíṃ góṣu staràmahe

Which miser shall we overthrow for cattle, with the missile of this Agni, who has eyes in [his] back ?

The ṛṣi of this hymn, Virūpa, praises Agni so that the god may leave the opposing camp and favor Virūpa's side (verse 15). The fight is for cattle (verse 11); the foe is the *paṇí*.
Sénayā: see 10.156.2, below.

40. A. A. Macdonell, *Vedic Mythology* (Strassburg, 1897), 148.

10.156.2 (To Agni)

yáyā gā́ ākárāmahe sénayāgne tā́votyā́
tā́m no hinva maghā́ttaye

With the missile, with which we drive the cattle together, O Agni, with your protection,
Send that forth, for us to receive wealth.

sénā: Agni's missile refers to his flame, much as *hetí* f. 'missile, weapon' (M-W *Dict.*) may designate Agni's flame (10.142.3). *Sénā* may be some sort of fiery projectile weapon (cf. 6.6.5) used by the cattle fighter to collect the herd to his side. Renou (*EVP* 14, p. 100): "*sénā* "armée," mais l'autre acception, "arme de jet", est postulée concurrement par *hinva c.*"
Sāyaṇa: *gaḥ — dakṣiṇā*
Singh[41] mentions the use of fire in warfare. He conjectures that flaming arrows were used; however the passages from the RV he cites are not so specific on this detail; (cf. Blair, *Heat*, p. 84).

6.28.4 (In Praise of Cows)

ná tā́ árvā reṇúkakāṭo aśnuten á saṃskṛtatrám úpa yanti tā́ abhí
urugāyám ábhayaṃ tásya tā́ ánu gā́vo mártasya ví caranti yájvanaḥ

The steed, with dust-covered neck, does not reach them, nor do they go to the saṃskṛtatrá.
The cows of the man who sacrifices roam over a wide and secure [path].

Unequivocally, it is the cows of the *yájamāna* who are kept safe from danger. It is hoped that they will be protected from horses used in cattle fights (pāda a; cf. 4.38.4).

reṇúkakāṭa: RV hapaxl. Mayrhofer, I (under *kakā́ṭikā*), suggests that *kṛkāṭam* is to be associated with *kakāṭa*. So also Geldner *HOS* 34, p. 127. Whitney[42] in the commentary to AV 4.21.4 cites that *kakāṭa* is explained by *udbhedaka* *saṃskṛtatrá*: RV hapaxl. M-W *Dict.* derives the term from *sám* $\sqrt{}$*kṛ*. Sāy.: slaughtering block. This meaning (from $\sqrt{}$*kṛt* 'to cut'), is not accepted by Debrunner (*AiG* II_2, p. 78); he offers "das Zugerichtete (*saṃskṛtá-*) schützend" (*-tra-*).

41. *Anc. Ind. Warfare*, p. 126.
42. *Atharva-Veda Saṃhitā, HOS* 7, 187.

pánthām is understood: cf. 8.68.13
In the above examples, cows certainly are the contested object of a fight. But is this a secular or a religious fight ? The question is part of a larger problem. Are we justified in giving a secular interpretation to parts of the Rig Veda, or, should we assume that this text is solely concerned with material of a religious nature?

In my reading of this text, it does seem to me that activity from daily life is occasionally woven, without hesitation, into the hymns. Section D below, on similes using *gó* etc. demonstrates this tendency. To be sure, these images from actual life are introduced into the text for the purpose of clarifying the mysterious, numinous powers of the transcendental.

The robust quality which presumably characterized Vedic life, may also be reflected in the above references to cattle contests. Taken as allusions to actual fights between supporters and non-supporters of Vedic conventions, the above verses would represent requests to specific gods to assist the worshippers in secular skirmishes. The frequent mythic terminology and imagery met with in these verses would call into activity those powers which the god(s) used in winning 'cattle' as a result of a cosmic conflict. Understood in this way, the references to cattle wars act quite differently in the text than those other secular references, the *gó* similes. For whereas the latter act as the known quantum (i.e. customary activity in an agricultural society) used to elucidate the unknown (i.e. supra-normal activity of the divine), in the former, the known quantum (i.e. earthly cattle wars) stands to gain through establishing a correct correlation between this activity and divine activity.

Kuiper in "The Ancient Aryan Verbal Contest" (*IIJ* 4, 117ff) raises serious objections to the introduction of secular ideas into the Rig Veda. This important paper prepares the groundwork for ascribing many seemingly secular references to a religious context. If, through further corroborating evidence, Kuiper's hypothesis (an expansion on Hillebrandt's winter solstice theory) proves to be correct, namely that much of the Rig Veda, especially the oldest section, is "a textbook for the new year ritual" (p. 222), and, that this ritual comprized word-contests, chariot contests and potlatch ceremonies, then numerous passages, including those on cattle fights, will require a different interpretation.

According to Kuiper, the cosmological event which the new year's festival celebrates is the critical transition from the old to the new year; the hymns to Indra describing his combat with Vṛtra, and, the freeing of sunlight, recount this contested event (see Kuiper, p. 221). At the time of the festival, this cosmic fight was ritualized and imitated on earth so as "to assist Indra in his fight against Death and Darkness. . ." (p. 221). (On other examples of a symbiotic relationship between Vedic myth and ritual, see Kuiper's remarks on the Mahāvrata ceremony, p. 221; also D. Srinivasan, "Saṃdhyā: Myth and Ritual" *IIJ* 15.1 [1973], pp. 161-178).

Eliminating all secularism and following these suggestions, the above references to cattle fights would probably not describe mock battles, but rather actual ritualized combats between Aryans and non-Aryans at the time of the new year ritual. Kuiper cautiously suggests: "Although it is advisable in principle to omit all reconstructions of possibly underlying ideas which are not explicitly stated in our texts, the fact that the Rigveda often associates the ideas of war and contests allows us to conjecture that war, no less than present-giving, contests and chariot-races, was thought of as stimulating the creative forces of the Cosmos during the winter ritual" (p. 269).

The Old Aryan winter ritual, according to Kuiper, was a replica of the primordial contest between the powers of the nether world and upper world; as such, it is a ritual celebrating the original creation to effectuate annual re-creation. The argument goes that since the new year's ritual aims to reiterate the cosmic creation act, a nd, in this, is supported by an actual ritualized ombat the prize of battle can consist of elements both necessary for creation and for daily well-being (p. 270).

There is much evidence in the 'cattle fighting' passages to support Kuiper's hypothesis:

1. The image of a formal ritual combat between two organized

groups rather than an impromptu cattle raid could be advanced by 5.34.8; 8.75.7,15.

2. Terminology parallel to Kuiper's examples
   a) *párye dyóḥ* (6.66.8)
   b) *sūnṛ́ta* (3.31.2) see Kuiper p. 232, 236; *maghávan* (5.34.8) see Kuiper, p. 238.
   c) *gó* (cf. Kuiper, p. 272) and *vā́ja* (3.30.21): "as the wealth and prestige won in the ceremonial contest" (Kuiper, p. 240; 239).
   d) *svàr*-(6.35.2) see Kuiper 220.
   e) *toká, gó, tánaya, áp* (etc. see 6.66.8); cf. Kuiper p. 268; 270.

3. The correlation between the Indra mythology and cattle fighting themes, brought about through interweaving imagery (3.31.21) and terminology (3.30.21; 6.35.2; 5.34.8; 6.66.8) would be explained thus: the ritual combat, in which Aryans fought to capture the actual goods of their enemies, reenacted the cosmic battle. Whereas actual cattle are among the prize of the ritualized war, 'cattle' symbolizing 'dawn's light' were won on the cosmic plane.

4. *The Sacrificer Gains the Protection of his Cows*

9.11.3 (To Soma)

sá naḥ pavasva śáṃ gáve śáṃ jánāya śáṃ árvate
śáṃ rājann óṣadhībhyaḥ

Purify yourself [to bring][43] well-being for our cow(s), well-being for our people, well-being for our horse(s),
Well-being, O King,[44] for the plants.

Sám with *gó*, common phrase to express the wish for the health and safety of the herd (so also 1.43.6; 7.35.12; 8.5.20; 9.11.7; 9.61.15). All these verses except 7.35.12, use the dat. of *gó*; dat. also with *śárman* (8.30.4).

10.106.11c (To the Aśvins)

yáśo ná pakvám mádhu góṣv antár

43. Cf. 1.43.6 $\sqrt{}$*kṛ* and *śám*.
44. Soma.

[Put] cooked sweet [milk], as splendour, inside the cows.

Pakvám mádhu refers to the cows' milk (Blair, *Heat*, p. 133), most often said to be 'put' in the cows (Blair, ibid.).
yáśas is defined as 'beauty, splendour, glory, fame, favor' (Mayrhofer 18, p. 12). See Renou's notes (*EVP* 3, 38) on *yáśas*, properly "marque distinctive". The etymology is not clear (see A. Walde, J. Pokorny, *Wörterbuch*, 195). Renou (p. 38) postulates the root *√ *yaś*-from which the term would be derived. 'Milk' considered as *yáśas*, is both a splendour in the sense of a brilliant substance (cf. p. 49 ff), and, following Renou's suggestion, the distinctive attribute of the cow.

Of interest are occurrences of *yaśás*[45] and derivatives with words signifying 'light'. *Yáśasvat* modifies *uṣás* in 1.79.1 and 10.11.3. In 4.1.16 *yaśás* is used in connection with dawn's red glow: the red (dawn) became apparent by the glorious (light) of the cow (i.e. Uṣas)[46]; Renou (*EVP* 3, 7) and Geldner (*HOS* 33, p. 415) believe *yaśása góḥ* = milk. I would add that this 'milk' is to be taken metaphorically for 'the light of Dawn'[47]. Renou's understanding of *yáśas* clarifies all these occurrences. In the economic sphere, the milk[48] is the cow's *yáśas*; in the mythology, the *yáśas* of the cow Uṣas is her light which may be symbolically referred to as her 'milk' (see under 3.30.14). On the conceptual association between 'milk' and 'brightness' see p. 49 ff.

5. *Divine Protection Sought for Cows*

6.28.8 (To the Cows)

úpedám upaparcanám āsú góṣúpa pṛcyatām
úpa ṛṣabhásya rétasy úpendra táva vīryè

Let this mixture be mingled in these cows,
Mingled in the semen of the bull, mingled in your virility, Indra.

The function of the repetition (*úpa* and *upapárcana*) may be to focus magic power on the concept expressed by *úpa* √ *pṛc*. (Cf. J.

45. On the oxytonic accent see Debrunner, *AiG* II/2, 231.
46. *Āvír bhuvad aruṇī́r yaśásā góḥ*.
47. Cf. 2.34.12.
48. Or, sour milk, mixed with *soma*: 9.81.1 *dadhnā́...yaśásā gávām*.

Gonda, *Repetitions*, p. 185). *Upapárcana* is a RV hapax legomenon; it is used in AV 9.4.23, a hymn to accompany the gift of a bull. In verse 8 it should connote some sort of fructifying ritual oblation. *Upapárcana* as 'fertility agent' would be asked to make the cows, the actual bull of the herd and the god Indra more productive (on the divine bull or Lord of Cattle, see *Epithets;* cf. 4.19.7; also cf. 8.15.6 where the Cosmic Waters, often symbolized as 'cows' are said to be the wives of bull, Indra). 'Fertility' here also implies 'liberality'. *Upapárcana* could also refer to the *gávāśir* made by blending cows' milk (pāda b) and soma juices (pāda c); when imbibed by Indra (cf. 6.28.1d) it blends with, and heightens thereby, his virility (pāda d).

D. SIMILES

1. *Introduction*

For the analysis of conceptual development and transference, the most important part of this chapter is the present section dealing with similes. Through the use of a simile construction, associations are established which reveal the values and thought patterns peculiar to a people. The following similes demonstrate a particular cultural reaction to the economic usefulness of the cow. The cultural attitudes are reflected in the choice of imagery and in the selection of subjects these images are compared with.

The similes (*upamānas*) depict the sights and sounds familiar to the herder engaged in his daily routine;[49] indeed these similes should have entered the hymns from demotic life. From these similes it is learned that early in the morning the cattle stream from their pens and are driven with sticks[50] presumably unto the grazing grounds. There they wander freely about searching for food with apparent relish. In the pasture, mother cows low to the calf[51] and lavishly protect, nourish and fondle it. The scene of the grazing milk cow suggests the streams of milk that will soon flow when she is affectionately called with song to release her

49. C. R. Lanman, "Sanskrit Diction as affected by the interests of Herdsman, Priest and Gambler," *JAOS* 20 (1899), 12-17.

50. 7.33.6: *daṇḍā́ ivéd goájanāsa.*

51. 2.2.2; 8.88.1. On *svásara* see L. Renou, "Vedic svásara," *Vishveshvaranand Indological Journal*, Vol. I, pt. 1 (March 1963), 37-39. Cf. *Ved. Index* I, 232.

food. As dusk approaches, the cattle are led back to the warmth of the covered stalls; by the time it is dark they have settled in the pens.[52]

These rather ordinary sights gain in significance because they illustrate phenomena in nature, procedures in the ritual, and sentiments of gods and sacrificers. Thus, as illustrations taken from easily apprehended visual experiences, they serve to clarify those mysterious powers and sentiments which pertain to, or are released by, nature and the rite. Had Vedic thinkers explored the root cause of phenomena through systematic and objective study, their observations would have been marked by a greater degree of abstract conceptualization.[53] As it is, they chiefly broadened their scope of knowledge through the use of concrete analogies. The similes discussed in this section are in the main employed to bring some power or sentiment to the same level of understanding as the phenomenon to which it is compared.[54]

In order to use one concept to clarify another, the literal and suggestive capacity of the clarifying agent must necessarily be unambiguous. The *gó* similes are no exception; they demonstrate that a set of sympathetic feelings such as joy, tenderness, maternal love and generosity are regularly attributed to the cow.

On occasion, these comparisons reveal the thought progressions whereby 'cow' comes to symbolize a great variety of mythological ideas. In these instances, it is possible to watch the expansion of an image; the simile becomes the transitional point of reference in tracing the progression of a concept from the literal to the symbolic plane. For instance, in a cattle oriented economy, it is quite natural for the cow's milk to inspire a variety of illustrative and picturesque expressions. A Vedic example would be that light, like milk, is bright, radiant, glowing. This association developed into a singular pattern of conceptualization represented in similes which describe the rays of light as streams of milk (*góarṇas*). This analogy explains the inner logic of the mythological

52. 1.191.4: evening images; cf. verse 5: *pradoṣá*. On *ketú* "signes de la vie consciente" (Renou, *EVP* 16, p. 95; see also *EVP* 7, pp. 47,73).

53. Cf. J. Gonda, *Remarks on Similes in Sanskrit Literature*, Orientalia Rheno-Traiectina Vol. I (Leiden, 1949), pp. 12-13.

54. True also of 8.41.1; 6.6.5; 4.13.2; 5.63.5; 10.79.6.

representation of the sunrise. Sunrise is thought to occur when the goddess of the dawn (the Mother of the cows) rides through the heavens on a chariot pulled by milk cows.

In the RV similes[55] studied below the terms (*gó, dhenú, sudúghā, vāśrá* and *gó* compounds) as well as the context, are to be taken literally.

The similes have been divided into two main groups. The first consists of formulaic similes (No. 2). These passages are highly conventionalized expressions which may function as charms. They clearly indicate that the cow is conceived as the summation of feminine bounty, freely and lovingly bestowed. The similes in the second group are arranged according to the subject they modify (Nos. 3-6). The comparisons in this group are vivid and imaginative; in most cases, the underlying rationale for a particular metaphorical usage of cow is revealed. This often turns out to be the image of the flow of the cow's milk; so for example rain, light and water come to be associated with the cow.

2. *Formulaic Similes*

(a) The movement of the grazing herd

The coming and going of the herd should have been one of the most common sights in a Vedic community.[56] The following three similes refer to this event, in particular, the size and home-coming of the herd.

8.46.30a (To Indra)
gā́vo ná yūthám úpa yanti vádhrayaḥ
the geldings come as a herd of cattle.
Geldner (*HOS* 34, 363) and Patel[57] consider this verse part of the dānastuti. The simile is used to indicate quantity. Note that the two terms of the comparison instead of being in

55. For 'cow and her calf' similes in the AV see H. D. Velankar, "Similes in the Atharvaveda," *Journal of the Asiatic Society of Bombay*, N.S. Vol. 38, (1963), 25.

56. For reference to Vedic grazing and milking customs see *Vedic Index* I, 232.

57. M. Patel, *The Dānastutis of the Rig-Veda*, trans. B. H. Kapadia (Vallabha, Vidyanagar 1961), p. 26.

different cases to indicate relationship (i.e. *gónām*) are in the same nom. case (see Bergaigne, "Syntaxe", 92-94).

10.4.2ab (To Agni)

yáṃ tvā jánāso abhi saṃcáranti gắva uṣṇám iva vrajáṃ yaviṣṭha
You whom the people seek, as cattle a warm stall, O Youngest One,

Uṣṇám...vrajám: clearly indicates that enclosed and covered stalls were built (*LRV*, IV, 399; the collection of cattle in the stall is compared in 8.41.6 to the gathering of horses which are to be harnessed). In this and the following verse, Agni is praised as the protective, domestic fire.

1.66.9 (To Agni)

táṃ vaś carắthā vayáṃ vasatyắstaṃ ná gắvo nákṣanta iddhám
To him your [Agni] kindled, we, the wanderers [approach] for the sake of a resting place [for the night] as cattle approach [their] home.

The comparison is between *vayám* and *gắvaḥ*; note that the verb is placed with the subject of the simile (Bergaigne, "Syntaxe," 81). The meaning of the simile is much the same as the simile in 10.4.2.

The first part of the verse is uncertain; it can be translated in a variety of ways since the word sequence is difficult. *Carắthā* is problematic and there seems to be the need for some insertion for the sake of intelligibility. Renou (*EVP* 12, 14) translates: "Cet (Agni une fois) allumé, nous (autres l'atteignons) [pour vous], (soit) dans (sa) marche, (soit) dans (sa) demeure (fixe), tout comme les vaches atteignent le gîte-du-retour." *Carắthā* is an instr., correlative with *vasatyắ* (*EVP* 12, 87). Geldner (*HOS* 33, p. 88): "Zu diesem eurem (Agni) kommen die Wanderer (und) wir mit der Hausgenossenschaft wie die Kühe nach Hause, wenn er angezündet ist —". *Carắthā* is tried as nom. pl. and instr. s. in Oldenberg's two translations: "As cows go to their stalls, all that moves and we, for the sake of a dwelling, reach him who has been kindled."[58] "Diesen, den entflammten, erreicht—wie Kühe das

58. H. Oldenberg, *Vedic Hymns*, in *SBE* 46 (Oxford, 1897), 57.

Heim — euer Sichregen (und) wir mit unserm Verweilen" (*Noten* 11, p. 67; perhaps *caráthā* cf. 1.68.1; 1.70.3,7). Ludwig (*RV* I, p. 290; IV, p. 259) offers three possibilities, but discounts the third. "Zu disem euren mit allem sich regenden [gott], in der nacht wie zur wonung komen die Kühe dem entzündeten"; "Zu disem euren entzündeten gotte wie mit dem wanderer [Vāyu] des nachts zum stalle die rinder wir zur wonung [gelangen]". "Zu disem entzündeten mit dem wanderer zusammen komen wir euch um zu nächtigen wie die Kühe nach hause".

Both 1.66.9 and 10.4.2. feature the same sort of simile in association with Agni. The general meaning for both seems to be that people search out the domestic fire at night, as cattle their stalls. For cattle, this was routine (cf. 1.191.4). Cattle are not expected to wander about at night; should they be seen in the forest at night, it is a mirage caused by darkness (Geldner, *HOS* 35 on 10.146.3,4). According to 5.6.1, cows return at dusk to *agní*, the heating agent in their stall (?).

(b) As above, used as a Charm

In the next three examples, the same type of simile functions as a magical expression used to promote success.[59] Presumably, the herder's routine of taking the cattle out to graze at sunrise, and returning them home before sunset, had come to represent an event so repetitious and unfailing that it became expressive of, and associated with, the element of certainty and success. The simile in these examples confers success upon the subject which is in each case significant in the ritual.

10.97.8 (In Praise of Herbs)

úc chúṣmā óṣadhīnāṃ gāvo goṣṭhād īverate
dhánaṃ saniṣyántīnām ātmánaṃ táva pūruṣa

The powers of the plants stream forth as cattle from the stall,
Granting wealth, and your life O Man.

The simile describes how the juices extracted from plants stream forth; these are asked to cure the ailing man and bestow a reward upon the healer.

59. Also 10.149.4: *gávą iva grámam.*

9.66.12 (To Soma)

ácchā samudrám índavó 'staṃ gávo ná dhenávaḥ
ágmann ṛtásya yónim á

The (soma) drops have gone to the sea, as milk cows to their home,

To the womb of the *ṛtá*.

Dhenú—appositional modifier of *gó*.

6.41.1 (To Indra)

áheḷamāna úpa yāhi yajñáṃ túbhyaṃ pavanta índavaḥ sutásaḥ
gávo ná vajrint svám óko ácchéndrá gahi prathamó yajñíyānām

Being not displeased, approach the sacrifice; the pressed drops cleanse themselves for you.
As cattle to their own pen, O Thunder-wielder, come, O Indra, first to those worthy of sacrifice.

Uncertainty as to Indra's presence at the ritual is assuaged by offering his favorite oblation (ab). To paraphrase cd: May there be as much certainty in your coming to the sacrifice O...., as cattle returning to their pen.

(c) Calling the Cow for Milking

The following similes compare the calling of the cow at the time of milking[60] to the calling of Indra at the time of sacrifice. Milking is of course the action most representative of the cow's usefulness. In effect, calling a cow to milk may, in a general sense, be equated with asking someone to be beneficial. Asking the gods to be beneficial is the purpose of the *ṛṣi*'s invocation, and the

60. The verses do not indicate whether the cow is milked for the ritual oblation or for daily food. Ludwig (*RV*, V p. 2;118) favors the ritual context for 1.4.1 and 6.45.7. The four similes analyzed in c) are not repeated in the Śrauta literature. 10.42.2 (*dóhena gám úpa śikṣā sákhāyam*; Roth's emendation: *dóhe ná gám*..) reoccurs in Śāṅkhāyana Śrauta Sūtra 5.10.8 when the cow is milked in the Agniṣṭoma. It is possible to take *gám* in 10.42.2 as an appositive to *sákhāyam* (i.e. Indra); note that Indra is called a cow when his liberality is emphasized (6.45.26; cf. 8.14.3). On this vs. see Geldner (*HOS* 35, p. 196, fn. 2a).

desire to win favors from a god is referred to as 'milking him like a cow'.[61]

8.52.4cd (To Indra)

táṃ tvā vayáṃ sudúghām iva godúho juhūmasi śravasyávaḥ

Wishing to praise, we call you thus, as the milkers call to a good milking cow.

6.45.7 (To Indra)

brahmā́ṇaṃ bráhmávāhasaṃ gīrbhíḥ sákhāyam ṛgmíyam
gā́ṃ ná doháse huve

To the brahman, to whom the prayer is offered, with songs I call to the praiseworthy friend, as to a cow to be milked.

8.65.3 (To Indra)

ā́ tvā gīrbhír mahā́m urúṃ huvé gā́m iva bhójase
índra sómasya pītáye

With songs I call to you, the great, the expansive, as to a cow to be used [for milking],

O Indra, to drink the soma.

Bhójase: cf. *doháse* in 6.45.7, above.

1.4.1 (To Indra)

surūpakṛtnúm ūtáye sudúghām iva godúhe
juhūmási dyávi-dyavi

Assuming the right form, we daily call (him, i.e. Indra) for help. As (one calls) a good milk cow for the milker.

Godúh: used here as in 8.52.4; 1.164.26 where it means "the milker." Oldenberg (*Noten* 11, p. 3) suggests *godúhe* possibly under the influence of *ūtáye* and should read *godúhaḥ*, as in 8.52.4.

(d) Using the Ox to Plow

1.23.15 (v. 15 to Pūṣan)

utó sá máhyam índubhiḥ ṣáḍ yuktā́n̐ anuséṣidhat
góbhir yávaṃ ná carkṛṣat

61. i.e. 7.18.4.

And may he, driving forward six yoked ones, due to the soma drops,
Plow for me as [he would plow] barley with oxen.

Gó as 'ox' in the context of plowing.[62] (Cf. comments under 5.27.1). The priest hopes that by offering soma to Pūṣan he will be rewarded as one succeeds in getting a harvest when oxen are used to plow.

Anusidh - "l'implication d'un profit et d'un succès" (see Renou, *EVP* 17, p. 79). Atkins[63] suggests the following interpretation of the verse: "The bard asks Soma to drive, as a plowman drives his team of oxen when plowing the field, a team of six (composed of deities and set of deities) to the Soma-sacrifice." This interpretation is based on taking *sá* to refer to Soma (if *sá* were to refer to Pūṣan then Atkins states, "he would be asked to drive a team, one member of which would be himself), and changing *anuséṣidhat* to *ánu seṣidhat* and *carkṛṣat* to *cárkṛṣat*.

(e) Cows in the Pasture

In each of the four occurrences of the upamāna 'as cows in the pasture', the main verb √ *ran* compares some expected enjoyment of the gods (Soma: 1.91.13; Indra: 8.92.12)[64] or mortals (see 10.25.1; 5.53.16 below) to that of the cows, who delight in eating in the pasture (cf. 10.100.10).[65]

10.25.1 (To Soma); 5.53.16 (To the Maruts)

ráṇan gắvo ná yávase

they should delight as cows in the pasture

Ráṇan: subject for 10.25.1, perhaps the priests or the desires (*kắmaḥ*) in verse 2; for 5.53.16, the Maruts and the sacrificers (*LRV* V, 247).

62. So also *gắḥ* in 8.20.19.

63. *Pūṣan*, 31ff for complete exegesis.

64. "As cows (delight) in the pastures, we gladden you...with our praises". Cf. W. P. Schmid, "Die Kuh auf der Weide", *Indogermanische Forschungen* 64 (1958) 1-2. Note that Bergaigne ("Syntaxe", 88) considers *gắvaḥ* as *tvā*, dependent upon *raṇayāmasi*, and thus expects *gắḥ*.

65. Schmid, *op. cit.* 2.

The above examples permit us to understand the ellipsis occurring in 1.38.2. Pāda c reads: *kvà vo gā́vo ná raṇyanti.* Gonda[66] translates: "where do they take pleasure in you like the cows [t. p., viz. in pastures]" ?

The shepherd routinely accompanies the cows to pasture. The opposite situation (i.e. the cows leaving the pasture without their herder) is used as a simile to illustrate the unorderly departure (of an enemy ?, of the Maruts ? in 7.18.10, see Geldner *HOS* 34, p. 196).

(f) The Cow and her Calf

In the Rig Veda, pious devotion or human longing is evoked by the image of the cow with her calf. This image expresses maternal affection[67]; the cow, tender, abounding in milk and protective of its young, is the embodiment of maternal energy (e.g. 1.38.8; 9.12.2; 3.33.1). However, the simile based upon this image has already lost the specific meaning of motherly love, and acts more as a cliché to connote abundant devotion.

The expression 'as the cow to the calf' is an example of Gonda's type of simile which supplants an adverb.[68] 'Unfailingly', possibly 'affectionately' (10.145.6), 'reverently' (2.2.2; 9.12.2), 'munificently' (10.149.4) could well replace, yet keep the value of the simile. It will be noticed that the original 'motherly' quality has, with the possible exception of 10.149.4, been elaborated upon.

10.149.4 (To Savitṛ)

gā́va iva grā́maṃ yū́yudhir ivā́śvān vāśréva vatsáṃ sumánā dúhānā
pátir iva jāyā́m abhi no ny ètu dhartā́ divaḥ savitā́ viśvávāraḥ

As cattle to the village, as the fighter to his horses,
As the lowing cow, pleased and yielding milk, to the calf,
As husband to wife, so let Savitṛ, the supporter of heaven, bestower of all desires, approach us.

66. J. Gonda, *Ellipsis, Brachylogy and Other forms of Brevity in Speech in the Ṛgveda, Verhandeligen der Koninklijke Nederlandse Akademie van Wetenschappen, Afd. Letterkunde,* N. S. Vol. 67, No. 4. (Amsterdam 1960), 65.
67. Bloomfield, *RV Rep.* (*HOS* 24), 583.
68. Gonda, *Similes*, 28ff.

Each simile describes how the god is to approach the worshippers:

(1) unfailingly (having the same value as group 2b)
(2) resolutely
(3) munificently
(4) lovingly

Gáva á ná dhenávaḥ in 9.68.1 also belongs to this category: 'To the god (i.e. Soma) the drops containing sweetness have flowed as milk cows[69] [speed to their calves]. Cf. 1.32.2 also implying that the milk cows approach some thing. 8.22.4 suggests the same image: Let your benevolence, O Lords of Splendour, (speed) to us as a milk cow [to its calf].

In 7.103.2 the effect of the simile is adjectival (*gávām áha ná māyúr vatsínīnām*) expressing the 'joyous' sounds made by frogs with the coming of the rain.

(g) The Cow filled with Milk

The above similes could not be formulated were the cow not a symbol of motherhood. The cow's maternal nature, as well as the related quality of beneficence etc. is axiomatic in similes describing the 'cow filled with milk'.

The cow's copious stream of milk is compared to a variety of different situations: as the cow's udder is filled with milk, so should the priests fill Indra with soma (see 2.14.10); the swollen soma stalks, like cows with distended udders, are milked (i.e. pressed 8.9.19). As the udder of the cows [wherein the milk is cooked by Agni; cf. Śata. Br. II, 2,4,15] Agni is the seasoning of food (1.69.3).[70]

These comparisons show that the milk cow exemplifies overflowing abundance. Further, to be teeming with milk is concep-

69. *Dhenú* is an appositional modifier of *gó*.

70. *Vedhā́ ádṛpto agnír vijānánn ū́dhar ná gónāṃ svā́dmā pitūnā́m*. This trans. associates the miracle of the 'cooked' milk in the 'raw' cow with Agni (see p. 35). *Svā́dmā pitūnā́m* cf. 5.7.6. Another possibility is to understand this simile as Geldner (*HOS* 33, p. 90): as the udder ripens the milk and makes it tasty, so does the fire act upon food. This interpretation eliminates the 'miracle element' so consistently employed in the RV with the phenomenon of the already prepared food in the cow.

tualized in the RV as unbridled generosity. As such, liberality is characteristic of a milk cow (cf. 4.1.6 *maṅháneva dhenóḥ*), and this results in her becoming identified with Indra's *sūnṛ́tā*, as 8.14.3 demonstrates:

8.14.3 (To Indra)

dhenúṣ ṭa indra sūnṛ́tā yájamānāya sunvaté
gā́m áśvaṃ pipyúṣī duhe

Your liberality O Indra [is] a milk cow for the sacrificer who presses (soma);
Overflowing, (soma) it milks forth cow (s) and horse (s).

Sūnṛ́tā: Renou's study of this word (*Étude Voc. RV*, 84ff) shows that its original meaning ('gift, liberality') extends to signify the special gift of inspiration, i.e. poetic inspiration. As the beginning of this hymn speaks of material wealth (cf. vss. 1,2,4) *sūnṛ́tā* is here taken in its original sense.
Note in 1.8.8 *gómatī* describes Indra's *sūnṛ́tā*; for *gā́m* (pāda c) see pp. 9; 13.

3. *Deities Compared to gó, dhenú, usrā, vāśrā*

(a) Similes comparing Indra to *dhenú* and *gó*

The passages in which Indra is compared to a milk cow are probably in consequence of his liberality being considered a *dhenú* (see 8.14.3 above)[71]:

7.18.4ab (To Indra)

dhenúṃ ná tvā sūyávase dúdukṣann úpa bráhmāṇi sasṛje vásiṣṭhaḥ

Desiring to milk you, as a milk cow, in befitting pasturage,
Vasiṣṭha has showered prayers [upon you].

Sūyávase: with regard to Indra, 'at the sacrifice'. The whole comparison is most interesting: asking boons of Indra at the rite is likened to milking a cow in the pasture. There is no need to understand *ná vatsám* after *bráhmāṇi* (Geldner, *HOS* 34, p. 195). There is no similar example in the RV.

71. See also 6.45.26: Indra is a cow (*gaúḥ*) to him who longs for cattle (*gavyaté*). Cf. 8.1.10.

More often Indra is likened to *gó* meaning 'bull'. As might be expected, it is the strength of the bull which accounts for the comparison. Being mighty (*śākín*) as a bull (6.45.22), he prevails over men (*carṣaṇīsáh*) as a bull (8.1.2).[72] Indra is terrible (*bhīmá*) as a bull when he wishes to give (8.81.3). In addition to his physical power, Indra's *krátu* is also compared to a bull:

3.45.3ab (To Indra)

gambhīrā́n̐ udadhī́n̐r iva krātum puṣyasi gā́ iva

Deep as the seas, you possess an effective power, as bulls.

Gā́ iva: this simile may be explained by the simile occurring in 8.33.6 (*krátvā gaúr iva śākináḥ*). Perhaps it is due to his effective mental power (*krátu*) that Indra is also physically mighty as a bull.

(b.) Pṛśni as a Cow; the Maruts as Cattle

1.38.8 (To the Maruts)

vāśréva vidyún mimāti vatsáṃ ná mātā́ siṣakti
yád eṣāṃ vṛṣṭír ásarji

The lightning bellows as a lowing cow; it follows (the rain) as a mother her calf,
When their rain has been shed.

To shed rain is one of the Maruts' main function.

I understand the lightning to refer to Pṛśni (cf. 1.23.12 — the Maruts are born from the laughter of lightning). For Pṛśni as mother of the Maruts see Macdonell, *Ved. Myth.* p. 78. The lightning is said to follow the rain as a mother her calf, or, Pṛśni follows her offspring the Maruts. (For Pṛśni as 'cow' see Chap. 5). The Maruts, mainly because of their birth and strength, are likened to bulls and cattle. The troop is like a herd of cattle of equal zeal (8.20.21; 5.56.5); their excellent horn [symbol of strength ?, *LRV* V, p. 252; also Geldner *HOS* 34, re: 8.86.5] is made for prosperity [?][73] as that of cattle (5.59.3). As cows, as bulls, they are worthy of praise (see 1.168.2). Their force is

72. His *krátu* is *carṣaṇīsah* (5.35.1); cf. 8.33.6.

73. *Śriyáse:* cf. Gonda's remarks on *śriye* 5.55.3 (*Aspects of Early Viṣṇuism*, p. 181).

dreadful like a wild bull (5.56.3), or, as oxen difficult to yoke they shatter with their strength (5.56.4). Nevertheless the troop is said to be playful as a bull among the cows (1.37.5).[74]

(c) Apsarases as Cows

In 10.95.6,[75] a group of celestial Apsarases sped like ruddy colored (cows) and sounded as milk cows (i.e. as mother cows sound when calling to their calves, cf. 9.12.2). The term connoting a ruddy cow is *aruṇá*; *aruṇá* frequently describes the rays of dawn: 1.124.11; 5.80.3; 6.64.3. This description of the Apsarases emphasizes their feminine charm and their fertility (cf. Renou, *Vedic India* Vol. 3 in *Classical India* [Delhi, Varanasi] p. 72).

(d) Heaven and Earth (Rodasī, so Renou, *EVP* 12, p. 97 and Geldner *HOS* 34, p. 124 fn. 6a) like lowing cows approached Agni (1.95.6). The simile suggests that the Rodasī came to Agni with generosity and affection (cf. 10.149.4; 10.119.4).

(e) Uṣas as a cow (see Chaps. III and IV).

(f) The Demoness Dānu compared to *dhenú*

Dānu, the mother of Vṛtra, lies like a milk cow (*dhenú*) with her calf (i.e. Vṛtra 1.32.9).

4. *The Cow's Milk is compared to Light*

1.66.2b (To Agni)
páyo ná dhenúḥ śúcir vibhā́vā
like the milk (of) the cow, bright and shining

Śúcir and *vibhā́vā* refer to Agni.

Páyo ná dhenúḥ: both nouns are in the nominative; the simile is of the same type as *síndhur ná kṣódaḥ* in verse 10 (Bergaigne, "La Syntaxe", 95; Oldenberg, *Noten*, 11, p. 66).

74. See Geldner, *HOS* 33, p. 46. On *góṣv ághnyam* cf. Schmidt, *aghnya* - p. 24.

75. *Śriyé gā́vo ná dhenávo 'navanta*. On *śriyé*: Renou (*Étude Voc. RV* 37): "à l'envie"; Geldner (*HOS* 35, p. 301) "um die Wette"; Ludwig (*RV* II, p. 634) "zu glücke"; H. Oldenberg ("Vedic Words for 'Beautiful' and 'Beauty' ..." trans. from the German in *Rupam* No. 32, Oct. 1927, 101): 'beauty'. Gonda see fn. 73. For a discussion on the literary development of Urvaśī and Purūravas see D. D. Kosambi, *Myth and Reality*, 1962.

Verses 1 and 2 conserve the tenor of the preceding hymn, starting out with a poetic thrust which gradually diminishes (Renou, *EVP* 12, p. 86). Through a series of similes, different characteristics of the fire are described. Pāda b dwells on the radiant aspect of fire, comparing this aspect to the milk of the cow. The association established in this simile is important for the understanding of the whole series of *gó* similes and metaphors associated with the concept of light. What we have here is a comparison between fire and milk based upon the radiance of each element. While it is easy to admit of *śúci-* and *vibhā́va-* as descriptive of fire, it is not at all obvious how these adjectives are to be understood in relation to the cow's milk. *Śúci-* is derived from √*śuc* and means "leuchtend, strahlend, hell, rein (RV usw.)..." Mayrhofer Lief. 22, p. 377. *Vibhā́va-* from √*bhā* has much the same meaning in the RV (Mayrhofer II, p. 493: "strahlend, leuchtend"). However, the juxtaposition of 'cow's milk' and 'radiance' seems usual enough judging from the number of passages which associate the milk cow and her milk with the concepts of 'brightness' and 'light'.

The whiteness of milk should have prompted such descriptions as 'the white milk cow' (4.33.1 *śvaitarīṃ dhenúm*; i.e. the cow is described by what she contains), or, 'the white form' of soma (9.74.7 *śvetáṃ rūpáṃ kr̥ṇute yát siṣāsati*: 'when he wishes to acquire [a form] he assumes a white form'. Image of the *gávāśiḥ*: soma juice covered with milk). Soma becomes white because his goal is the *kaláśa* pot, itself white having been decked with milk (*ádha śvetáṃ kaláśaṃ góbhir aktáṃ* 9.74.8; 4.27.5). It is noteworthy however, that there are no passages in the RV describing *páyas* as *śvetá etc.* Instead, numerous passages insist upon another factor, namely that of the 'brightness' of milk, and, by extension, the 'brightness' of the milk cow. Examples are cited below:

1.137.3 *dhenúṃ ná vāsarī́m*. Sāy. *vāsarī́m bahukṣīrām*
5.1.3 see p. 61
6.35.5 *śukradúghasya dhenór*[76]
9.19.5 the soma cows (i.e. *vr̥ṣaṇyát-*) yield *śukrám...páyaḥ*

76. *Dhenú* may be taken both literally as the milk cow desired by the worshipper and metaphorically as Uṣas who produces morning light which is like a stream of milk (cf. 2.34.12).

9.91.3 *rúśat...páyaḥ* (more likely 'shining milk' than 'white milk' as transl. by Geldner; Renou).

3.58.4; 6.23.7; 7.21.1 *górjīka*. On *ṛjīkáḥ*: 'whose aspect is radiant, foam' see Mayrhofer II, 120. Cf. Wackernagel II, 102; II/2, 428. Thus *goṛjīka* could mean 'radiant with milk'. This description could well apply to the libation (*mádhu* 3.58.4), the soma (in 6.23.7 and 7.21.1 where *ándhas* refers to soma). The last two examples could refer to the *gávāśiḥ*

9.107.26 *jyótiḥ* could refer to the milk of the *gávāśiḥ* (cf. 3.30.14 ab: 'a great light has been placed in [her] udders; the raw cow wanders carrying about the cooked [milk]'. The cow is Uṣas; her rays of light are conceived as 'milk'. See Chap. III, The Myth of the Paṇis.

4.1.19 "Il a taraudé pour ainsi dire la clair mamelle des vaches...." (Renou, *EVP* 13, p. 3; *śúcy ū́dho atṛṇan ná gávām*....). The udder is bright since it contains the bright milk.

Why is 'brightness', 'radiance' a dominant characteristic of milk ? The conceptualization may reflect what was surely a marvel to Vedic man: that 'prepared' food is in a 'raw' animal. The phenomenon of 'cooked' milk in the 'raw' cow is brought about through divine power, most often that of Indra (see Blair, *Heat*, p. 133-4). It may be that 'brightness' represents 'the warmth' of the extracted milk, which thus appears to have been 'cooked'; 'brightness' may also represent 'the power of heat' (belonging to Indra, Blair, *Heat*, p. 134; or Agni, *Heat* p. 134, fn. 2, and note the Śata. Br. II, 2, 4, 15 reference) which 'prepared' the milk. In either case, it seems that a source of heat 'cooked' the milk in the 'raw' cow, thus making the milk ready for use; the heat also made the milk 'bright' in the sense of 'heated' or 'warm' when extracted. The conceptual relationships existing among 'bright' milk, 'heated' milk and 'cooked' milk may indicate why the figurative use of 'cow' and 'milk' appear so regularly and so prominently in the mythological descriptions of sunlight. This association appears to give rise to an image that assumes great importance in the mythology of Uṣas. The radiance of the early morning rays are considered to be like streams of milk (4.51.8; 4.52.5).

4.52.5 (To Uṣas)

práti bhadrā adṛkṣata gávāṃ sárgā ná raśmáyaḥ
óṣā́ aprā urú jrāyaḥ

The beautiful rays have appeared like streams of milk;
Uṣas has filled out the wide expanse.

Gávāṃ sárgā ná: 'like herds of cows' also possible, though probably not preferable, cf. 2.34.12 below.

2.34.12 cd (To the Maruts)

uṣā́ ná rāmī́r aruṇaír áporṇute mahó jyótiṣā śucatā́ góarṇasā

As Uṣas uncovers the nights with ruddy (beams) with a great light shining (as) a stream of milk.

If the rays of Uṣas are likened to streams of milk (*góarṇas* see Renou *EVP* 10,77) cannot the goddess herself be visualized as a cow ? This is precisely the analogy established by the simile in 1.92.4, below.

1.92.4b (To Uṣas and the Aśvins)

áporṇute vákṣa usréva bárjaham

She displays her breast as a cow her udder.

Possibly *rúśat—ū́dhaḥ* 10.31.11 also refers to the breast of Uṣas which contains *jyótiḥ* (3.30.14). Whereas Uṣas is likened to a milk cow (also 5.1.1 *dhenúm ivāyatī́m uṣā́sam*), her sister Night is compared to a barren cow (*stari* 1.122.2); ostensibly the absence of light is like the inability to conceive and produce milk. But when both sisters are mentioned in the dvandva *uṣā́sānáktā*, they are likened to a milk cow (cf. 1.186.4 and 7.2.6).

The similes of Uṣas clarify those epithets of Uṣas which single her out as a cow, and, the mother of cows.

5. *Milk Cows are compared to Water*

Streams (i.e. rains) having rent the sky with a rush of water poured forth, as cows which have milk (*dhenú* 5.53.7); rivers flow...as lowing (*vāśrā*) cows (*dhenú*) with their milk (10.75.4);[77] the Vípāś and Śutudrí, also rivers, press forward with their waters as two beautiful mother cows (*mātṛ́ gó*) licking their calf (3.33.1).[78]

It is of interest to note that in each of the above cases the flow of water is compared to some action of the mother cow. Though it is tempting to interpret the juxtaposition of water and mother cows as a result of their both being fertility symbols, the thrust of water, more than the fertilizing power of water is being emphasized here.

However, maternal energy is certainly a fundamental cause for the association of the Cosmic Waters with mother cows. In Vedic mythology, this flood represents a life-giving force essential for the creation of the universe.[79] In it are contained elements necessary for existence, namely moisture and light. Because the Waters beget life itself, they are called most motherly (6.50.7). In the creation myth, cows are the metaphorical equivalent for the Cosmic Waters; in the two similes below, cows exemplify a maternal, sustaining force, and as such are compared to the same concept in the cosmogonic realm.[80]

1.32.2cd (To Indra)
vāśrā́ iva dhenávaḥ syándamānā áñjaḥ samudrám áva jagmur ā́paḥ
As lowing milk cows flowing [with milk], the Cosmic Waters quickly descended to the ocean.

1.130.5 (To Indra)
tváṃ vṛ́thā nadyà indra sártavé 'cchā samudrám asṛjo ráthāñ iva vājayató ráthāñ iva
itá ūtī́r ayuñjata samānám ártham ákṣitam

77. Pāda 4b = 9.77.1d.
78. 'Calf' to be supplied as object of *rihāṇé*; cf. 1.186.7 and Nirukta 9.39c.
79. Brown, "Creation Myth," 97.
80. But note, 7.23.4a (*ā́paś cit pipyuḥ staryò ná gā́vo*). The *áp* are the Cosmic Waters. The meaning of the simile is difficult since these Waters, when released, are found to be pregnant. A usual mythic occurrence for *starī́* is in the Śayu legend (1.116.22; 1.117.20; 7.68.8); in this legend the Aśvins perform the miracle of making Śayu's barren cow productive. Perhaps *starī́* retains its association with the miraculous here, in which case, the Waters swelled as if by a miracle, that is, as if barren cows became fruitful.

dhenū́r iva mánave viśvádohaso jánāya viśvádohasaḥ

You O Indra, released the Waters to flow easily to the ocean, as cars, even as racing cars;
You O Indra, released the Waters to flow easily to the ocean, as chariots, even as chariots which contest for gains.
Hence they have applied [their] aids to one everlasting task,
They, as milk cows who yield all their milk for mankind, [giving] all milk to the people.

This entire verse is about the Cosmic Waters (*nadī́*) which Indra released. They are likened to milk cows because (a) each in its way supports life, and (b) in so doing, each exemplifies 'munificence' etc. *Dhenú* comes very close to the concept of Kā́madhenu. *Viśvádohas* means 'giving everything' (cf. 7.18.40).

6. *Similes comparing the Milk Cow to Religious Thought*[81]

One association contributing to a comparison between 'the cow' and 'the hymn' has already been mentioned, namely that hymns are thought 'to milk' the god as if he were a cow.[82] Another is based on savouring enjoyment: priests gladden Indra with prayers as cattle delight in the pastures (see 8.92.12).

The poet of 4.41.5 compares the ability to conceive 'visions' (*dhī́-*) which are fashioned into hymns, with a milk cow: "O Indra and Varuṇa, be ye lovers of this *dhīḥ* like two bulls of a cow; may she yield us milk, having gone as it were over the pasture..." (Gonda, *Visions*, p. 126). Sacred speech, product of *dhī́-*, personified as Vāc, is herself identified with the milk cow (8.100.11); it is she who is the *mahī́ gaúḥ* with a thousand streams of milk (4.41.5d; 10.101.9d; 10.133.7d) and who swells with everflowing udder (10.133.7).

Both 'cows' bestow a gift. To produce the regular milk, a cow goes to pasture. To produce the hymns ('milk') which flow from

81. A number of similes which feature *gó* and a term signifying 'prayer' do not illustrate the ideas given above: 10.127.8; 1.114.9 (see Schmid, "Weide" p. 2, fn. 7); 8.24.6; 8.43.17 are similes based on the to and fro movement of the grazing herd; 1.186.7; 10.119.4; 6.45.28; 4.41.8 are similes used to suggest 'devotion'.

82. 7.18.4.

Sacred Speech ('*mahī́ gaúh*'), this cow must be well attended and well fashioned, also needing, as it were, the right herder and the right pasture. (Gonda, *Visions*, p. 126). Such analogies prompted the following comparisons: "my *dhītayaḥ* ('materialized visions') go along like cows along the pastures..." (1.25.16; Gonda, *Visions*, p. 187); *dhiyaḥ* which swell like cows in the pasture (9.94.2).

CHAPTER III

THE COW IN THE VEDIC RITUAL

A. INTRODUCTION

The role of the cow in the Rig Vedic ritual[1] reaffirms the notions associated with her from the economic sphere, namely that she is the embodiment of feminine abundance. The varied and vital uses the cow serves in the rites sustain this notion.

To some extent the cow is the animal sacrificed and proffered to the gods.[2] In this capacity, care was taken to specify what sort of cow is to be sacrificed. That particular type of cow is called *vaśā́*. While the precise meaning of this term is elusive, it does seem to specify the cow reserved for the Brahmans. Mayrhofer[3] declines to accept the meaning 'sterile cow' for *vaśā́*. It is found, however that terms for economically profitable cows are not used in contexts implying that they were sacrificed.[4]

The essential function of the cow in the ritual is to provide for the offering. She is the supplier of the milk and milk products which are used for the oblation (cf. 1.187.11: *táṃ tvā vayám pito vácobhir gā́vo ná havyā́ suṣūdima*). Her importance in this capacity is singled out by the term *havyasū́d*, 'providing the oblation' (1.93.12; 4.50.5) used only to describe the milk cow (*usríyā*).

The cow yields her milk while other offerings are being prepared (*sākáṃ gā́vaḥ súvate pácyate yávo* 1.135.8). The milk, considered to be the cow's gift (*niṣṣídh* 3.55.8[5]; *saní* 3.1.23[6]) is poured into the

1. *Gó* as 'ox' also occurs in the ritual context (see 10.155.5; 10.165.5).

2. For a comparative study of cattle as the sacrificed animal among the Indo-European peoples, see E. Mayrhofer-Passler, "Haustieropfer bei den Indoiraniern und den anderen Indogermanischen Völkern", *Archiv Orientalni* 21 (1953), 182ff.

3. Mayrhofer, Lief. 20, p. 169.

4. See fn. 12.

5. For a different interpretation see Geldner, *HOS* 33, p. 400.

6. *Íḷām agne...saníṃ góḥ...hávamānāya sādha:* advance the oblation, the gift of the cow, for the invoker O Agni. The image is one of the flames sending upward, to the gods, the milk oblation. This verse is frequently found in hymns to Agni (3.5.11; 3.6.11; 3.7.11; 3.15.7; 3.22.5; 3.23.5).

sacrificial fire. Agni is said to value highly the cows and wood (1.70.9) whose milk and timber he feeds upon. These are expected to be present in a sacrifice to Agni.[7]

The priests' chanting accompanies the pouring of the milk. That is, the prayer interweaves with the oblation (*antár* √*car* 3.55.8). Hymns unaccompanied by oblations would be quite unacceptable. Thus the cows, whose milk is used in the offering, are said to season (√*svad* 8.49.5) the praises, that is, heighten their appeal.

It is in connection with the preparation of soma that *gó* is most frequently mentioned in the ritual context. *Gó* may represent the cow which supplies the milk, or, the milk itself, which mixes with the soma juices. This blend, the *gávāśiḥ*, is one of the common ritual oblations (e.g. 1.137.1; 9.64.28).

The cows who furnish the oblation have a special hold upon Indra. They tempt him to attend the rites—he can be pursued with cows, caught with milk cows (8.2.6).[8] The cows provide the milk for Indra's oblation (cf. 8.69.6); in this capacity, each cow is at his service when, through mental stimulation, he comes among his patrons (1.173.8).[9]

Together with the concept of abundance, another concept is emphasized in the ritual context: the cow in the soma rite is the embodiment of fecundity. This becomes apparent from the manner in which the theme of the *gávāśiḥ* preparation is described.

These two concepts, fecundity and abundance, are among the major concepts associated with the cow in the RV. Both these

7. Cf. 8.102.19 where the sacrificer has neither the expected cow (*ághnyā*) for milk, nor axe for timber for the sacrifice. Perhaps this is a reference to a mental sacrifice (Geldner, *HOS* 34, p. 433).

8. *góbhir yád īm anyé asmán mṛgáṃ ná vrā́ mṛgáyante/abhitsáranti dhenúbhiḥ*. Since there is no recurrence of either of the verbs, nor of pādas a and c, and since the context is not limiting, *gó* and *dhenú* could take one of several meanings. They could mean 'cows'; 'milk'; *gó* could also be used figuratively, for the soma juice (Sāy.), as may be the case in 5.30.7. *Gó* and *dhenú* could be in apposition, or different concepts.

9. Geldner (*HOS* 33, v. cit.) follows Sāy., in considering the cow to represent the hymn.

concepts, encompassing as they are, do not however entirely account for the usage of 'cow' as a figurative appellation for goddesses, and, on occasion, gods. The cow's central role in the ritual, as the supplier of offerings and as the coveted prize of the priests should have added a special dimension to her stature. Her complete utility in the sacred rites should have provided the added stimulus needed to associate the cow, the female force of creative and sustaining energy, with the divine.

The ensuing discussion examines the cow's utility in the Rig Vedic ritual. The analysis is based upon the ritual contexts mentioning 'cow' terms, with emphasis on *gó*. The variety of contexts is noteworthy. The numerous functions performed by the cow enable the orderly procedure of the rites. Lack of milk for the oblation, *dákṣiṇā* for the priest, hide for the soma preparation and funerary wrappings could seriously hamper, if not halt the ritual proceedings. Absence of a cow, killed as offering to honor a god, or, as food to honor guests, would likewise hamper both state and household ceremonies. Thus, the notion, developed in the preceding chapter, namely that the cow is considered as a sustaining force, is reffirmed in the ritual context.

It is the figurative applications of 'cow' terms which predicate creative force to her. She is a symbol of fertility in connection with the *gávāśiḥ*. She is the stick which kindles Agni, thus giving birth to fire. Cows, as press-stones, cause the appearance of soma juice, as, analogously, they yield milk.

It is through analysis and understanding the concepts associated with the cow in the Rig Vedic economic and ritual spheres that a background is formed to determine the meaning and origin of figurative uses for 'cow' terms in Rig Vedic mythology.

B. CONTEXTS

1. The Cow as the Sacrificed Animal : *vaśā́*

Cows were used as the sacrificial offering, or, as expressed in the words of the RV, "they cast themselves to the gods' (10.169.3). *Gó* is rarely if ever used in the RV to denote this cow.[10] *Vaśā́*,

10. But note 10.90 which considers the sacrifice of Puruṣa as the instrument of creation. From this sacrifice, the cows as a group were created.

the food of Agni (*vaśánna* 8.43.11) is the term used for the cow offered into the ritual fire (2.7.5; 6.16.47; 10.91.14).

What sort cow does the term *vaśá* ("Vielleicht mit lat. *vacca* 'Kuh' ursprungsgleich", Mayrhofer, Lief. 20, p. 169) designate ? The term should carry a special meaning since it appears in a distinctive context. A *vaśá* is offered to Agni in four out of the five occurrences of the term.[11] It is the only term denoting 'cow' so used.

The suggestion that *vaśá* designates an unproductive cow does not go unchallenged (see Mayrhofer, ibid). One can say that *usrá, usríyā, ághnyā,*[12] all terms for a fruitful cow, are not mentioned in the RV as sacrificed animals. Also, there is some evidence in the AV to indicate that *vaśá* connotes a barren cow.[13] AV 12.4.16 has been interpreted to show that a *vaśá* has some recognizable defect[14]; AV 7.113.2 compares *parivṛktā* to *vaśá* (Macdonell

W. Norman Brown in "The Sources and Nature of *pūruṣa* in the Puruṣasūkta", *JAOS* 51 (1931) 117, considers *gó* as well as the other animals mentioned in 10.90.10, to refer to the creation of sacrificial animals. The phrase *śásā góḥ* in 5.41.18 offers another problem of interpretation in this area. The meaning of *śásā* is uncertain. Debrunner (*AiG* II/2, 247) takes *śásā* as the inst. from "**śása-* Schlachtung". Thus verse 18 could signify that through the killing of *gó*, the sacrificers would wish to attain favor, food, from the gods. As such, this would be the only occurrence where *gó* is the sacrificed animal. Another explanation for *śásā* is possible. The term can be taken from √ *śaṅs* (see K. L. Janert, Sinn und Bedeutung des Wortes "*dhāsi*.." [Wiesbaden, 1956] 39ff), with *śás* possibly a variant of *śáṃsa* 'recitation'. He also takes *góḥ* with *íṣam*: "die (Trank-) labung der Kuh," and cites 3.1.23 as analogous in syntax (i.e. *íḷām..góḥ*. This syntax is doubtful for both 3.1.23 and 5.41.18.

However, *śásā* from √*śaṅs* offers another interpretation for *śásā góḥ*, namely: "through the praise of the cow", or, "by the words of the *gó*" (*gó* being an epithet according to Renou *EVP* 5, p. 21: "grâce à l'instruction [impartie] par la Vache"). This last suggestion has much merit since it presumes a relation between *gó* in 'b' with...*sudánur mṛḷáyanti deví práti drávanti* ...in 'cd'. The divine cow seems to be Vāc (so also Janert, ibid. p. 40). In form and meaning *gór óhena* (1.180.5) is analogous to *śásā góḥ*. Possibly this 'cow' is the goddess Dakṣiṇā.

11. In the fifth case (6.63.9), a *vaśá* is given as *dákṣiṇā* (see p. 76).
12. See H. P. Schmidt. "*aghnya-*," *Zeitschrift für vergleichende Sprachforschung auf dem Gebiete der Indogermanischen Sprachen*, 78, 1/2 Heft (1963), 7. W. Norman Brown, "La vache sacrée dans la religion hindoue," *Annales*, IV (1964), 664.
13. So, J. Gonda, *The Savayajñas*, p. 332; Bloomfield in his translation of AV 12.4 (*SBE* 42) translates *vaśá* as 'sterile cow'.
14. Schmidt, "aghnya," 39.

and Keith, *Vedic Index* II, 273). However, this evidence is inconclusive since the AV can also use the term to signify a productive cow. In AV 10.10 *vaśā́* is a cow which, upon being offered, becomes transfigured as some cosmic material which gives rise to worldly forms and conventions. *Gó*, used interchangeably with *vaśā́* in AV 12.4 does not aid in determining the meaning for *vaśā́*. That only indicates that *vaśā́* is a bovine (*gó*, the most general term for cow, is non-restrictive).

Perhaps the most one can conclude from the evidence in the RV and AV is that *vaśā́*, taken literally, designates the cow reserved for the Brahmans, whether for their offering or their *dákṣiṇā*. The term may designate a barren cow although the texts do not directly state this.

2. *Gó* as 'ox' in the Ritual

The literal use of *gó* as obj. of *pári* $\sqrt{}$*nī* occurs only in two RV vss: 10.155.5; 10.165.5. AV 6.28 brings these vss. together (AV 6.28. 1b [variant *nayāmaḥ*[15]] = RV 10.165.5b, and AV 6.28.2b = RV 10.155.5a). It thus seems likely that the meaning for *gó* is the same in both RV passages.

Parallel passages to 10.155.5 show that other Vedic texts and commentators understand *gó* as 'ox'. VS[16] 35.18 includes the verse: Mahīdhara in his commentary explains *gām* with *anaḍvāham*. Griffith[17] associates the ox in verse 18 with *anaḍvah... saúrabheya* in verse 13. AG[18] 4.6.14 also quotes 10.155.5. AG 4.6.15 appears to elucidate the preceding verse: *piñgalenaḍvān pariṇeyaḥ syādityudāharanti*.

The context for both RV verses is ritualistic. Bṛh. D. 8.60 states that 10.155 is for the destruction of bad luck[19]; Bṛh. D. 8.69 states that 10.165 is used for expiation.[19] AG 4.6.14 is also included in a ceremony to remove an unlucky *gṛhya* fire.[20]

15. *Atharvaveda* (Śaunaka), ed. V. Bandhu (Hoshiarpur, 1961).

16. *Vājasaneyi Sanhitā*, ed. A. Weber (Berlin, London, 1852).

17. R. T. H. Griffith, *The White Yajurveda* (Benares, 1899), p. 290.

18. *Āśvalāyana Gṛhya Sūtra*, ed. R. N. Vidyaratna, *Bibliotheca Indica*, New Series CII (Calcutta, 1866).

19. A. A. Macdonnel, *Bṛhad Devatā*, *HOS* 6 (Cambridge, 1904), p. 309; p. 312.

20. See H. Oldenberg, *The Gṛhya Sūtras*, *SBE* 29 (Oxford, 1886), fn. 6,2. p. 246.

From the above evidence, it may be concluded that *gó* in 10.155. 5 and 10.165.5 is an ox, led about during a ceremony to avert or destroy misfortune.

3. *Gó* as Metonymy for the Milk Oblation

The milk oblation may be offered alone or in combination with the soma juice. Because of the elaborate and costly procedures of the Soma sacrifice, the simpler sacrifices, using milk, curds, ghee, grain, barley, and rice as offerings were probably more common and frequent. However, since the hymns of the RV deal in the main with the Soma rite, there are comparatively few references to the simpler offerings. This is especially true of the milk offering[21]; very few examples can be cited for *gó* as 'milk', outside of the soma preparation (vss. 1.95.8[22]; 1.151.8 [*gó* could also be metonymy for 'ghee']; 5.1.3; 5.3.2 may be considered as such examples).

5.1.3ab (To Agni)

yád īṃ gaṇásya raśanā́m ájīgaḥ śúcir añkte śúcibhir góbhir agníḥ

When she has awakened the line of the assemblage, bright Agni is anointed with bright streams of milk.

The entire verse is generally considered obscure in meaning and has thus been dealt with in a variety of ways. The various interpretations of pādas ab result from differences of opinion on *gaṇásya raśanā́m*, terms not easily associated with Agni (see G *Wö*). Also, it is difficult to relate interpretations of this phrase to Agni, as subject of *ájīgaḥ*. For Agni cannot be said to awaken[23] a 'row of flames' (Gr. *RV*), a 'line of priests' (Ludwig, *RV*), the 'rubbing cord of the fingers which rub the kindling sticks together' (Geldner, *HOS* 34); 'the sacrifice' (Renou, *EVP* 13, p. 103) since n the 'logic' of mythopoeic thought, it is Agni who is aroused by any one of the above. Oldenberg (*Noten* 11, p. 311) takes *raśanā́m* $\sqrt{}$*gṛ* as arousing prayer, citing 7.10.1 as a similar example (*dhī́* $\sqrt{}$*gṛ*). However, there is no other instance where *raśanā́* has

21. This offering may be mixed with other ingredients, such as honey (8.4.8).

22. Since Soma as well as the sacrificial fire receive milk and water, the wording of 1.95.8 (To Agni) and 9.68.9 (To Soma) is very similar.

23. So also Renou (*EVP* 13, p. 103) on *ájīgaḥ*.

the connotation of prayer. The following interpretation is suggested:

Pāda a — *ájīgaḥ*: It has been assumed in the above translations that Agni ought to be the subject of this verb. However, in 1.113.9 we find a very good parallel to pāda a which has Uṣas as the subject of *ájīgaḥ* (*yán mā́nuṣān yakṣyámāṇān ájīgas*...[24]). *Gaṇásya* in 5.1.3 refers to the human sacrificers, also called *gaṇá* in another hymn to Uṣas (5.79.5). Thus, pāda a could mean when Uṣas awoke the group of worshippers who wished to perform the sacrifice.

Pāda b — *śúcibhiḥ*: bright (see p. 49 ff); *góbhiḥ*: metonymy for either 'ghee' or 'milk'. Geldner (v. cit.) and G*Wö* understand *gó* to be the clarified butter, influenced perhaps by the phrase *śúci ghṛtá* occurring in 4.1.6; 6.10.2; 9.67.12. Also, there is one example of Agni being anointed (√*añj*) with *ghṛtá* (10.118.4). However, the combination we have here, √*añj*...*góbhiḥ* occurs at least 10 times in a context where *gó* represents the milk added to the soma juice (see p. 64) making *gó* as 'milk' more likely (so also for 5.3.2).

The general sense of the first two pādas seems to be: At daybreak, that is, when Uṣas has awakened the worshippers, Agni is given the oblation by the attending sacrificers.

The same phrase, *góbhiḥ*...√*añj*, occurs in 1.151.8, a hymn to Mitra-Varuṇa. Again, 'milk' could be applied here but since *ghṛtá* seems to be the usual type of oblation offered to these dual divinities (cf. Geldner, *HOS* 33, p. 210) *gó* in this verse is probably a metonymy for 'ghee'.

4. *Gó* etc. in the Soma Preparation

The preparation of the soma offering is a well defined procedure in which the cow and her products play an important part.

The stalks of the soma plant are prepared for the pressing by being first bathed in water; this causes them to swell.[25] Next the

24. On Uṣas plus causative √*gṛ* cf. also 1.113.4-6; 3.58.1; 6.65.1; 7.75.1.

25. Geldner, *HOS* 35, 5; the RV may know of this practice but does not use it regularly (A. Hillebrandt, *Ved. Myth.*, I, 1950.

priests pound the extended stalks with stones to extract the juice. This process takes place above a skin of cow-hide. The juice which collects upon the hide is then poured through a sieve made of sheep's wool. This is done to remove any gross particles. The resultant liquid is clear, and in this pure state it is spoken of as Pavamāna.

Soma may also be blended with a number of ingredients. It is then poured into wooden vats laden with water.[26] To this, the blend is added. It may consist of milk (3.35.8; 6.40.2; 2.36.1; 9.82.3; 6.47.14) or sour milk, or barley.[27] Adding milk to soma makes it palatable, sweet (*svādú* 8.2.3; √*svad* 9.62.5), perhaps milder, though still powerful (*śuṣmín* 9.14.3) and capable of arousing elation (*máda* 9.45.3; 9.43.1; 8.82.5).

This is the extent of the preparation of soma in the RV; later texts indicate further elaborations.[28]

(a) *Gó* as Metonymy for the leather material of the hide which catches the soma drops

Extracting the juice from the stalks is envisioned as soma playing with the press-stones upon the hide of leather (9.66.29), or as the press-stones chewing soma upon the hide of leather (9.79.4). These two passages contain the usual expression for the leather material of the spread: the genitive of *gó* and the locative singular of *tvác* (so also for 1.28.9; 9.65.25; 9.101.11). Once *gavyáyī tvác* is used (9.70.7). In two verses, *tvác* is absent and *gó* alone, in the rarely used locative singular, stands for the leather skin (10.94.9[29]; 10.116.4).

(b) *Gó* as the milk used in the *Gávāśiḥ*

Book IX frequently described this particular soma blend. These descriptions are prosaic, not so much due to paucity of imagery as lack of variety in expression. Uniformity of text is characteristic of this book.[30] The uniformity results from the repetition

26. Hillebrandt, *ibid.*, 212ff.

27. These are the three admixtures of soma (5.27.5). Soma may also be mixed with *ghṛtá* and *mádhu*.

28. Hillebrandt, *ibid.*, 117-266.

29. See Nirukta 2.5.

30. Renou, *EVP* 9,5.

of key words rather than complete pādas. The following verses, all illustrating the use of *gó* as the milk mixed with soma, are grouped according to the repeated element associated with *gó*.

Gó itself assumes a characteristic handling. It is found that *góbhiḥ* is by far the most frequent form; synonyms of *gó* in parallel passages likewise take the instr. pl. (cf. 9.72.1 *dhenúbhiḥ*; 9.93.2 *usríyābhiḥ*).

It is the meaning of the repeated elements which favors taking *gó* as a metonymy. I emphasize this point because in another group of verses, discussed below, the imagery prescribes translating *gó* as 'cow' even though 'cow' stands for the milk used in the soma blend.

Verb Repetitions.

√*añj*—anoint, besmear, decorate; closely associated with the milk admixture. *Góbhir* √*añj* is used to describe soma as it mingles with the milk[31]: 4.27.5; 9.10.3; 9.32.3[32]; 9.45.3; 9.50.5[33]; 9.74.8; 9.85.5; 9.96.22; 9.103.2; 9.107.22; possibly 10.31.4; 9.86.47 *sam* √*añj* (the blend is made in the two *camū́* vessels and in the *kalaśá* container); also *dhenúbhiḥ sám* √*añj* 9.72.1.

√*kṛ*-

1.134.2 (*índavaḥ*)...*góbhiḥ krāṇā́ḥ*; (the soma drops) prepared with milk.

3.35.8 *sám indra góbhir mádhumantam akran*; O Indra, they have prepared the sweet (draught) with milk.

9.61.13 (*índum*) ...*góbhir*...*páriṣkṛtam*; (Indu) adorned with milk.

√*kṣar*-

9.107.9ab: *anūpé gómān góbhir akṣāḥ sómo dugdhā́bhir akṣāḥ*;

31. In 8.20.8a *góbhiḥ*. .*ajyate* is said of *vānā́ḥ*...*sóbharīṇām*; see Geldner for the interpretation of this line.

32. For *ajyate* in pāda c, Geldner (*HOS* 35) suggests either √*aj* or √*añj*.

33. Pāda b: *góbhir añjānó aktúbhiḥ* (soma) being anointed with milk (as) with ointment. Renou (*EVP* 8, p. 85): "on ne peut éviter ici le relativement rare *aktú* "onguent". "So also Geldner. Bhave (*Soma Hymns* II, p. 108): "being anointed (i.e. mixed with the besmearing milk..."). Cf. S. D. Atkins, "The Meaning of Vedic *aktú*", *JAOS* 70 (1950), p. 36: "... anointed (i.e. mixed) with streams of milk (lit. 'with milk, with streams')...".

The possessor of cows has flowed into the water with the milk, Soma has flowed with the extracted milk.

Ref. to *gávāśiḥ*. N. 5.3 offers the following interpretation of 9ab: "When the cowherd dwells with kine in a watery place, soma flows from the milked cows."[34] Geldner (*HOS* 35, p. 111) following this suggestion, states that a comparison is made between soma mixed with water and milk, and a cow owner who is in a region abounding in water. *Gómān* could well describe Soma, who, as a masculine symbol par excellence is frequently described as the bull, the warrior, the lord and master of the Soma cows (see below). *Dugdhā́bhiḥ* modifies *góbhiḥ* 'milk' appositionally; cf. 6.48.22; 7.74.3; 9.96.15 where *dugdhám* modifies *páyas*.

ab hí √dhanv-

9.24.2a *abhí gā́vo adhanviṣur*; The streams of milk have rushed forward.

Since *gā́vaḥ* is compared with *ā́paḥ*, the meaning 'milk' is preferable to 'cow' (Geldner, G*Wö*), although the nom. pl. of *gó*, in the context of the Soma rite, usually refers to the Soma cows. Cf. 9.66.6c (*túbhyaṃ dhāvanti dhenávaḥ*) where *dhenávaḥ* also means 'streams of milk'.

√dhā-

3.50.3 *góbhir mimikṣúṃ dadhire*...; With milk they made the blend (the soma).[35]

góbhiḥ—Sāy. *gomiśritaiḥ somaiḥ*

ádhi √dhṛ-

9.105.4 *śúciṃ te várṇam ádhi góṣu dīdharam*; Your pure color I place upon the milk.

Cf. 9.104.4

Śúciṃ várṇam refers to the appearance of the purified soma. *Śukrá*, when applied to soma, also has this meaning. *Góṣu*- one of the few instances where the loc. case signifies 'milk' in the ritual context.

√mṛj - rub, polish, cleanse; *√mṛj* may be used when either water

34. L. Sarup, *The Nighaṇṭu and Nirukta*, p. 73.

35. Sāyaṇa understands *índram* as object of *dadhire*. The above insertion follows Geldner (*HOS* 33, v. cit.), Ludwig (*RV*, v. cit) and G*Wö*.

or milk is added to soma (9.43.1) or, when both are added:
9.68.9c *adbhír góbhir mṛjyate ádribhiḥ sutáḥ*; He is embellished with waters, with milk, having been pressed with stones. 'Embellished' is preferable to 'cleansed' because the water and milk are additions to the 'pure' or 'cleansed' state of the soma juice.

√*vas* - to clothe.
góbhiḥ...√*vas* refers to the *gávāśiḥ* (9.2.4c = 9.66.13c; 9.14.3). So also 9.42.1 *vásāno gā́ apó háriḥ*; 9.8.5 *sáṃ góbhir vāsayāmasi*; 9.104.4 *góbhiṣ te várṇam abhí vāsayāmasi.*

pari ā √*vṛ* -
9.86.27 (*hárim*)...*pári góbhir*[36] *ā́vṛtaṃ*; (The Tawny One) enveloped in milk.

6.47.27 (*rátham* ?) *pári góbhir ā́vṛtam.*

pári √*vyā* -
9.107.18 *apó vásānaḥ pári góbhir úttaraḥ sídan váneṣv avyata;* Dressing himself in water, the excellent One, settling in the wooden vessels, has wrapped himself around with milk.

Allusion to the *gávāśiḥ*; the image of soma wrapped in the admixture like one who is covered by a garment is more frequently expressed by √ *vas*...*nirṇíj* (see below).

√ *śrī* - to mix, cook[37]; to fortify, to strengthen.[38]
góbhiḥ...√ *śrī*[39] is performed by the priests upon the extracted juice (8.2.3.; 8.82.5; 9.46.4[40]; 9.107.2; 9.109.17).

The problem is to determine the shade of meaning for √ *śrī* in this context. Ludwig (*RV*, ad 9.107.2d and e) translates √ *śrī* as 'to cook'; Geldner prefers 'to mix'. Renou (*EVP* 8, 26) in translating *śrīṇīta* (9.46.4) 'fortifiez-en-mélangeant' apparently wishes to indicate that √ *śrī* may refer not only to the mixing process, but also to the effect that the milk has upon the soma.[41] This seems to be appropriate since a number of passages tell

36. Bergaigne (*Rel. Véd.* II, 58) considers *góbhiḥ* as celestial cows.
37. For the relationship between √*śrī* √*śrai*, √*śrā* see Wackernagel, *AiG* I, 87.
38. 'kräftigen': Oldenberg, "Beautiful and Beauty", 98-121.
39. For *gā́vaḥ* √*śrī* see p. 71.
40. Nirukta 2.5.
41. In an earlier study by Renou (*Étude Voc. RV.*) √*śrī*, with soma and milk, is chiefly understood as 'préparer à point', 'cuire' p. 37.

us how the milk works upon the flavor of soma; with √ *śrī*, the effect is *svādú* (8.2.3) and *máda*[42] (8.82.5).

Noun Repetitions.

nirṇíj

1. *gó...ná nirṇíj*

 9.107.26cd: *janáyañ jyótir mandánā avīvaśad gā́ḥ kṛṇvānó ná nirṇíjam*

 He,[43] causing light to be brought forth, made the enraptured ones[44] bellow, assuming their milk as his robe.

 Perhaps a pun is intended with the term *jyótiḥ*. *Jyótiḥ* could refer to the cows' milk (cf. 3.30.14) with which the soma is mixed; *jyótiḥ* could also refer to the light with which the god Soma dispelled the darkness (1.91.22). The latter event is part of the myth dealing with the appearance of light. The cows represent the rays of light which await a god to release them. Occasionally, Soma is one such god (p. 102).
 pāda d = 9.14.5c.

2. In 9.86.26 and 9.95.1 *nírṇíjam* is in apposition to *gā́ḥ*.

3. *nírṇíj* as an appositive to *usríyā*: 9.68.1
 prá devám ácchā mádhumanta índavó 'siṣyadanta gā́va ā́ ná dhenávaḥ
 barhiṣádo vacanā́vanta ū́dhabhiḥ parisrútam usríyā nirṇíjaṃ dhire
 To the god, the drops containing sweetness have flowed as milk cows [speed to the calves].
 Seated on the *barhís*, eloquent, they[45] have put on the milk, the robe, inundated by (the milk of) the udders.

 Usríyā, as also *gó* in the above examples, is associated with *nirṇíj* and therefore is understood as 'milk' and not 'milk cow' (as suggested in G*Wö*).

42. *Máda* in this context is not used exclusively with √*śrī*: e.g., 9.45.3 (√*añj*), 9.43.1 (√*mṛj*).
43. Soma.
44. The cows.
45. The soma drops (Ludwig, *RV*, V, p. 357).

(c) *Gó* as 'Cow', figuratively referring to 'milk' mixed with soma.

The preparation of the *gávāśiḥ* is one of the favorite fertility themes of the Rig Veda. Why this should be so is clear enough. The ingredients of the blend are produced by two well established symbols of fertility: the cow and Soma. The cow, chief image of feminine virtues in the Rig Veda, sheds forth her milk, which is emblematic of the female element. Soma, acting as an invigorating stimulus, is a Rig Vedic male principle par excellence.[46] As bull or stallion, Soma unites with a bevy of females at the time of the sacrifice.[47] He unites with the fingers (which cleanse the stalk), the prayers (which accompany the juice) and the mixtures (with which the juice mingles in the vats).

Gávā́śiḥ verses refer to Soma as a bull at the time of mingling with *gó*. The words used are *vṛ́ṣan* (9.6.6;[48] 9.71.7; 9.97.13[49]), *vṛṣabhá* (9.96.7) and *ukṣán* (9.69.4). In the same vein, Soma is considered to be the beloved lord (*júṣṭa páti*[50] 9.97.22; *priyá páti* 9.72.4) of the cows; the Soma cows are *vṛṣaṇyántī* (9.19.5).[51] These passages suggest that the soma juice, as the god Soma, is referred to as 'a bull', just as the milk is referred to as 'cows'.

46. Thus, when soma drops are compared to *gā́vaḥ* (as in 9.41.1) the latter must be 'bulls'.

47. Bergaigne, *Rel. Véd.* II, 22ff.

48. *táṃ góbhir vṛṣaṇaṃ rásam mádāya devávītaye/sutám bhárāya sáṃ sṛja/ / vṛ́ṣaṇaṃ* is understood to be in apposition with *rásam*; so also Geldner (*HOS* 35, p. 14). Renou (*EVP* 8, p. 6) G*Wō*, Ludwig (*RV*, v. cit.) take *vṛ́ṣaṇaṃ* adjectivally. Perhaps 9.6.6 can throw light on *góbhiḥ* in pāda a of 9.84.3: *ā́ yó góbhiḥ sṛjyáta óṣadhīsv ā.* The points of comparison, besides the fact that both hymns are addressed to Sōma, rest on the use of the inst. pl. of *gó* in association with a form of $\sqrt{sṛj}$. On this basis, it might be ventured that pāda a pertains to the preparation of the *gávāśiḥ* and *góbhiḥ* is 'cows', used figuratively. (For a different interpretation see Bergaigne, *Rel. Véd.*, I, pp. 170, 172; II, p. 35; Hillebrandt, *Ved. Myth.* I, p. 343.) However *óṣadhiṣu* is still hard to explain. See Renou *EVP* 9, p. 9, fn. 1 and paragraph 9 on the treatment of ritual sequence in Book 9.

49. *vṛṣā śóṇo*...refers to soma; pāda a occurs in Pañcaviṃśa Brāhmaṇa 11.8.4. Section 8 is the midday pavamāna-laud of the second day of the Dvādaśāha (W. Caland, trans. *Pañcaviṃśa-brāhmaṇa* in *Bibliotheca Indica*, Work No. 255, Issue No. 1514 N.S. (Calcutta, 1931).

50. Soma is also the cows' protector (*gópati* 9.97.34).

51. Different interpretations for *vṛṣaṇyántī*: "prayers" (Renou, *EVP* 8,14; Geldner *HOS* 35, p. 23); "actual waters" milking out the shining juice (Bhave, *Soma Hymns* II, p. 13).

Further evidence to substantiate this use of *gó* comes from similes which sustain the fertility image. The preparation of the *gávāsíḥ* is compared to the theme of religious devotion (4.41.8) and mundane love (9.32.5; 9.93.2). These similes are used to describe the commingling of the male soma and the female milk in the ritual vats.

9.32.5ab

abhí gā́vo anūṣata yóṣā jārám iva priyám

The cows have called [to him] as a maid to her desired lover.

Gā́vaḥ: *Sāy. sábdāḥ*
Abhí anūṣata: cf. 9.26.2; 9.80.2.

9.93.2cd

máryo ná yóṣām abhí niṣkṛtáṃ yánt sáṃ gacchate kaláśa usríyābhiḥ

Like a youth approaching a maiden for the tryst, he[52] joins with the milk cows in the kalaśa container.

4.41.8cd (To Indra-Varuṇa)

śriyé ná gā́va úpa sómam asthur índraṃ gíro váruṇam me manī-ṣā́ḥ

As cows have come to soma to mix [their milk], my thoughts and songs [have gone] to Indra and Varuṇa [for their glory].

The simile is used to describe the devotion with which the sacrificer performs the rites. On the cows' disposition upon meeting soma, see 9.101.8 where they are said to be *priyá* and *ghṛ́ṣvi*.

Śriyé: The translation follows Geldner (*HOS* 35, v. cit.) and Renou, (*EVP* 1, 19; *Études Voc. RV*, 38) in assuming a double meaning for *śrī*.

By nature of the *gávāśiḥ* preparation, reference to motion, specifically that of meeting and joining, is found to be a characteristic and oft repeated description. With verbs meaning 'to approach, to unite, to impel' etc., the emphasis is on *gó* 'milk cow', figuratively applied to refer to the milk admixture. Listed below are some examples:

52. Soma, who is called *vṛ́ṣan* in pāda b.

9.64.13c *índo rucā́bhí gā́ ihi*
9.69.4a *ukṣā́ mimāti práti yanti dhenávo*
9.72.6c *sám ī gā́vo matáyo yanti saṃyáta*
9.72.3a *áramamāṇo áty eti gā́ abhí*
9.77.4d *gávām urubjám abhyárṣati vrajám*

vrajá—the ritual vat; the term is most frequently applied to the enclosure confining the mythical cows (see Geldner, *Ved. Stud.* II, 282-287). Perhaps *vrajá* is used intentionally here to allude to Soma's role in this myth (see p. 113).

9.78.1b *apó vásāno abhí gā́ iyakṣati*
9.87.9a *utá sma rāśím pári yāsi gónām*[53]

rāśím...gónām could equally well refer to the mythical cows mentioned in verse 8. Sāy. *rāśiṃ*: *samūhaṃ paṇibhirapahṛtaṃ*

9.96.8d *àṅśór ūrmím īraya gā́ iṣaṇyán*
9.97.9b *vṛ́thā krī́ḷantam...mimate ná gā́vaḥ*
9.97.22 *āyan júṣṭam pátiṃ kaláśe gā́va índum*
9.97.34c *gā́vo yanti gópatim pṛcchámānāḥ*

The sound produced as the milk and juice are jointly poured into the ritual vats sustains and enhances the fertility image; indeed, it is a characteristic feature of it. Upon meeting, the bull and cows call to each other (*abhí* √*nu* 9.26.2; 9.32.5; 9.71.7; 9.80.2[54]; *sám* √*nu* 9.101.8). More specifically, the cows bellow[55] (√*ma* 9.33.4) and the bull roars (√*krand* 9.33.4; 9.97.13; √*mā* 9.69.4). These vociferous greetings are mating sounds. This interpretation rests on the use of *vāvaśānáh* (9.96.14), *vāvaśānā́ḥ* (9.97.22,35) to describe soma and the cows, respectively, as they converge in the vat. *Vāvaśāná* is the perfect participle middle of

53. A. Hillebrandt ("Vedisch *dhāman*", *Indogermanische Forschungen* 44 [1927], 148) uses this pāda to comment on 9.97.31c. He translates *dhāman* in 31c as 'troop' and compares it in meaning to *rāśí*. Gonda's study on *dhāman* (p. 45) secures the meaning of 31c as: "O (Soma pavamāna,) thou clarifiest thyself like (and at the same time, as) the ghee (which is the location of the specific power of the cows)"....

54. Pāda a: *yáṃ tvā vājinn aghnyā́ abhy ánūṣata.* Professor Brown lists *aghnyā́* as possibly being an epithet of the Cosmic Waters ("Sanctity of Cow", 33). However, pāda a is such a close parallel to 9.26.2 and 9.32.5 that such an interpretation is doubtful. Cf. H. P. Schmidt, "*aghnya*," 18, who translates the term "Milchströme."

55. Soma has caused the cows to bellow (9.34.6c).

either $\sqrt{}$*vāś* 'to bellow' or $\sqrt{}$*vaś* 'to desire'. There is no need to prefer one root to the other.[56] The purpose lies precisely in the ambiguity.

The actual mingling of the two ingredients is described in language characteristic of the cattle fights (see Chap. II). Soma becomes the warrior who seeks to capture the cows, as the examples below show:

9.89.3c: *śū́ro yutsú prathamáḥ pṛcchate gā́*; First hero in battles, he seeks the cows.

Śū́ra also said of soma juice in the *gávā́śiḥ* in 9.62.19; 9.16.6; 9.87.7.

Whereas this pāda offers an explicit analogy with a cattle fight, other verses achieve the same end through the use of stylistic clichés peculiar to the theme of cattle wars:

9.86.12b *ágre vācó agriyó góṣu gacchati*; At the head of the hymn he goes first among the cows.

Note the similarity between *agriyó góṣu gacchati* and *prathamó góṣu gacchati* (1.83.1a; 2.25.4b), as well as *góṣu* $\sqrt{}$*gam* (4.38.4); the latter are stated in connection with a cattle contest. Further, since the loc. pl. of *gó* appears most frequently in the context of the cattle fight, the expression *góṣu* $\sqrt{}$*sthā*, said of soma (9.16.6; 9.62.19; 9.96.7) associates the theme of the *gávāśiḥ* with the imagery of the cattle wars.

(d) *Gó* (literal usage), as the 'Cow' in the Soma Ritual

Gó may be used in the literal sense to designate the cow which supplies the products to be mixed with soma; these are milk (9.97.43; 9.91.3), sour milk (9.81.1), and fat (9.31.5).

Cattle with their milk sweeten, 'season' ($\sqrt{}$*svad* 9.62.5), 'swell' ($\sqrt{}$*pī* 1.153.4), 'fortify' ($\sqrt{}$*śrī* 9.71.4; 9.84.5; 9.93.3), and 'refresh' (úpa $\sqrt{}$*av* 8.72.12) the soma.

RV 1.137.3a-e makes the analogy between the extraction of milk from the cow, and juice from the soma stalk:

56. Cf. Renou, *EVP* 9, 97-98, note 31.

tā́ṃ vāṃ dhenúṃ ná vāsarī́m aṅśuṃ duhanty ádribhiḥ sómaṃ duhanty ádribhiḥ

asmatrā́ gantam úpa no 'rvā́ñcā sómapītaye
As a bright milk cow, they milk with stones this stalk for you; they milk the soma with stones;

Tā́ṃ vāṃ dhenúṃ occurring in ŚS[57] 10.7.7 is to be pronounced in the morning service of the sixth day of the Dvādaśāha.

Vāsarí adj. 'bright, shining' (Hillebrandt, *Ved. Myth.* I, 25-26; Ludwig, *RV*). Cf. Geldner (*HOS* 33, p. 192) 'am Morgen'. The cow may be considered 'bright' because she stores the milk. (see p 50).

5. *Gó* in Other Śrauta Sacrifices

(a) *Gó* etc. in the Pravargya Rite

In the period of the Rig Veda, the Pravargya ceremony may have been a separate sacrifice performed once a day, in the morning.[58] The oblation used in the rite was milk. This was first heated in a special ritual vessel before being offered to the Aśvins. Textual evidence, states Keith, shows that the Pravargya rite "was understood as a sun spell, and this is directly indicated by the formulae used at the rite."[59]

RV 1.164.26-30 "report a celebration of the pravargya rite."[60] The first pādas of both v. 26 and v. 27 occur in AB 1.22.2 in connection with Pravargya rite. In v. 26 *sudúghāṃ dhenúm* refers to the cow whose milk is used for the oblation. The connotative value of the phrase does not end here, for, while vss. 26-30 describe the rite, they also act as a charm to aid the rise of daylight.[61] With this in mind, *sudúghāṃ dhenúm* could also designate Uṣas (cf. 1.186.4; 7.2.6; 2.3.6). The 'milk' of Uṣas, the cow, mentioned in this verse as well as 27 and 28, is her light (see 3.30.14). Verse

57. *Śāṅkhāyana-Śrautasūtra*, trans. W. Caland (Nagpur, 1953), p. 266.
58. A. B. Keith, *Religion and Philosophy of the Veda and Upanishads*, *HOS* 32 (Cambridge, 1925), 332. A recent comprehensive study on the rite is by J. A. B. van Buitenen, *The Pravargya*, Poona, 1968.
59. Keith, *ibid.*, 333.
60. W. Norman Brown, "Agni, Sun, Sacrifice and Vāc: A Sacerdotal Ode by Dīrghatamas (Rig Veda 1.164)", *JAOS* 88, 214.
61. See Brown, ibid. for exegesis on vss. 26-30.

27 continues the twofold allusion. *Aghnyā́* is both the cow at the rite and Uṣas. In verse 28, *gó* = Uṣas; 28c can be interpreted two ways depending upon whether the subject is understood to be the milk oblation or Uṣas. If Uṣas is subject of *abhí vāvaśānā́* then the participle comes from *abhí* √*vaś*, 'to long for', the sense being that Uṣas longs for the warm mouth of her calf the Sun. If milk is the subject, the participle comes from *abhí* √*vāś*, 'to low'; the pāda would then describe the heated milk lowing (i.e. bubbling) over the edge of the ritual vessel. *Gó* in v. 29 refers to the milk oblation.

(b) *Gó* in the Aśvamedha

The RV knows of the horse sacrifice; hymns 1.162 and 1.163 refer to this ceremony though in a manner differing from the later texts.[62] 1.163.8ab describes the train following the horse:

ánu tvā rátho ánu máryo arvann ánu gāvo 'nu bhágaḥ kanī́nām; *gó* is understood in the literal sense 'cattle'. This verse is repeated in VS 29.19, TS 4.6.7.3 and KSA 6.3; it is one of a series of verses recited by the Hotar in order to praise the horse.[63]

6. *Gó* in Household Ceremonies

On the occasion of a marriage, milk is poured into the ritual fire (5.3.2)[64] and cattle are slain (10.85.13). Perhaps we are to understand from 10.32.4b that milk cows led the marriage procession.

The corpse, on the funerary pyre, is covered with pieces of cows' omentum[65] (10.16.7).

7. *Gó* etc. as dákṣiṇā

The treasured gift, the most cherished prize of the officiating priests is the cows bestowed upon them as their *dákṣiṇā*. *Dákṣiṇā* is payment in kind (e.g., *gó*, *áśva*, *vásu*, *híraṇya* 7.90.6b[66]; also

62. A. B. Keith, *Taittiriya Sanhita*, in *HOS* 18 (Cambridge, 1914), cxxxii.

63. See P. E. Dumont, *L'Aśvamedha* (Paris, Louvain, 1927), p. 146, No. 444; p. 265, No. 10.

64. √*añj góbhiḥ*; see p. 62.

65. Sāy. *góbhiḥ: anustaraṇīgocarmaṇā*.

66. Cf. pāda b with 10.108.7b; the similarity between these two pādas is of considerable significance in furthering our understanding of *gó* in the myth

ánna 10.107.7, *rátha* 6.47.24) for services the priest renders the sacrificer.[67] *Dákṣiṇā*, be it translated 'fee' or 'gift' is the priest's reward for the accurate performance of the sacrifice. A well performed sacrifice is a potent sacrifice. That is, it becomes the proper and only instrument by which to approach the gods and inspire them to protect and enrich the life of the worshipper. The Rig Veda reflects the idea that if a man knows the nature of his god and tends carefully to his wishes, the godheads could be won over and asked to intervene in the earthly affairs of men. As a result, the sacrifice as reflected in the hymns, is fundamentally the presentation of offerings to the heavenly gods, and the request for security in terms of economic prosperity and social stability for the sacrificer. It is within the power of the priest alone to approach the gods for such blessings. His power works through the hymn. The giving of *dákṣiṇā* is done in recognition of the potential power inherent in the hymn and the accompanying ritual practices. RV 4.24.10, I believe, illustrates the last point.

ká imáṃ daśábhir máméndraṃ krīṇāti dhenúbhiḥ
yadā́ vṛtrā́ṇi jáṅghanad áthainam me púnar dadat
Who buys this Indra of mine for ten milk cows ?
When he has slaughtered foes, then he may return him to me.

It has been suggested that an image of Indra is being temporarily bartered off for ten cows (J. Kirste, 'Zum Citralakṣaṇa," *ZDMG* LXXIV [1920], 271). This opinion is difficult to maintain in view of there being, to my knowledge, no other passage in the RV which alludes to the making of images, nor has anything been found materially, to date, to indicate that images were made during the Rig Vedic period. The hymn itself suggests a different

of the Paṇis. *Góbhiḥ* in 7.90.6 denotes one of several forms of *dákṣiṇā*; *góbhiḥ* in 10.108.7 is used to indicate one of the several treasures that the Paṇis have robbed and concealed. For *gó* in this mythological context see below. The complete translation of 7.90.6 reads: The wealthy ones who bestow the light upon us with cattle, horses, riches, gold, O Indra-Vāyu, all through life may these lords, with horses and heroes, prevail in battles. *Iśānā́so yé dádhate svàr ṇo góbhir áśvebhir vásubhir híraṇyaiḥ/índravāyū sūráyo víśvam ā́yur ā́rvadbhir vīraíḥ pṛtanāsu sahyuḥ.* I adopt Geldner's interpretation (*HOS* 34, v. cit.) for svàr, namely that it is equivalent to *máhi jyótiḥ* of Dakṣiṇā in 10.107.1.

67. For a complete listing of the various kinds of *dákṣiṇā*, see M. Patel, *Dānastutis*, pp. 64-75.

approach. This hymn is addressed to Indra at the time of battle (v. 4). Each side invokes Indra (v. 3) but one side, because of the hymn's appeal will gain Indra, and thus victory, to its side (see v. 11d). For Indra will choose that side which literally offers him the most (see v. 7). Which hymn can draw Indra (v.1) ? Vāmadeva, the *ṛṣi* of 4.24 and the speaker of verse 10 indicates that he can produce such a hymn. He is quite forthright in declaring his fee for the hymn: ten milk cows. The situation could illustrate what Bloomfield (*Religion of the Veda*, New York, London, 1908, p. 185) so vividly describes as a "scramble for the gods."

While in later ritualistic texts the giving of *dákṣiṇā* may figure as a symbolic correspondence to the cyclic unfolding and dissolution of the universe,[68] in the RV and AV Saṃhitās, *dákṣiṇā* should be viewed primarily as the priest's honorarium, and as such synonymous with *pūrtí*, *pūrtá*.[69]

Cattle, due to their economic value, are most highly prized as *dákṣiṇā*; indeed the term *dákṣiṇā* may be used specifically with *gó* in mind (3.36.5cd). Requests for *dákṣiṇā* are incorporated within the body of the hymn (e.g. *ṣahásrāṇy asiṣāsad gávām ṛ́ṣis* 8.51.2). Large requests are in the main considered as exaggerations, meant to stimulate the patron's liberality. Equally, the *dāna-stutis* ('praise of gifts'), are used for the same purpose: "In dithyrambic language exorbitant gifts on the part of generous givers of old, mythic kings and patrons, are narrated so as to stimulate the potential patron of the present day."[70] The generous patrons, who 'share their stalls of cattle' are rulers of men, that is *kṣatríyas*.[71]

A *dānástuti*, according to the Bṛhad Devatā, is a verse or series

68. J. Heesterman, "Reflections on the Significance of dakṣiṇā," *Indo-Iranian Journal* III (1959): "dakṣiṇā is the material manifestation of the cyclic course of the universe as it is represented in the ritual," p. 257.

69. M. Bloomfield, "Contributions to the Interpretation of the Veda," *Amer. Journal of Philology* XVII (1896): "The root *par* (*pṝ*) means primarily 'to fill' and that was probably the extent of the original dákṣiṇā...," p. 410.

70. Bloomfield, *The Religion of the Veda* p. 196.

71. Cf. 7.16.7cd *yantā́ro yé maghávāno jánānām ūrvā́n dáyanta gónām.* Geldner (*Ved. Stud.* II, p. 273) cites this verse as having the only occurrence of *ūrvá* outside of a mythological context.

of verses which appear at the end of a hymn.[72] Or, it may comprise an entire hymn. The Anukramaṇī states that *dānástutis* are addressed to kings.[72] Listed below are those verses which conform with the traditional definition of a *dānástuti*, and which mention *gó* as the *dákṣiṇā*[73]; where possible, the number of cattle is also given.

6.27.8...*viṅśatiṃ gā́*...
6.47.24[74]...*sátáṃ gā́*...
7.18.22 *dvé*... *śaté gór*...
8.4.20 *ṣaṣṭíṃ sahásrā*...*yūthā́ni gávām*...
8.4.21[75] *gā́m bhajanta mehánā́śvam bhājanta mehánā*
8.5.37...*sahásrā dáśa gónām*
8.6.47...*sahásrā dáśa gónām*
8.46.22...*dáśa gávāṃ sahásrā*

The following two verses are taken from a hymn the whole of which is recognized as a *dānástuti*:

1.126.2 *śátáṃ*...*gónām*...
1.126.5...*aṣṭā́v*...*gā́ḥ*

Other verses, though not included in the traditional count, have been recognized as *dānástutis*[76]:

1.122.7...*gávāṃ śatā́*...
5.27.2...*śatā́ ca viṅśatíṃ ca gónāṃ*...
5.27.1 *ánasvantā*...*gā́vā*...
5.30.12...*gávāṃ catvā́ri*...*sahásrā* (v.15 *gávya*)
5.30.13...*gávāṃ sahásrai*...
5.33.10 *vrajáṃ ná gā́vaḥ práyatā ápi gman*
5.61.10...*dhenūnā́m śatáṃ*...
6.63.9...*dáśa vaśā́so*...
9.74.8[77]...*gónām*

Gó may also refer to the *dákṣiṇā* when it occurs outside of a *dānástuti*. Then it is somewhat more difficult to recognize, since

72. See *Bṛhad Devatā* 6.45; Patel, *Dānastutis*, p. 7.
73. Patel, *Dānastutis*, pp. 13-19.
74. Recognized only by the Anukramaṇī (Patel, *Dānastutis*, p. 20)
75. *gā́m*: used in collective sense (Geldner *HOS* 35, 345).
76. Patel, *Dānastutis*, pp. 20-30.
77. A rare Book 9 *dānástuti* (Renou, *EVP* 9, v. cit., p 87)..

gó is a form of wealth desired by priest and patron alike. Therefore, in order to establish whether *gó* is considered as the priest's *dákṣiṇā*, we must look either for points of comparison with the *dānástutis*, or for the mention of a priest as recipient. An aid in deciding who the recipient ought to be, comes from the series of terms itemizing the riches desired by the praisers of the gods. It is understood from the *dānástutis* that only certain items were considered appropriate for *dákṣiṇā*.[78] As indicated above, animals, chariots, golden objects, clothes and food are the usual honorarium; conspicuously absent from the *dānástutis*, is the mention of land. However, we do know that land was considered an important source of wealth, territorial acquisition being one of the main motives for a warrior's setting out to do battle (6.19.12). This point may be used to determine, in the following way, the intended recipient of wealth enumerated in a series: while the patron's requests are for land, heroic sons and herds, the *dákṣiṇā* of the priest is chiefly in produce and animals.

In the following verses, the priest expresses the desire to receive *gó* as *dákṣiṇā*:

1.10.7cd (To Indra)

gávām ápa vrajáṃ vṛdhi kṛṇuṣvá rā́dho adrivaḥ

Open the stall of the cattle, bring riches O Possessor of the Press-Stones.

Ápa- √*vṛ vrajám* and the genitive of *gó* is an expression used to indicate the giving of cattle as wealth. In that sense, the pāda is discussed on p. 18 under the heading : The Cow as Economic Wealth. The usage of *gó* in this and the following verse is probably literal and refers to cattle as the prize of war (vs. 10, *vā́ja*), or as the priest's *dákṣiṇā* (so Geldner, *HOS* 33, p. 11 and H.-P. Schmidt, *Bṛhaspati und Indra*, Wiesbaden, 1968, p. 154). Because of the possible meaning of *gó* as *dákṣiṇā*, the pāda is reiterated here. Note that *ápa* √*vṛ vrajá* reoccurs in the context of Indra's liberality in 4.20.8, where likewise *gó* signifies actual cattle wealth.

78. Patel, *Dānastutis*, pp. 64-75.

6.46.2c: *gā́m áśvaṃ rathyàm indra sáṃ kira.* *Naḥ*, (pāda a), indirect object of *sám* √*kir*, refers to the poets (*kārávaḥ*, v. 1). *Gó, áśva, rátha, rathín* are the usual *dákṣiṇā* given the priest (cf. 6.47. 24; 10.107.7; 6.27.8).

8.78.1,2: Verse 4 suggests that the preceding verses describe items desired as *dákṣiṇā*; the items mentioned in verses 1 and 2 are among the usual gifts presented (cf. 7.90.6).

5.42.4 in pādas ab, the priests ask for cattle, patrons (*sūrí*)[79] and prosperity.

10.97.4c *sanéyam áśvaṃ gā́ṃ vā́sa*; the priest wishes a horse, cow and dress for achieving a cure using plants. For dress as *dákṣiṇā*, see 6.47.23.

In 10.7.2 *rā́dhaḥ*, consisting of *gó* and *áśva*, may be used to describe the *dákṣiṇā* (cf. 5.79.7).

10.100.12 differs from vss. 1—11 with regard to meter and refrain. Geldner (*HOS* 35): *duvasyú*: 'Huldiger' or, Proper Name of poet; the request is for *dákṣiṇā*. For *góagra* in a *dákṣiṇā* context: 1.53.5; 1.90.5; 1.92.7.

8. *Gó* as the Cow Desired by the Sacrificer

Not only the wishes of the priest, but also those of the patron are incorporated into the body of the hymn. The patron has initiated the sacrifice to insure a period of well-being. The desires of the *yájamāna* are expressed in 8.97.2, and 9.91.6, the latter is cited below:

evā́ punānó apáḥ svàr gā́ asmábhyaṃ tokā́ tánayāni bhū́ri
śáṃ naḥ kṣétram urú[80] jyótīṅṣi soma jyóñ naḥ sū́ryaṃ dṛśáye ririhi

79. *sūrí*, related to *sū́ra, svàr*; liberality is associated with the concept of light. Cf. *máhi jyótiḥ*, said of *Dakṣiṇā* 10.107.1; 7.90.6.

80. Hillebrandt (*Ved. Myth.* III, 108, fn. 3). and Grassmann, (*Wö*, s.v. *urú*), understand *urú* to modify *jyótīṅṣi*.

So, being cleansed, [grant] us waters, sunlight, cattle, offspring, abundant progeny.
Grant us well-being, extensive land, light, O Soma [lit: for us to see the sun a long time] so that we shall see the sun for a long time.

Note the similarity between the valuables cited above, and those which the *yájamāna*, will fight to secure: 6.25.4; 6.66.8; 6.19.12.

Food (*íṣ*), waters, plants, non-poisonous forests, cattle, horses and men are asked for in 6.39.5. The problem is that although the items listed in pādas cd of that verse bespeak of the *yájamāna's* wishes, pāda a mentions the singer (*gṛṇát*) as the recipient. It may be conjectured that the priest is to obtain *íṣ* (in pāda b) and the *yájamāna* those items in c and d.

To have heroic sons is a hope characteristic of the *kṣatríya*. Thus, *gó* appearing in an enumeration together with *vīrá* (10.68.12) and *vīrávat* (9.9.9) is taken as the cattle desired by the *yájamāna*.

For a number of verses, all one can say is that *gó*, together with other objects of value, are desired by the praisers of the gods; the intended receiver is uncertain:

To Soma are directed pleas for:

...śatagvínaṃ[81] *gávām póṣaṃ sváśvyam* 9.65.17[82]
íṣam ū́rjam...áśvaṃ gā́m urú jyótiḥ...9.94.5
...gā́ḥ...9.96.16

To Indra go pleas for:

...góbhir áśvaiḥ...1.16.9[83]
gór áśvasya...8.52.5
...áśvāya...gáve 8.92.25 (probably for Ṛṣi Śrutakṣa)
piśā́...góbhir áśvais...7.18.2
...góṣv áśvesu...1.29. 1-7

81. For *śatagvín*, see Bloomfield, *Amer. Journal of Philology*, XVII, pp. 423-424. The author translates *śatagvín* as 'hundredfold' to bring out its generalized meaning and untautological aspect. Renou considers °*gvínaṃ gávām* redundant (*EVP* 8, p. 98).

82. pāda b—1.93.2d; also cf. 9.67.6.

83. Cf. with 6.45.21.

...góbhir aśvínā 1.53.4
góbhiṣ ṭaremā́matiṃ durévāṃ yávena...10.42.10

More pleas for cattle are directed to Indra than any other god, for it is known that Indra, when aroused by soma, gives cows (cf. 1.4.2) in large number (cf. 4.32.18; 7.18.1) to the one who presses the juice for him (2.30.7).

9. *Gó* and *starī́* figuratively used to connote ritual implements

(a) *starī́* as the kindling stick: 10.31.10 (to the All-Gods)
starī́r yát sū́ta sadyó ajyámānā vyáthir avyathī́ḥ kr̥ṇuta svágopā putró yát pū́rvaḥ pitrór jániṣṭa śamyā́ṃ gaúr jagāra yád dha pr̥cchā́n

When the barren cow [the kindling stick] on being anointed [with ghee] suddenly gave birth [=sprang into flame], she, who was her own herder, steadied the unsteady (flames).

When the son [Agni who is concealed in the *śamī* wood] was born before the parents, the full [Agni] swallowed the stick [i.e. the fire burnt up the stick] should they ask.

The meaning of this verse is uncertain though it is usually understood as an allusion to the kindling of the sacrificial fire. I agree with this interpretation, supported by 4.7.9. (There are no parallel passages for 10.31.10).

4.7.9cd (To Agni)
yád ápravītā dádhate ha gárbhaṃ sadyáś cij jātó bhávasī́d u dūtáḥ

(The other is) when the unimpregnated one bears the offspring, immediately [after] having been born, you become a messenger.

This verse describes the birth of Agni. The *ápravītā* may refer to the kindling stick (as suggested by Hillebrandt, *Ved. Myth.* II, p. 72). As such, *ápravītā* may be compared to *starī́*, and *dádhate ...gárbham* to *sū́ta*.

10.31.10c refers to Agni; cf. 10.32.3b

Gó in 10.31.10d is difficult. The term, if associated with *starí* (pāda a), would make for a curious situation. How would the cow, being the stick, consume the stick ? One would expect that of Agni (so also Oldenberg, *Noten, loc. cit.*). Cf. 10.79.4.

Perhaps *gó* ought to be taken as a masculine, and epithet of Agni. Agni is often described as a bull (see Macdonell, *Vedic Mythology*, p. 89); *vṛ́ṣan* and *vṛṣabhá* are commonly used. *Gó* 'bull' is a less frequent epithet of his.[84] Less likely is that *gó* means 'cow' and still refers to Agni. But, cf. 10.5.7, where Agni as a creative principle is both *dhenú* and *vṛṣabhá*; this is, however, a very different type of conceptualization and does not permit understanding Agni as solely 'cow' in other contexts.

Sāy. *gaúḥ*: earth; the female of the two sticks. On *śamyā́m*, see Geldner (*HOS* 35, *loc. cit.*).

(b) *gó* in 9.99.3 (*yáṃ gā́va āsábhir dadhúḥ*) could be used figuratively for the stones which press the soma stalks. We may compare pāda c with 10.76.7 where it is said that these stones, as men, cleanse the oblation with their mouths; the same verse states that the press-stones 'milk' the soma stalks (also 1.137.3).

A translation of 'cows' or 'bulls' is possible for *gó* in 9.99.3. Note that the press-stones (*grā́van*) are referred to as *vṛ́ṣan*.[85]

Sāyaṇa and Ludwig (*RV* v. cit.) take *gó* literally, as the cattle which have tasted soma in the plants.

84. See *gó* as epithet of Agni, p. 142.

85. S. G. Oliphant, "The Vedic Press-Stones", *Studies in Honor of Maurice Bloomfield*, (New Haven, 1920), p. 244.

Chapter IV

'COW' IN VEDIC MYTHOLOGY

The symbolic use of 'cow' terms occurs in two major Rig Vedic myths as well as numerous minor mythic contexts. One of the major mythic themes deals with creation of the universe; the other most likely deals with its preservation. Both major and minor themes involving 'cow' terms are discussed in this chapter.

A. 'COW' IN THE INDRA-VṚTRA MYTH, THE MYTH OF CREATION

The Rig Veda contains several theories to explain the origin of the universe and all living things. The variety of explanations is due both to the formulation of different theories as well as to the conceptual developments within a particular theory.[1]

The Indra-Vṛtra myth presents a rather anthropomorphic statement of a theory viewing creation as a differentiation process.[2] Fundamental to this theory is the idea that cosmogony is due to the differentiation between organized and unorganized matter.[3] This myth "opens with the state of precreation. The material constituents of the universe seem already to have been in existence then, but there was no warmth in the universe, no moisture, nor any organization of the material elements, that is, no order or system. There was only chaos, without the principles of cosmic truth or order, or ordered movement (*ṛta*) to regulate all. There existed, however, powerful beings with life who were called Asuras...The Asuraṣ were of two kinds, the Ādityas, led by

1. For developments within different theories see W. Norman Brown, "Theories", 23ff; on the emission process as a theory of creation, see D. Srinivasan, "The Religious Significance of Multiple Bodily Parts to denote the Divine: Findings from the Rig Veda", *Asiatische Studien* XXIX, 2 (1975), 137-179.

2. Interpretation of this myth rests mainly on the studies of W. Norman Brown, "The Creation Myth of the Rig Veda", *JAOS* 62 (1942), 85ff; H. Lüders, *Varuṇa* I, 183ff. Recently F. B. J. Kuiper ("Cosmogony and Conception: A Query" *IIJ* 10 [1970] 91-138) suggests that the Indra-Vṛtra myth of creation has some resemblance to human conception.

3. Brown, "Theories", p. 24.

Varuṇa, and the Dānavas or the Dānava, led by Vṛtra...".[4] Vṛtra, by enclosing the Cosmic Waters, is obstructing the process of creation. The Ādityas call upon Indra to aid their cause and defeat the chief of the Dānavas. Indra's might, gained by drinking soma and enhanced by his weapon the *vájra*, triumphs: he slays Vṛtra,[5] the dragon (*áhi*), thereby releasing the Cosmic Waters. With the release of these Waters (*ā́pas*, fem.), actual creation is able to proceed. The Waters provide the necessary moisture for life; they also make heat and light available. Once released, the Waters are found to be pregnant and their embryo is the Sun.[6] Thus in this myth of creation, the Cosmic Waters represent the generative and fructifying principle, containing as they do powers to produce and sustain life.

The Cosmic Waters which stream out of Vṛtra are said to be like cows (1.32.11; 1.61.10).

1.61.10 (To Indra)

asyéd evá śávasā śuṣántam ví vṛścad vájreṇa vṛtrám índraḥ
gā́ ná vrāṇā́ avánīr amuñcad abhí śrávo dāváne sácetāḥ

Even with his might, with the *vájra* Indra cut Vṛtra, absorbing (moisture), into pieces,
He, inclined to give, released the streams, pent up like cows, for glory.

On pāda c, cf. Geldner (*HOS* 33, v. cit.).
Śuṣántam: from √ *śvas*, √ *śuṣ* (Whitney, *Roots*); Ludwig (*RV* v. cit.): "den aussgetrocknenden Vṛtra"; Lüders (*Varuṇa* I, 182): "den schnaubenden Vṛtra".

1.32.11 (To Indra)

dāsápatnīr áhigopā atiṣṭhan níruddhā ā́paḥ paṇíneva gā́vaḥ
apā́ṃ bílam ápihitaṃ yád ā́sīd vṛtrā́ṃ jaghanvā́ñ ápa tád vavāra

Having the *dāsá* as lord, the dragon as keeper, the Waters remained confined as the cows by the *paṇí*.

4. Brown, "Theories", 23-24.
5. He is to tear Vṛtra across as the limbs of an ox (see 1.61.12).
6. Brown, "Creation Myth", 97.

The cave of the Waters which was shut, that he opened when he had slain Vṛtra.

Niṛukta 2.17 considers *paṇi* in this verse to mean 'merchant'. More likely, the reference is to another demon called Paṇi who also withholds cows (see p 100). Indeed this verse indicates that in spite of the similarity of 'withholding cows', both myths were distinct enough to permit of a comparison. Bergaigne (*Rel. Véd.* II, 319) has already observed this. Cf. remarks by Strauss (*Bṛhaspati im Veda*, p. 34, fn. 1) and H.-P. Schmidt (*Bṛhaspati und Indra*, p. 182, fn. 38; p. 244).

The use of *gó* etc. in economic and ritual contexts discussed above, helps in some measure to explain why 'Cosmic Waters' and 'cows' may be compared. It is suggested that on occasion imagery from the daily routines of these farming-herding peoples makes its way into the sacred literature. Thus, for example, cows, flowing with milk, may be likened to rushing waters such as rains and rivers.[7] In addition to this comparison between 'waters' and 'cows', which springs from a comparison between observable phenomena, there exists a connection between the symbolic value of the 'Cosmic Waters' and 'cow'. Each in its own frame of reference represents maternal vital energy. Like the 'Waters' whose flood contains elements for life, so the 'cow' contains milk, considered in the Rig Veda as the female principle of life.[8] Each, on that account, represents a force having the capacity to create and sustain life. This underlying conceptual similarity may account for the similes noted above and, for the metaphorical use of 'cow' in the verses to be discussed below. These verses contain terminology characteristic of the Indra-Vṛtra myth. Such terms are: *vṛtrá* (1.61.10); *áhi* (1.32.11; 5.29.3; 8.96.5, see Bergaigne, *Rel. Véd.* II, 203ff on the identification of Vṛtra with *áhi*); *vájra* (8.96.5). √*Han* typically describes the action taken against Vṛtra (Indra's chief epithet is *vṛtrahán* 1.32.11; 5.29.3; 8.96.5); √*muc* (1.61.10) and *ápa* √*vṛ* (1.32.11) are used to describe the release of the Waters. These are most often called *áp* (1.32.11; 7.23.4) though they may also be named *saptá síndhavaḥ* (see 1.32.12).[9] Since Indra is mentioned in another

7. See p. 52ff.

8. Brown, "Creation Myth", p. 87; cf. pp. 53-54 above.

9. See Hillebrandt, *Ved. Myth.* III, 174ff on further terminology pertaining to the Indra-Vṛtra myth.

myth as a 'releaser of cows', mention of this god's feat is not enough to assure the context. However, mention of Indra's helpers, the Maruts and Rudra, does provide a reliable and discerning indicator. These helpers may be the anthropomorphic representations of the power in the atmosphere which comes to Indra's aid. The forces prevalent in this region, symbolized by the Storm gods and the *vájra* constitute an essential feature of this myth.[10] Other helpers of Indra are Viṣṇu, Agni, Soma;[11] Soma is drawn into the myth since the drink empowered Indra to slay Vṛtra.

In the following verses, a term for 'cow' is used figuratively to denote 'the Cosmic Waters' appearing in the Indra-Vṛtra myth:

5.29.3 cd: (To Indra)

tád dhí havyám mánuṣe gā́ ávindad áhann áhim papivā́ñ índro asya

For this oblation found the cows for man; Indra, having drunk it, slew the dragon.

Asya: Oldenberg (*Noten*) rather *asyá*.

In the sense that the soma draught enables Indra to defeat Vṛtra, the soma oblation may be considered as having found 'the cows', that is, the Cosmic Waters.

2.19.3abc: (To Indra)

sá mā́hina índro árṇo apā́m prairayad ahihā́chā samudrám
ájanayat sū́ryaṃ vidád gā́

The mighty Indra, the slayer of the dragon, sent forth the flood of Waters to the Ocean.
He produced the Sun; he found the cows;

The terminology of pādas ab clearly belongs to the Indra-Vṛtra myth.

10. On a more abstract level, the myth is a "symbolic representation of Potentiality" (i.e. Ādityas) "striving with Inertia", (i.e. Dānavas) "and overcoming Inertia through the aid of the Power or Energy existing in the universe, especially in the atmosphere where the mighty winds blow, the thunder rolls, and the lightning strikes". Brown, "Theories", p. 24.

11. W. Norman Brown, "Creation Myth", p. 96.

Pāda b relates that the Cosmic Waters, once released, made their way to the heavenly ocean (*samudrá* cf. 1.32.2; note Brown, "Creation Myth", p. 97). For an analysis of *samudrá* as (1) a real body of water, (2) the ocean which surrounds the world, (3) the heavenly ocean, see Lüders, *Varuṇa* I, 92-121. If pāda c is understood as part of the context established in the first hemistich, then *gó* = 'cows' as 'Cosmic Waters'. But, pāda c, taken with pāda d, could also apply to Indra's feat in the myth of the Paṇis. Pāda c could be taken, therefore, as a more general reference to Indra's cosmic feats. As such, *gó* could be 'Waters' as well as 'rays of dawn' (cf. 10.68.11). So also Bergaigne (*Rel. Véd.* II, 191); H. P. Schmidt (*Bṛhaspati und Indra*, p. 244 fn. 113). Grassmann (*Wö*) takes *gó* as 'rays of the sun',[12] or 'flames of Agni'. Sāy. *gó*: *paṇibhirapahṛtā*.
Cf. Oldenberg, *Noten*.

8.96.5 (To Indra)

á yád vájram bāhvór indra dhátse madacyútam áhaye hántavā u
prá párvatā ánavanta prá gā́vaḥ prá brahmā́ṇo abhinákṣanta índram

When you O Indra take the *vájra* in your arms, (the *vájra*) moved by [your] intoxication to slay the dragon,
The mountains sounded and the cows, the brahmans approaching Indra.

Brahmā́ṇaḥ could refer either to the Aṅgirases or the Maruts (cf. Geldner, *HOS* 34, v. cit.; cf. 5.29.3); the latter group is preferred since the key words (*vájra, áhi,* $\sqrt{}$*han*) indicate that this verse describes the Indra-Vṛtra myth; the Aṅgirases are not connected with this myth (cf. Brown, "Creation Myth", 96; A. Venkatasubbiah, "On Indra's Winning of Cows and Waters", *ZDMG* 115 [1965], 127). The Maruts, are not characteristic helpers in the myth of the Paṇis. One verse (2.34.1) has been interpreted by several scholars as the only reference to the Maruts in the myth of the Paṇis (Lüders, *Varuṇa* II, 530;

12. This meaning for *gó* seems doubtful. *Gó* is the usual metaphor for Dawn's rays, as 'horses' are for the sun's rays. *Gó* in 1.164.7 probably refers to the rays of Dawn, though these are situated on the head of the bird, Sūrya. The image relates to a rain theory, see Brown, "1.164", p. 212.

Renou, *EVP* 10 ad 2.34.1; Geldner, *HOS* 33, p. 318), but the terminology is not precise enough to warrant this conclusion. 2.34.1d mentions that the Maruts disclosed 'the cows', and this could mean that Indra's helpers released from Vṛtra's hold the Cosmic Waters.

10.89.7cd (To Indra)

bibhéda girím návam ín ná kumbhám á gá índro akṛṇuta svayúgbhiḥ
He split the mountain like a new jug; Indra brought forth the cattle with [his] allies.

This verse seems to be another example mentioning, in each hemistich, a major cosmic deed of Indra. So also H.P. Schmidt (*Bṛhaspati und Indra*, p. 244 fn. 113). Thus, pādas ab refer to the killing of Vṛtra; cd could refer also to that myth, or, to the myth of the Paṇis. √*Bhid* is used with both myths (e.g. 1.52.5; 2.11.20; 2.15.8; 3.34.10; 10.62.2; 10.68.6 have √*bhid* and *valá*; 1.52.10; 2.11.18 have √*bhid* and *vṛtrá*).

Svayúgbhiḥ: either the Maruts or Aṅgirases (cf. 10.67.8); Sāy. *marudbhiḥ*. Therefore, *gó*, as in 2.19.3, could mean 'Cosmic Waters' as well as 'rays of dawn'. Bergaigne (*Rel. Véd.* II, 220) considers the 'cows' as 'Waters'; so also Sāyaṇa. Venkatasubbiah (op. cit. p. 121) takes pādas cd as part of the Indra-Vṛtra myth.

4.19.7cd (To Indra)

dhánvāny ájrāñ apṛṇak tṛṣāṇáñ ádhog índra staryò dáṃsupatnīḥ

He satisfied the thirsting deserts and plains; Indra milked the barren cows, they who have a lord who does wonders.

Pāda c: cf. Bergaigne (*Rel. Véd.* II, 184).
Dáṃsupatnīḥ: pada pāṭha—*dám-supatnīḥ*. Cf. 6.3.7 *dáṃ supátnī*. Cf. Geldner (*HOS* 33, v. cit.) and Mayrhofer, Fasc. 9, p. 10. Renou (*EVP*/ I, 52, fn. 1): *dáṃsu* is loc. pl. of *dám* 'house'. *Starī*: metaphor for the Cosmic Waters; cf. 7.23.4 (see fn. 80, p. 53). Indra caused the 'cows' to become fruitful (Brown, "Creation Myth" 97). The Waters were barren until Indra caused their maternal state, released them and made it possible for them to give birth to the Sun. As a result of this, Indra is said to have

put the milk in the cows. Achieving this, Indra is the lord who works wonders. Bergaigne (*Rel. Véd.* II, 497) offers "les eaux du ciel, qui, avant d'être 'traites' par Indra, étaient appelées indifféremment vierges ou stériles.." See also Geldner in *Auswahl* II, ad 4.19.7 and Hillebrandt, *Lieder*, p. 46.

The creation of the universe may be attributed to Indra without referring specifically to the Indra-Vṛtra myth. In such cases allusions to the creation theme are generalized. That is, Indra as the All-maker (*viśvákarman* 8.98.2), gives shape to the universe, and creates and controls the forms which fill the world. Thus, Indra is said to have 'found' (i.e. created) the cattle (*gó*), horses, plants, waters and woods (1.103.5); in his control are horses, cattle (*gó*) troops, all chariots; he creates the sun and dawn; he is the leader of the waters (2.12.7). He designates the wealth of cattle (*gó*) for booty (1.121.2).[13] In the above verses, ***gó*** is used literally.

In 6.60.2 Indra-Agni cause the appearance of some of the basic elements of existence; cows are included among these:

tā́ yodhiṣṭam abhí gā́ indra nūnám apáḥ svàr uṣáso agna ūḷhā́ḥ
díśaḥ svàr uṣása indra citrā́ apó gā́ agne yuvase niyútvān

O Indra, Agni you fought now to gain cows, waters, sun, the dawns which were carried off.
The directions, the sun, the bright dawns O Indra, the waters the cows you gain, O Agni, having a team.

This verse has allusions to both the Indra-Vṛtra myth and the myth of the Paṇis. *Uṣásaḥ ..ūḷhā́ḥ* could belong to the Paṇis' myth.[14] However, the phrase occurs here together with ***áp***, evocative of the Cosmic Waters. These are probably not a primary feature of the myth of the Paṇis (see p. 125); ***díśaḥ*** in pāda c is likewise not found in this myth. ***Díś*** and ***áp*** belong to the creation theme. 6.60.2 seems to contain a general statement on the cosmic feats of Indra-Agni, mixing themes and termino-

13. *Góḥ* in b is used in a collective sense. The translation follows Geldner's (*HOS*, 33). Cf. Oldenberg, *Noten*, v. cit. and Ludwig, ***RV***, v. cit.
14. So also Sāyaṇa; for 'dawns' in the myth of the Paṇis, see under B.3. c. The Treasure of the Paṇis.

logy in so doing. The meaning of *gā́ḥ* in 6.60.2a and d probably does not alter (not so Grassmann, *Wö*, *gā́ḥ* in 'a' = oxen; *gā́ḥ* in 'd' = rays of Sun or Agni) for the major terms in ab are repeated in cd. *Gó*, occurring as it does with *áp* and *uṣás* in both sections of the verse is therefore unlikely to be a metaphor for the Cosmic Waters or the rays of Dawn. Perhaps we are to understand *gó* in the literal sense. That is, *gó* are the cows which contribute so amply to the daily needs of Vedic man,[15] especially the dakṣiṇā cows and the oblation-giving cows which also figure in the myth of the Paṇis (*gó* in 3.34.9 may have this connotation too).

A number of other deities are drawn into Indra's creative feats; as above, *gó* represents in these verses the actual cow created when the world took shape. Mitra-Varuṇa caused the plants to grow, the cows to stream with milk and they send the rain (5.62. 3). Soma produced all these plants, cattle and the waters (1.91.22). Viśvedevas gave birth to the formula, the cow, the horse, plants, forest trees, the earth, mountains and waters (10.65.11).

B. 'COW' IN THE MYTH OF THE PAṆIS

There appears to be in the Rig Veda, a narrative which expresses Vedic man's ideas concerning the re-establishment of world order. The ideas are contained in a story focusing on the Paṇis, the chief demons in this account. Their demonic act is that they withhold 'cows' and other essential items from those championing the Vedic sacrifice. In order to determine the meaning of 'cows' in this context, it is necessary to analyze the entire situation surrounding this demonic deed of the Paṇis. Accordingly, this chapter[16] discusses in detail those verses which mention the Paṇis, and the events and personages characteristically associated with them. In so doing, a legend exhibiting internal logic and cogency develops; it has the Paṇis' deed as its core and is called the myth of the Paṇis.

15. So also for *gó* in 5.14.4 (to Agni) and 9.90.4 (to Soma). Both have a series of terms similar to 6.60.2. 5.14.4c: *ávindad gā́ apáḥ svàḥ*; 9.90.4c: *apáḥ síṣāsann uṣásaḥ svàr gā́ḥ*. Cf. 9.91.6 for literal use of *gó* in a similar series. In the same way, *áp* in 6.60.2; 5.14.4; 9.90.4 could be the 'actual waters' with allusion to the 'Cosmic Waters'.

16. This chapter is an extended treatment of the study discussed in "The Myth of the Paṇis in the Rig Veda", *JAOS* 93 (1973), 44-57.

The myth of the Paṇis tells the story of the Paṇis who, as anti-sacerdotal forces, withhold a treasure mainly from mythical priests. The treasure consists of horses and cows offered as the priests' honorarium (*dákṣiṇā*), the oblation-giving cows, the rays of dawn, dawn itself, the ritual fire, the sun, the path of light and the day. What the Paṇis are in fact doing is to withhold items essential to the performance of the sacrifice. The rite may not begin in darkness nor can it proceed smoothly with neither the oblation nor the honorarium. However, should the sacrifice not be performed, disorder and chaos would engulf the world of men and gods, for the performance of the sacrifice promotes the *ṛtá*, a force which causes order to prevail throughout the organized universe. Therefore, for an ordered world structure to exist, a force is needed to release the Paṇis' treasure. Mere physical force will not work against them; the Paṇis are nearly indomitable due to the nature of the treasure they withhold. However, their great vulnerability stems from the fact that they have no magic power, or as the Veda says, their "words are no weapons" (10.108.6). The priests, on the contrary, have the most potent magical power at their command. Their chantings evoke that power, the *bráhman*. With their hymns and songs, the priests and their divine allies triumph over the Paṇis and cause the treasure to be released. Thus commences the unfolding of daylight: dawn's rays emerge from darkness; these are followed by the sunlight. Day begins. The ritual fire is lit. The oblation milk is available, as well as the most esteemed *dákṣiṇā*. Conditions are now such that the sacrifice may begin.

This story is not presented in its entirety in any single place in the Rig Veda; rather it must be pieced together. To select the pieces which are likely to constitute the distinctive elements of this myth, a method must be followed which is able to isolate those elements forming the nucleus of the myth. In this way only the primary elements will enter into the interpretation. We are fortunate in having one hymn which devotes itself entirely to an episode in the story of the Paṇis. RV 10.108 is recognized by the Indian tradition as relating a legend dealing with the Paṇis. Nirukta 11.25, in commenting upon 10.108.1 states that "there is a legend that the bitch of the gods" [i.e. Saramā] "sent forth by

Indra, conversed with the demons called Paṇis".[17] Also in connection with 10.108, the Bṛhad-Devatā cites the legend in 8.24-36.[18] Thus, due to this testimony within the tradition, we can be reasonably sure that the majority of features found in RV 10.108 are germane only to the myth of the Paṇis. This hymn thus serves as a reliable standard upon which to base the distinctive features of the myth.

1. Synopsis of RV 10.108

The core of the myth described in 10.108 tells the story of the Paṇis who, having withheld a herd of cows, horses and other riches kept them hidden in a rock (10.108.7) on the other side of the River Rasā (10.108. 1,2). Determined to free the treasure, Indra sends his messenger Saramā to trace the whereabouts of the wealth and arrange for its safe return (see 10.108.2). Saramā, flying around to the ends of the sky (10.108.5), finds the demons and their treasure. The Paṇis however seem to be in no mood to release it; they would make Indra their cowherd (10.108.3), or offer to make Saramā a sister (10.108.9), but would not surrender their wealth without a fight (10.108.5). The demons do not change their stand even though Saramā gives them ample warnings: that they lack the decisive weapon—holy utterance (10.108.6) that Bṛhaspati will not spare them (10.108.6), that they will be killed by Indra (10.108.4), that Bṛhaspati together with Soma, the Pressing Stones and the wise Ṛṣis will let the lowing cows come out (10.108.11), and that their cows will be divided up by the Ṛṣis, Ayāsya, the Aṅgirases and the Navagvas (10.108.8). 10.108 leaves off at this point. We are able to pursue the story further if we isolate the distinctive features of the myth as found in 10.108 and then analyze those Rig Vedic passages wherein these features reappear.

These are :

demons : Paṇis, Vala[19]

demons' opponents : Indra, Bṛhaspati, Aṅgirases, other mythic priests, Soma.

17. L. Sarup, *The Nighaṇṭu and the Nirukta*, p. 177.

18. Macdonell, The *Bṛhad-Devatā*, Paragraphs 30-36 deal with events not mentioned in the RV; a variation of these events occurs also in the Jaiminīya Brāhmaṇa (see H. Oertel, "Contributions from the Jāiminīya Brāhmaṇa to the history of the Brāhmaṇa literature", *JAOS* 19 [1898], 97-103).

19. See exegesis of 10.108.9.

the weapon of victory : holy utterances
the withheld treasure : cows, horses, riches

The findings, using this approach, are discussed below. The translation and exegesis of 10.108 directly follow. Next, the detailed philological analysis of the distinctive features is presented. Based upon this evidence and a comparison between the myth of the Paṇis and the Indra-Vṛtra myth, certain conclusions on the significance of the myth of the Paṇis are proposed.

2. Translation[20] and exegesis of 10.108

1. (Paṇis)

kīṃ icchántī sarámā prédám ānaḍ dūré hy ádhvā jáguriḥ parācáiḥ
kásméhitiḥ ká páritakmyāsīt katháṃ rasáyā ataraḥ páyāṅsi

Seeking what has Saramā reached this place ? The road is diminishing far into the distance.
What is [your] message for us ? How was [your] wandering ?
How did you cross over Rasā's waters ?

Jáguriḥ : Mayrhofer—'steep', with *guráte;* Whitney (*Roots*) from √*jṛ*, √*jur*, so also Oldenberg (*Noten*). Nirukta 11.25 takes it from √*gam*. Wackernagel (*AiG* I,22) from √*gṛ* 'to sing'. Cf. Hillebrandt, *Lieder*, p. 147.

Páritakmyā : A. Debrunner, J. Wackernagel, *AiG* II_2, 810 : "Angst verursachend"; fem. "Irrfahrt, Gefahr"; see Mayrhofer, II, 218.

Rasā—"name of a mythic stream at the ends of the earth which as well as the atmosphere it encompasses" (Macdonell and Keith, *Vedic Index* II, 209).

2. (Saramā)

índrasya dūtír iṣitá carāmi mahá icchántī paṇayo nidhín vaḥ
atiṣkádo bhiyásā tán na āvat táthā rasáyā ataraṃ páyāṅsi

20. Translations of this hymn are found, outside of the standard translations of the entire Rig Veda, in: A. Hillebrandt, *Lieder des Ṛgveda* (Göttingen, Leipzig 1913), p. 147; K. Geldner and A. Kaegi, *Siebenzig Lieder des Rigveda* (Tübingen, 1875), p. 78; L. von Schroeder, *Mysterium und Mimus im Rigveda*, (Leipzig, 1908) p. 173ff. E. J. Thomas, *Vedic Hymns*, in *Wisdom of the East* (London, 1923) 51ff. Hanns-Peter Schmidt, *Bṛhaspati und Indra*, (Wiesbaden, 1968), 185-187.

I come, sent [as] messenger of Indra, seeking O Paṇis, your great treasures.
Due to fear of leaping over, this[21] helped us. Thus I crossed over Rasā's waters.

Sāy. *nidhīn : bṛhaspatergonidhīn*
Pādas cd : Ludwig (*RV* II, 636), Geldner (*HOS* 35, 329) and Hillebrandt (*Lieder,* 147) have Rasā the subject of *āvat.* This interpretation results from the account given in Jaiminīya Brāhmaṇa 2,439, 2-3 (see H. Oertel, *JAOS* 19, p. 101). See Oldenberg's criticism of this position (in *Noten* v. cit.) which my translation follows.

3. (Paṇis)

kīdṝññ índraḥ sarame kā́ dṛśīkā́ yásyedáṃ dūtī́r ásaraḥ parākā́t
ā́ ca gácchān mitrám enā dadhāmā́thā gávāṃ gópatir no bhavāti

What [is] Indra like O Saramā ? what [is his] appearance, for whom you now travelled far [as] messenger ?
Should he come, we will form a friendship with him; then, may he be the herder of [our] cows.

4. (Saramā)

nā́háṃ táṃ veda dábhyaṃ dábhat sá yásyedáṃ dūtī́r asaram parākā́t
ná táṃ gūhanti sraváto gabhīrā́ hatā́ indreṇa paṇayaḥ śayadhve

I know him [to be] not injurable; he harms, [he] of whom I came [as] messenger from afar.
Deep rivers cannot hide him; you will lie killed by Indra, O Paṇis.

5. (Paṇis)

imā́ gā́vaḥ sarame yā́ aīcchaḥ pári divó ántānt subhage pátantī
kás ta enā áva sṛjād áyudhvy utā́smā́kam ā́yudhā santi tigmā́

These [are] the cows O Saramā which you sought, flying around to the ends of the sky, O Lovely One.
Who would surrender them to you without a fight, and our weapons are sharp.

21. i.e. being Indra's messenger.

Pāda b : cf. 5.47.4

6. (Saramā)

asenyā́ vaḥ paṇayo vácāṅsy aniṣavyā́s tanvā̀ḥ santu pāpī́ḥ
ádhṛṣṭo va étavā́ astu pánthā bṛ́haspátir va ubhayā́ ná mṛḷā́t

Your words [are] no weapons, O Paṇis. Though your evil bodies may be immune to arrows,
or the path insuperable to approach, in either case Bṛhaspati would not spare you.

Pāda a is in response to 5d. Thus *vácāṅsi* refers to their previous words. Cf. Sāy. *vácāṅsi : purvoktāni.* In addition, *vácas* may also = *ā́yudha* in 5d, for in this myth the significant weapons are holy words. The Paṇis believe that their weapons are potent; Saramā knows better. It is with the priests' *vácas, bráhman, arká, ráva* and *ukthá* that the Paṇis will be defeated.

Asenyā́ : hapax legomenon in the RV. *Sénya :* in RV 1.81.2 Indra called *vīra sényo.* AV 1.20.2 : *sénya* modifies *vadhá* (so also in AV 6.99.2 which Bloomfield [*AV* in *SBE* 42, p. 123] translates "hostile weapons"). In AV 18.1.40: *sénya* is used with *ní* √*vap.* All three AV verses ask protection from the effect of *sénya.* I concur with Bloomfield[22] that *asenyā́* has the sense of 'weak, feeble' etc.

Pādas bc are the two suppositions denied by pāda d. Each supposition has its own main verb; *santu* and *astu* are both employed as the concessive use of the imperative.

Aniṣavyā́s : "cowardly; not inured to arrows"—Bloomfield.[23]

Ubhayā́ : Bloomfield[24] : "in either case"; he makes abc dependent upon d.

For Vedic adverbs in *ayā́* see T. Burrows, *The Sanskrit Language p.* 281; see also Wackernagel *AiG,* II/1, 21; II_2, 917.

There has been general disagreement as to how this verse ought to be understood. For other opinions see Bloomfield,[25] Oldenberg (*Noten,* N. F. 331-2); Geldner (*HOS* 35, 329) also

22. Bloomfield, "Some Cruces in Vedic Text, Grammar and Interpretation," *American Journal of Philolophy*, 38 (1917), 11-13.

23. *Ibid.*

24. *Ibid.*

25. *Ibid.*

considers 6a as the answer to 5d, and *ubhayā́* as referring to pādas bc.

7. (Paṇis)

ayáṃ nidhíḥ sarame ádribudhno góbhir áśvebhir vásubhir nýr̥ṣṭaḥ
rákṣanti táṃ paṇáyo yé sugopā́ réku padám álakam ā́ jagantha

This treasure [chamber] in the base of a rock, [is] filled with cows, horses, riches, O Saramā.
The Paṇis who [are] good herders, guard it; you came to this deserted place in vain.

Pāda b : Cf. 7.90.6b; 4.17.11

Sugopā́ : i.e. careful guardians

Réku : A. Debrunner and J. Wackernagel, *AiG* II_2, 470 : "freilassend"; Mayrhofer, Fasc. 18, p. 72 : "ergiebig; reich; from *riṇákti*". Geldner (*HOS* 35, 330) : "falsche"; Ludwig (*RV* II, 636) : "weit entfernten". Hillebrandt (*Lieder* p. 147) : "vollen Ort".

Pāda d : Geldner (*HOS* 35, 329) : 4.5.12.

8. (Saramā)

éhá gamann ṛṣayaḥ sómaśitā ayā́syo áṅgiraso návagvāḥ
tá etám ūrváṃ ví bhajanta gónām áthaitád vácaḥ paṇáyo vamann ít

The *ṛṣis*, aroused by soma, will come here, Ayāsya,[26] Aṅgirases, Navagvas.
They will divide this stall of cattle among themselves; then will the Paṇis repent this talk.

Ūrvám : means both 'a body of water' and 'an enclosure' (*PW;* Mayrhofer I, p. 117) *Ūrvá* frequently occurs in this myth where it is translated as 'cowstall' (Ludwig, *RV* II, 636; Grassmann, *RV* II, 388; Schroeder, *Mysterium,* p. 175). This meaning is rejected by Thomas (*op. cit.* p. 53) and Geldner, (*Ved. Stud.* II, 269 ff). Geldner suggests 'herd' and 'mountain con-

26. See Keith and Macdonell, *Vedic Index* 1, p. 32. Bergaigne (*Rel. Véd.* II, 292 fn. 2) states that *ayā́sya* is an epithet, not a proper name. He believes it refers to Bṛhaspati in v. 8. H. P. Schmidt, (*Bṛhaspati und Indra,* p. 189) considers *ayā́sya* as an epithet of Indra.

taining a herd'; for 10.108.8c he prefers 'herd'. My own preference is to keep the idea of a container (*ūrvá* from √*vṛ* 'to cover') and to understand pāda c as referring to the partition of the treasure chamber (cf. 7.27.1: *gómati vrajé bhajā*; 5.34.5 : *bhajati gómati vrajé*). However *abhajat* (*gā́ḥ* understood) in 2.24.14 favors Geldner's interpretation.
Vácaḥ : without magical connotation.

9. (Paṇis)

evā́ ca tvám sarama ājagántha prábādhitā sáhasā daívyena
svásāraṃ tvā kṛṇavai mā́ púnar gā ápa te gávāṃ subhage bhajāma

Since you came O Saramā urged on by divine force,
let me make you a sister; do not go again; we will share cows with you, O Lovely One.

Sáhasā daívyena : see Chap. IV, fn. 91.
Subject of *kṛṇavai* is *Vala;* see below.

10. (Saramā)

nā́háṃ veda bhrātṛtváṃ nó svasṛtvám índro vidur áṅgirasaś ca ghorā́ḥ
gókāmā me acchadayan yád ā́yam ápā́ta ita paṇayo várīyaḥ

Neither brotherhood nor sisterhood know I, Indra and the fearful Aṅgirases, they know [it].
When I left, they seemed to me eager for cows; go away from here O Paṇis, farther away.

11.[27]

dūrám ita paṇayo várīya úd gā́vo yantu minatī́r ṛténa
bṛ́haspátir yā́ ávindan nigū́ḷhāḥ sómo grā́vāṇa ṛ́ṣayaś ca víprāḥ

Go far away O Paṇis; let the lowing cows come out according to the *ṛtá,*

27. Speaker ? Hardly the Paṇis; possibly Saramā. Were the P myth a reoccurring event, then Saramā, in v. 11, could be telling the Paṇis to do that which they have done in the past. Cf. Thieme's view ("Agastya und Lopāmudrā", *ZDMG* 113 [1963], 69ff: He does not think that the Aṅgirases could be the speakers since the finding of the cows is referred to by a verb in the imperfect, the tense of the distant past in the Veda. He considers the verse to be a spell ("Legendenzauber") and spoken when an actual event parallels the mythic situation described in the body of the hymn.

Which Bṛhaspati found hidden, and Soma, the Pressing Stones and the wise Ṛṣis.

Minatī́r : possibly *mimatīr* Bloomfield (*Ved. Concordance* p. 261). Schmidt (*op. cit.* p. 187) and Thieme (*op. cit.* p. 71) "tauschend". Oldenberg (*Noten*) adds that shouting is characteristic of this scene.
For the role of *ṛtá* in this myth, see p. 114.
3.44.5d (*ū́d gā́ háribhir ājata*) could be another reference to the release of the cows by the Pressing Stones. *Hári* may refer to the Stones (*ádri*) as is the case in pāda c (*ápāvṛṇod dháribhir ádribhiḥ sutám*). *Ádri* and *grā́van* (10.108.11) are the two common terms for the Vedic press stones (Oliphant, "Press-Stones", p. 225ff). Oliphant notes that *ádri* is modified by *hári* three times (p. 244). Possibly 'cows' in connection with the Press Stones are the oblation-giving cows (see p. 117). Sāyaṇa : *gā́ḥ*—those stolen by Paṇis. Ludwig (*RV* II, p. 85), Geldner (*HOS* 33, p. 386) and Sāyaṇa take *hári* as 'horses'.

The ruin which Saramā predicts for the Paṇis does come about as the gods set out to conquer them. Saramā found the cows going to the *ṛta* (see 5,45.7) and the Aṅgirases sang with the cows (5.45.8). The Fathers (i.e. the Aṅgirases) who drove out the wealth consisting of cows, by means of the *ṛta,* broke through Vala in one year (10.62.2); they had found all the Paṇi's nourishment (1.83.4). The singers aided Indra as he slaughtered Vala (2.15.8; 2.11.20), and burst the foundations of the mountain (2.15.8). Indra entered into the fight with other mythical priests as well; the Navagvas, the Seven Seers, the Daśagvas were by his side as he, with sound (*ráva*) rent through Vala (1.62.4).

When Bṛhaspati entered the battle, he also brought forth the cows from Vala, who has cow forms (*góvapus*) in his own body (see 10.68.9). He cleft Vala with the chant (*arká* 10.68.6) and with *bráhman* (2.24.3); he split the rock and found the cows (10.68.11d = 1.62.3c).

After the rock was cleft and the Paṇis were vanquished, the entire treasure which they had been withholding streamed forth.[28]

28. Cf. H. Lüders' discussion (*Varuṇa* II, 532) on the released treasure.

Bṛhaspati found the dawn (*uṣás*), sun (*sū́rya*) and *gó* (10.67.5)[29]; he found *uṣás*, the sun (*svàr*) and fire (*agní*) (10.68.9). Brahmaṇaspati drove out cows (*gó*) and caused *svàr* to appear (2.24.3). Indra created *sū́rya*, *uṣás*, a path (*gātú*)[30] and *agní* (3.31.15); together with the Aṅgirases he dispelled darkness by means of *uṣás*, *sū́rya* and cows (*gó*) (1.62.5). The Aṅgirases, in 1.71.2 found the day (*áhar*), *svàr* and the light of the cows (*ketú usrā́*).

3. Analysis and Interpretation of the myth

a. Personages in the myth

1. *Paṇis* : In 10.108 the term *paṇí* occurs in the plural and is used in the mythic context. The term is not always so used. Outside of this myth, *paṇí* in the RV designates someone who is a miser (cf. 8.64.2 and 10.60.6 : *paṇí...arādhás*) especially in ritual affairs.[31] A *paṇí* stints with regard to the *dákṣiṇā* and is therefore thought of as one who does not patronize the Vedic sacrifice.[32] Indeed he is the very antithesis of the devout sacrificer (cf. 8.97.2). A *paṇí* does not press soma (4.25.7); he does not seem inclined to present offerings in general (cf. 6.53.3; 8.64.2). Consequently, the priests have no praise for him (5.61.8). Since he is stingy and thus impious, he is to be kept away from the ritual. Uṣas,

29. Two meanings could be argued for *gó* in the enumeration *uṣásam sū́ryam gā́m* in 5c. *Gó* masc. could refer to Agni (cf. 3.31.15; 10.68.9); *gó* masc. occurs as an epithet for Agni (e.g. 10.31.10; 8.74.10). Or, *gó* could be used in the collective sense to signify 'rays of light' (cf. 1.62.5). *Arká* in 10.67.5d is understood as 'light', referring, in the collective sense to *uṣás, sū́rya gó* in pāda c. In general, as well as in this myth, *arká* may mean 'hymn' and 'light'. Naighaṇṭu 2.20 indicates that *arká* may also mean *vájra*. Possibly in 10.67.5d, *arká* connotes both 'hymn' and 'light' (cf. Renou, *EVP* 15, 17 ad 10.67.5).

30. *gatú*- Renou (*EVP* III, 72): "voie tracée dans l'espace indifférencié, pour marquer l'issue hors des ténèbres; aussi fig., voie vers le bonheur, le salut: équivalent archaïque de *gáti*, mot presque inconnu du RV". Cf. 1.71.2. Ludwig (*RV*): 'gesang'. See also Geldner (*Auswahl*, v. cit. and *HOS* 33, v. cit.).

31. On the meaning of *paṇí* see Schmidt (op. cit. p. 209ff); Mayrhofer (Fasc. 9, 195); Debrunner and Wackernagel (*AiG* II/2, p. 297).

32. Bloomfield (*Rigvedic Repetitions*, 287) lists the following terms as being synonyms for *paṇí* : *aśraddhá, ápṛṇat, ayajñá, áyajyu, áditsant, árāvan, kṛśá, ádāśuri, áyajvan, ásunvant, kavārí, ádāśvas, ásuṣvi, ádevayu, ádevayant, anindrá, etc.*

who heralds in the sacrificial day, is asked to awaken only the generous and let the stingy, called Paṇis, sleep (1.124.10). It is not that a *paṇi* is too poor to give; on the contrary, he is described as prosperous (4.25.7). His niggardly ways make him contemptible to the Ṛṣis.[33]

The character of an actual *paṇi* accords closely with that of the mythic Paṇis. RV 7.6.3 gives a succinct description of the demons. They are without spiritual insight (*akratú*), false (*grathin*),[34] speaking contemptuously (*mṛdhrávāc*),[35] bereft of faith (*aśraddha*),[36] not strengthening (*avṛdhá*)[37] the gods by means of the offering, and abstaining from the sacrifice (*ayajñá*).

It would indeed seem that the Paṇis in 10.108 are a mythic intensification of an actual *paṇí*.[38] A paṇí in daily life should

33. One indication of this attitude is provided by the adjectives modifying *paṇí*. Such a list is provided by B. H. Kapadia, "Paṇis in the Ṛg-Veda", *Poona Orientalist*, Vol. 27, 1 and 2 (1962), 54.

34. Debrunner, Wackernagel *AiG* II_2 342; Geldner (*HOS* 34, p. 186): "zugeknöpften"; Hillebrandt (*Ved. Myth.* I, 90) agreeing with Sāyaṇa's interpretation of *grathín* as *jalpaka*, elaborates in taking the term to signify the flow of speech in a foreign tongue and thereby creating the impression that the words run together. Cf. Oldenberg, *Noten*, N.F. 13, p. 9.

35. See Mayrhofer, Fasc. 9, p. 595 for the literature which discusses other meanings; Hillebrandt (*Ved. Myth.* I, 89-90): speech of a foe, a barbarian. (So also Renou, *EVP* 13, 57).

36. Bloomfield ("Contributions"): "...the epithet *aśraddhá* 'devoid of *śraddhā* used of the Paṇis in 7.6.3, amounts in the end to their characteristic designation 'stingy' " p. 412. The author shows how the term *śraddhā* whose primary meaning is 'faith', assumes in the Vedas the extended meaning of 'faith which manifests itself through work'. Thus, having *śraddhā* is in effect having a state of mind which desires to sacrifice and give. There is a "frequent juxtaposition of *śraddha*...with *yajña*, or derivatives of the roots *yaj* and *hu*...with *dákṣiṇā* and the root *dā*..." (p. 411).

37. *Avṛdha* is a *RV* hapax legomenon; it is understood as the negation of *vṛdhá*, which is a derivative of the root *vṛdh*. √*Vṛdh* means 'to strengthen', especially in the sense of increasing the power of a god through the strengthening agents of the sacrifice (cf. Bergaigne, *Rel. Véd.* II, 272ff). *Avṛdhá* refers to one 'who does not increase, i.e., who does not strengthen the gods through offerings'.

38. The close connection between the two has already been noticed by a number of scholars: Bergaigne, *Rel. Véd.* II, 319; A. B. Keith, *The Religion and Philosophy of the Veda and Upanishads* I, 128; O. Strauss, *Bṛhaspati im Veda*, p. 35 and fn. 2 on that page for further references.

have been an actual enemy who opposes the Vedic sacrifice by refusing to honor the rites and priests. Similarly, the group of Paṇis attempt to thwart the sacrifice by withholding conditions vital to its performance.

If this be the unique character of the mythic Paṇis, it is equally informative to note what they are not. Nowhere in the text are they associated with the Dānavas. Epithetical qualifiers are restricted to one: *dásyu* (7.6.3). *Dásyu*[39] means 'demon, enemy of the gods, impious man, foreigner'. Since *dásyu* is applied to a wide range of Rig Vedic demons, the term is not helpful in associating the Paṇis with another set of demons.

2. *Vala*: If the Paṇis constitute a group, then who is the speaker of 10.108.9 ? And who is the Paṇi mentioned in 1.83.4; 1.93.4; 6.44.22; 10.67.6 ? These verses describe the same myth as 10.108; however they use *paṇí* in the singular to distinguish one member from the group. Do the Paṇis have a leader ? 10.67.6 seems to indicate so:

índro valáṃ rakṣitā́raṃ dúghānāṃ karéṇeva ví cakartā rávеṇa
svédāñjibhir āśíram ichámānó 'rodayat paṇím ā́ gā́ amuṣṇāt

Indra cut through Vala, the guardian of the milk cows, with sound as with the hand.
He, desiring milk, together with those who glisten with perspiration, caused the Paṇi to weep; he stole his cows.

Ravеṇa: as in 4.50.1,4; 1.62.4; 1.71.2 in the same myth (Geldner, *HOS* 35, p. 242).
Svédāñjibhiḥ: Geldner (ibid.); the Aṅgirases; cf. v. 7. Sāy.: the Maruts. C. J. Blair (*Heat in the Rig Veda and the Atharva Veda*, p. 111) translates "bathed in sweat", and suggests that the sweat generated by the Aṅgirases was proof of their devotional fervor.

This passage permits us to draw the conclusion that *paṇí* in the sg. refers to Vala; this is the only passage where Vala is called a *paṇí*. In 6.39.2 he is mentioned together with the group of Paṇis

39. See Mayrhofer; also see Macdonell, *Vedic Myth*. p. 158 for the extensive use of *dása, dásyu*, applied to the enemies of the gods.

in a manner suggesting that Vala is the personification of the enclosure in which the Paṇis have kept the cows:

6.39.2 (To Indra)

ayám uśānáḥ páry ádrim usrā́ ṛtádhītibhir ṛtayúg yujānáḥ
rujád árugṇaṃ ví valásya sā́nuṃ paṇī́ṃr vácobhir abhí yodhad índraḥ[40]

This one,[41] desiring the cows, the one united with the *ṛtá* joined around the rock by those having knowledge of the *ṛtá*,
He broke the unbroken ridge of Vala; Indra vanquished the Paṇis with spells.

Ádrim: refers to Vala; cf. 1.62.4; *ádribudhna* 10.108.7 also refers to Vala. Additional verses where *ádri* refers to Vala are: 1.7.3; 1.71.2; 1.62.3;[42] 3.31.6,7; 4.1.15; 5.45.1; 6.17.5; 6.32.2; 10.68.11. Vala is also designated by terms which are synonymous with *ádri*: *párvata* (2.15.8; 2.23.18; 10.68.3,7); *áśman* (10.68.4).[43]

The etymology of the term *valá* bears out its significance in the myth. Bailey[44] suggests that *valá* is a dialect form of Indo-Iranian *vara* 'enclosure'. *Valá* is a derivative of Skt. √*vṛ*[45] 'to enclose, to cover' and literally means 'the covering'.

The picture which thus far emerges is that the Paṇis have withheld a treasure and have kept it hidden inside a rocky enclosure. Vala is the personification of this enclosure. He is the subject of *kṛṇavai* in 10.108.9.

The personification remains quite transparent.[46] Thus Vala, the demon, is called the 'guardian of the milk cows' (10.67.6), and

40. Oldenberg (*Noten*): read *indra*; could it be an epithet of Soma ?
41. Geldner (*HOS* 34, p. 135) and Lüders (*Varuṇa* II, 513) have Soma as the subject of pādas abc. So also Schmidt (*Bṛhaspati*, p. 150).
42. Cf. 2.24.3: *ábhinad...valám*.
43. On this subject cf. Hillebrandt (*Ved. Myth.* III, 263).
44. H. W. Bailey, "Analecta Indoscythica II", *Journal of the Royal Asiatic Society*, Parts 1 and 2 (1954), 26-34.
45. Wackernagel, *AiG* I, 220.
46. Hillebrandt (*Ved. Myth.* III, 261-264) demonstrates how the choice of verbs associated with *valá* shows that the personification is not fully developed. In fact Hillebrandt believes that *valá* is most frequently 'cave', but appears as a proper noun in 10.67; 10.68.

the one 'whose nourishment is cows' (*gó-dhāyas* 10.67.7); in 1.11.5, the cave (*bíla*) opened by Indra belongs to Vala who is rich in cows (*gómat*). And, *valá*, the rocky confinement, is described as a *vrajá*,[47] that is 'a pen' filled with cows (*vrajá gó*[48] 3.30.10; cf. 1.130.3 and *vrajá gómat* 4.1.15; 4.16.6; note *áśma-vraja* 4.1.13; see also 1.132.4), as well as 'a stall' *gotrá*[49] (2.17.1; 2.23.18;[50] 4.16.8) and *ūrvá*. *Ūrvá* is closely associated with the myth of the Paṇis. It occurs in 10.108.8,[51] and reoccurs in numerous other verses which deal with this myth (1.72.8: *vidád gávyaṃ sarámā dṛḷhám ūrváṃ*; 6.17.6: *aúrṇor dúra usríyābhyo ví dṛḷhód ūrvắd gắ asṛjo áñgirasvān*).

Further evidence to support the belief that Vala and the Paṇis belong to the same myth comes from a listing of their respective opponents; these demons are the enemies of nearly the same gods. The principal destroyers of Vala are: Indra (e.g. 3.30.10; 6.39.2; 8.14.7), Bṛhaspati (e.g. 2.24.3; 10.68.5,6,9,10), the Añgirases (e.g. 2.11.20; 2.15.8), the Daśagvas and the Navagvas (1.62.4). Likewise, the Paṇis are defeated by Indra (e.g. 6.20.4; 10.108.4), Bṛhaspati (e.g. 10.108.6), the Añgirases (10.108.8) and Navagvas (10.108.8). Agni (7.6.3) and Soma (9.22.7; 9.111.2; 10.108.11) also join in the battle against the Paṇis.

The above distribution assumes its full importance if we take note that all these deities, with the exception of Indra, Agni and Soma achieve their main eminence in the RV through their suppression of these demons.

On the basis of the foregoing analysis, the Rig Vedic verses pertaining to both Vala and the Paṇis are used to comment upon the mythic events outlined in 10.108.

47. Cf. Geldner's study on *vrajá* in *Ved. Stud.* II, 282ff; note *vrajá* (in pl.) *gómat* in 6.73.3. For pādas with *vrajá gómata*, see M. Bloomfield, *RV Rep.*, 211.

48. Perhaps *ródhanā góḥ* in 1.121.7 is synonymous with *vrajá gó*. *Ródhana* is a place of confinement. *Gó*, in both 3.30.10 and 1.121.7 could be used in the collective sense.

49. Cf. fn. 36, Chap. II.

50. *Gávāṃ gotrám ud √sṛj* could also mean 'to release the herd of cows'.

51. Cf. Geldner on *ūrvá* (*Ved. Stud.* II, 269ff); he takes *ūrvá* in 10.108.8 as 'herd' and considers 'herd' the meaning of *ūrvá* in the P myth. Oldenberg ("Ṛgveda VI, 1-20", *ZDMG* 55 [1901], 316ff) reviews this view; he takes *ūrvá* as 'enclosure' in this myth. Cf. Renou on *ūrvá* (*EVP* III, 7, fn. 2). Cf. Janert (*Dhāsi*, p. 10. fn. 10) who also understands the term as 'enclosure'.

RV 10.108 suggests that a specific region is to be associated with the Paṇis. Verse 1 mentions that Saramā had to cross Rasā's waters to get to the Paṇis; verse 5 adds that she had to fly around the ends of the sky. The identity and location of the Rasā is uncertain. Keith and Macdonell[52] identify the Rasā as a "mythic stream at the ends of the earth, which as well as the atmosphere it encompasses." Bhave suggests (re. RV 9.41.6) that the Rasā may be a heavenly stream.[53] In the Epic and Purāṇic literature rasā-tala denotes the lower world.[54] The image may be that the Rasā encircles the hemispherical parts (i.e. the upper and lower worlds) constituting the Vedic universe. This cosmological feature has also been noticed in RV 1.164.[55] Additional information concerning the Paṇis' domain comes from 7.6.3 where they are associated with a western region. From 7.6.4 the implication is that the Paṇis' enclosure extends to the East since exit on that side is barred for the treasure they withhold.[56] It is conjectured therefore that the Paṇis are associated with a mountainous enclosure spanning from West to East in the region surrounded by the nether part of the Rasā. Further, this enclosure (i.e. Vala) in the lower world ought to have its entrance in the West and its exit in the East.[57] The conjecture that the Paṇis occupy a region of chaos in the lower world accords well with their status as Dasyus (7.6.3). A description of the inhabitants of this world agrees remarkably well with what we know of the Paṇis: "Those who reach this place are actively anti-divine creatures... All the asuras and the dasyus are driven there...so too,...conspirers against the sacrifice, those who would injure the pious and cheat them of the fruit of their good works."[58]

3. *Indra*: 10.108 identifies the Paṇis' chief opponents.[59] However they are not involved with the demons to the same

52. *Vedic Index* II, 209.

53. S. S. Bhave, *The Soma-Hymns of the Rigveda*, Pt. II in *M. S. Univ. of Baroda Research Series* 5 (Baroda, 1950), p. 81.

54. Mayrhofer, *KEWA* 18, p. 48.

55. See Brown, "1.164", 203.

56. See Schmidt, *Bṛhaspati und Indra*, pp. 190; 241-242.

57. Schmidt, ibid.

58. W. Norman Brown, "The Rigvedic Equivalent for Hell", *JAOS* 61 (June, 1941), 78-79.

59. See Bergaigne's interesting analysis of the personages in 10.108 (*Rel. Véd.* II, 307ff).

degree. Indra's warrior talents are not exclusively confined to the Paṇis, yet he is mentioned as their opponent more frequently than any of the other gods. Indra cut through Vala; he caused the Paṇi to weep by taking away his cows (10.67.6). He made a path[60] easy to traverse, to drive out the cows (3.30.10). He drove out the cows and opened Vala (2.14.3).[61] Indra becomes the master of the self-luminous stall (*gotrásya...svarā́jaḥ*[62] 10.120.8); the dawns, knowing him, spread forth, and Indra became the sole master of the cows (3.31.4). But as often as not, he gets assistance in the fight.[63] And this is a crucial point. In scanning those verses which mention Vala, Paṇi, Paṇis together with their adversaries, it is noteworthy that in about half the cases, Indra is assisted by helpers; Bṛhaspati, the Aṅgirases, the Navagvas and the Ṛṣis come to his aid. These helpers are mainly committed to the destruction of the Paṇis, and moreover they can often do the job alone. Thus Indra's warrior talents are not of prime importance in this myth.[64] The reason, not hard to find, is that physical force is not the decisive weapon against the Paṇis (see The Weapon of Victory, below). Lüders too considers Indra as a secondary personage in this myth (*Varuṇa* II, 531), noting that he has almost no direct connection with the important weaponry in this myth (i.e. *ṛta* and chants).

How are we to explain that the mighty Indra relies so heavily upon helpers in this myth ? What powers do these personages possess that enable them, with or without Indra, to slay the Paṇis ?

60. *Patháḥ*—cf. 10.108.6.

61. Cf. 2.12.3; on *apadhā́* see Oldenberg, (*Noten*, v. cit.); he suggests "durch Aufdeckung des Vala". Geldner (*HOS* 33, v. cit) proposes "nach Beseitigung", or "der Beseitiger".

62. *Gotrá*=Vala; *svarā́j* because he contains 'cows', i.e. the rays of dawn. *Gotrá* could also be 'herd' (the term vacillates between 'stall' and 'herd') in which case the above phrase would describe the rays as self-luminous herd of cattle.

63. Unassisted, Indra uses might (5.30.4) derived from soma (2.17.1; 6.17.1,5; 6.43.3; 8.32.5) and the hymns. Though he also uses potent words, namely the ritual chants (3.31.11; 6.39.2), this is a priestly weaponry which Indra makes use of.

64. Schmidt holds that Indra is the chief hero of this myth (*Bṛhaspati und Indra*, p. 237ff). For the main objections to this view see Srinivasan "Myth of the Paṇis", 50, fn. 46.

4. *Bṛhaspati*: Bṛhaspati's name, as well as the doublet, Brahmaṇaspati, delineate the god's realm of potency; he is lord (*páti*) of the mystic power (*bráhman*) found in the universe.[65] *Bráhman* causes augmentation: "...in the RV *bráhman* repeatedly appears as a vardhanam, i.e. as something that causes to increase, that grants prosperity, that strengthens, animates".[66] The *bráhman* is somehow imminent in the prayer.[67] The prayer taps as it were this mystic force and attempts to control it for the welfare of those who believe in the Vedic rites. Thus the *brahmán*, through the efficacy of his hymns is able to evoke and control the *bráhman*.

Bṛhaspati/Brahmaṇaspati, a *brahmán* (2.1.3) and *puróhita* (2.24.9) of Indra, is the chief divine priest and master of the *bráhman* (cf. 2.23.1). As progenitor (2.23.2) king (2.23.1) and guide (2.23.19 = 2.24.16) of the *bráhman*, Bṛhaspati holds a key position in the sacrifice. Without him the sacrifice does not succeed (1.18.7); his call reaches to heaven and earth (1.190.4); both gods and men listen (1.190.1).

65. Bṛhaspati is a compound having an accent on both the first and second member (*bṛ́has* and *páti*). It has been determined by Strauss that all but two occurrences of compounds ending in *páti* and having a double accent, use the genitive form in the first member (Strauss, op. cit. 14ff; cf. Wackernagel, *AiG* II/1, p. 246). Strauss as well as other scholars place *bṛ́haspáti* into this group and consider *bṛhas* as the genitive of the reconstructed stem *bṛh* (see L. Renou, "Sur la notion de '*bráhman*,'" *Journal Asiatique* 237 (1949), 10, fn. 1; J. Gonda, *Notes on Brahman* Utrecht, [1950], 67. *Bṛh* like *bráhman* is from the root *bṛh* 'to strengthen, to increase etc.' See Gonda, *Bráhman*, 18ff; Renou, *EVP* I, 12, fn. 2). For a different approach see P. Thieme, "Bráhman", *ZDMG* 102 (1952), 91ff. The author understands the term *bráhman* as "Formulierung, Gestaltung, Formung" p. 102; he derives *bráhman* from **mrégʷh-men-*"Formung" p. 127. This meaning is supported by Schmidt (*Bṛhaspati*, pp. 16-22) who reviews the evidence on the meaning of *bráhman* and on the relation between **bṛh* and *bráhman*. His conclusion is "eine Entscheidung der Frage, ob **bṛh* mit *bráhman* etymologisch verwandt ist, aufgrund des Vergleichs mit möglichen Verwandten in anderen Sprachen nach dem Stand unseres gegenwärtigen Wissens nicht möglich ist."

66. Gonda, *Bráhman*. p. 40.

67. Renou ("Bráhman," 8ff) notes that an initial approximation of *bráhman* is 'formula' and subsequently 'recitation, hymn'. Verbs of speaking, singing, fashioning are associated with the term. However *bráhman* has a wider meaning than that. For Renou it means 'enigma'.

Bṛhaspati is thus an hieratic deity, conceived of as the glorification of the Vedic litany. As such, his place beside Indra in the battle with the Paṇis represents the power inherent in the ritual prayer which toils for Indra. It gives the god the might needed to conquer this foe.[68]

But why is the *bráhman* and not the *vrája* the crucial weapon against the Paṇis ? Why is this mystic power so efficacious when turned against them ? These questions can only be answered by reverting our attention once more to the type of opponents the Paṇis represent. It is my belief that this myth casts the demons as the supreme enemies of the sacrifice. They have posed a threat to the ritual by the nature of the wealth they have kept, thereby making it necessary for those desirous of safeguarding the sacrifice to bring into operation the *bráhman* and cause it to work against the Paṇis. That is one reason why priests are so closely identified with the myth. They, being most eager for the survival of the ritual, have the power to defeat the Paṇis and preserve the rite since they have the ability to evoke the *bráhmān.*

The lord of the *bráhman* takes on a leading role in safeguarding the sacrifice. Several hymns addressed to Bṛhaspati (e.g. 2.24; 10.67), recount in detail his role in the myth; verses from these hymns need thus to be analyzed.

10.67.3.

haṅsaír iva sákhibhir vā́vadadbhir aśmanmáyāni náhanā vyásyan
bṛ́haspátir abhikánikradad gā́ utá prā́staud úc ca vidvā́ṅ agāyat

With friends shouting like geese, shattering the bonds made of stone
Bṛhaspati shouting to the cows, sounded forth and chanted (as) one who knows.

Sákhibhiḥ—the Aṅgirases
Aśmanmáyāni náhanā = *valá*

68. Bergaigne (*Rel. Véd.* II, 275-276) has pointed out that 'prayer' increases Indra's might also for the slaying of Vṛtra (2.11.2; 5.31.4; 8.96.5). Lüders (*Varuṇa* I, 22) believes that a god's 'growth' by means of the hymn is equivalent to 'growth' by means of the sacrificial offering proffered during the ritual.

Prá √*stu* and *úd* √*gī* represent the singing of the Prastoṛ and Udgātṛ (Geldner, *HOS* 35, p. 242; Renou, *EVP* 15, 70). Schmidt (*Bṛhaspati*, p. 225): "sang Bṛhaspati Stomas und Sāmas, der Wissende."

10.67.4

avó dvā́bhyāṃ pará ékayā gā́ gúhā tíṣṭhantīr ánṛtasya sétau
bṛ́haspátis támasi jyótir ichánn úd usrā́ ā́kar ví hí tisrá ā́vaḥ

Down with two, up with one [thus the three] cows secretly standing in the bonds of *ánṛta* (Bṛhaspati drove out).
Bṛhaspati, seeking light in darkness drove out the cows; he has indeed disclosed the three.

Aváḥ—paráḥ see Geldner (*HOS* 35, 242)

In the myth of the Paṇis, the 'cows' are frequently called *usrā́ḥ* (1.71.2; 4.1.13; 6.39.2; 10.138.2). Note that in this verse *usrā́h* (as elsewhere *uṣā́sah*, see p. 119) is in apposition with *gā́ḥ*.

Tisráḥ refers to *usrā́ḥ*: three *usrā́ḥ* could be the three dawns or the three types of 'cows' withheld by the Paṇis (see pp. 116-21, and cf. Hillebrandt, *Ved. Myth* II, p. 33 fn. 3; Bergaigne, *Rel. Véd.* I, 314, 322). Three *uṣás* are mentioned in 3.17.3; 8.41.3 (see also Renou, *EVP* 3, 10 on this subject).[69] Other opinions on *tisráḥ*: Ludwig (*RV* V, 479) compares vs. 4 with 4.58.3,4. He takes *tisráḥ* to refer to the sky, atmosphere, earth and suggests that pāda a could mean: underneath the atmosphere and sky, above the earth. The cows are the rays of light which Bṛhaspati drove forth with the two Uṣas and Sūryapatnī. For Geldner (*HOS* 35, 242) *tisráḥ* means 'three doors'; cf. 6.18.5; 10.120.8d; so also Oldenberg (*Noten*, v. cit.), Renou (*EVP* 15,70) Schmidt (*Bṛhaspati*, p. 225). The major difficulty with this position is that the number 'three' is closely associated with 'cows', not 'doors' in this myth.

69. In the following vss., *gó* may = the three dawns: 5.47.4—'Threefold are his highest cows; they go round the ends of heaven daily'. (For *gó* as 'rays of dawn': 7.79.2). Geldner (*HOS* 35 ad 10.108) compares 5.47.4 with 10.108.5. *Tridhā́tu gā́ḥ* in 6.35.2 could be an allusion to the three Uṣas; note that the request in pāda d is for *dyumnáṃ svàrvat*. The allusion is in the language of cattle wars. (Cf. *tridhā́tubhir áruṣībhiḥ* 9.111.2 which Ludwig identifies as the three Uṣas; see also Renou, *EVP* 9, 118).

Ánṛtasya ṣétau in 'b' is situated in *támas* of 'c'. Cf. 4.51.2. (It is to this place that Saramā has to fly to the ends of the sky and cross the Rasā). This terminology further supports the belief that the Paṇis are situated in the Vedic underworld, that is, the Asat (see Brown, "Rigvedic Equivalent for Hell", esp. pages 76-79 and see 7.104.3,8).

10.67.8

té satyéna mánasā gópatiṃ gā́ iyānā́sa iṣaṇayanta dhībhíḥ
bṛ́haspátir mithóavadyapebhir úd usríyā asṛjata svayúgbhiḥ

They, with true will, approaching the Lord of the Cows for cows, incited themselves with poetic visions.
Bṛhaspati released the cows with allies who guard each other from blame.

Té: the Aṅgirases; Sāy.: the Maruts.
Gópatiḥ: usually describes Indra; here Bṛhaspati.
Usríyāḥ common term for 'cows' stolen by the Paṇis. In the mythology of the RV, *usríyā* is associated with two concepts: milk and light. *Usríyā* designates the cow in which the gods place the cooked milk (see p. 135). *Usríyā* is also mentioned with deities of light; in those instances the term signifies 'rays of light' figuratively called 'cows' (e.g. 7.81.2 *úd usríyāḥ sṛjate sū́ryaḥ sácām̐*; 7.75.7 *rujád dṛḷhā́ni*[70] *dádad usríyāṇām práti gā́va uṣásaṃ vāvaśanta*; 3.1.12 *úd usríyā jánitā yó jajā́na*).[71] In the myth of the Paṇis, *usríyā* is both the milk cows who provide the oblation (4.50.5) and the rays of light released from the Paṇis' hold (v. 8 above; 1.62.3; 10.68.6,7).

2.24.14cd

yó gā́ udā́jat sá divé ví cābhajan mahī́va rītíḥ śávasāsarat pṛ́thak

(He) who drove out the cows, and allotted them to heaven; as a great stream it[72] dispersed with might in all directions.

70. *Dúr* is to be understood with *dṛḷhá*. Cf. 6.17.6. The doors which need to be opened belong to Vala; cf. 6.18.5; 6.39.2. In 7.75.7 it is Uṣas who breaks the doors of Vala and releases the cows.

71. The image is ritualistic: Agni gives birth to dawn's rays because they appear after he has been kindled.

72. The light.

Bṛhaspati released the rays of light, placed the light in heaven whence it emanates along a course comparable to radiating streams. The course of the soma juice flowing from the strainer spreads in the same way. Cf. Renou, *EVP* 15, 59. It is also possible that *mahī́va rītíḥ* carries with it an allusion to the streams of milk which are compared to the rays of light (see pp. 51-52). On *divé*, cf. Schmidt, *Bṛhaspati*, p. 235.
Ud √aj—characteristic in this myth (10.68.7; 2.24.3).

5. *The Aṅgirases*: The bond between Indra and the Aṅgirases alluded to in 10.108.10b rests upon their complementary function in this myth.

The Aṅgirases are *brahmáns* (7.42.1) *ṛṣis* (10.62.4) and knowers of the words (*padajñā́ḥ*[73] 1.62.2). Thus, they are chiefly characterized as singers and in this capacity enter into a special relationship with Indra. The lauds sung by the Aṅgirases accompany Indra as he performs the major deeds associated with this myth: while being praised by the Aṅgirases, Indra splits Vala (2.15.8); shattering the stalls, he splits open a great treasure (4.16.8) and illumines the darkness with the dawn (Uṣas), the sun (Sūrya) and the cows (1.62.5). Indra opened the doors,[74] the massive ones for the cows; accompanied by the Aṅgirases, he released the cows from their stall (6.17.6).

The voices[75] of the Aṅgirases appear to help him (cf. 3.30.10). 2.17.1 indicates how. In this verse, the priests who consider the Aṅgirases as forefathers (cf. 1.62.2; 1.71.2; 10.14.6) begin the hymn addressed to Indra as follows:

tád asmai návyam aṅgirasvád arcata śuṣma[76] *yád asya pratnáthodī́rate*
víśvā yád gotrā́ sáhasā párīvṛtā máde sómasya dṛṅhitāny aírayat

73. Also 'knowers of the path'; see L. Renou, *Études Voc. RV*, p. 22, I agree with Geldner (*HOS* 33, 80) that *pada* conveys both meanings here.

74. *Dúr*=doors of Vala; fn. 70, above.

75. The *vā́nīḥ* in 3.30.10 belong to the Aṅgirases (Ludwig, *RV* V, 64); Geldner, (*HOS* 33, 364): to the Maruts. Contextually, the voices ought to be those of priests. So also Schmidt (*Bṛhaspati und Indra*, p. 141).

76. *Śúṣmāḥ*: "...the entire range of meanings covered by the word is comprised easily within the ideas 'lightning' and 'fire', in the literal and applied senses of the word ('vigor, force')". Bloomfield, "Contributions" 6th series, *ZDMG* 48, 574. Cf. Renou, *EVP* 7, 57.

Sing this new [song] to him as the Aṅgirases, so that, as formerly, his energies surge up,
As when with might, all the covered, firm stalls, he, in soma's exhilaration, shook.

Pāda b clarifies the Aṅgirases' position beside Indra: their chant acts as a stimulant, as a strengthener which increases his power. As in the case of Bṛhaspati, the Aṅgirases are prominent as Indra's helpers because they control *bráhman* effectively and cause it to make Indra more mighty.

It is through the power of their chanting that the Aṅgirases can perform the feats of the myth alone.

1.62.2 (To Indra):

prá vo mahé máhi námo bharadhvam āṅgūṣyàṃ śavasānā́ya sā́ma
yénā naḥ pū́rve pitáraḥ padajñā́ ārcanto áṅgiraso gā́ ávindan

To the Great bring your great homage, to the Powerful One [bring] a lauding Sāman,
With which our ancient Fathers, the Aṅgirases, knowing the word [and place], found the cows (while) singing.

My interpretation of this verse rests on *yénā* which I take as referring to the Sāman (so also Lüders, [*Varuṇa* II, 518] and Ludwig, [*RV*, V, 20] who cites Śatp. Br. 4,6,7,2 to illustrate the power of the Sāman). Sāy. *yéna* = Indreṇa.

Padajñā́ḥ: double entendre; the Aṅgirases found the cows because they knew both the correct words and place to defeat the Paṇis.

For cd, cf. 9.97.39 cd (*yénā naḥ pū́rve pitáraḥ padajñā́ḥ svarvído abhí gā́ ádrim uṣṇán*).[77] According to Sāy. the *pitáraḥ* in 3.39.4 are also the Aṅgirases and *góṣu* are the cows stolen by the Paṇis.

1.71.2 (To Agni)

vīḷú cid dṛḷhā́ pitáro na ukthaír ádriṃ rujann áṅgiraso rávena
cakrúr divó bṛható gātúm asmé áhaḥ svàr vividuḥ ketúm usrā́ḥ

Our Fathers have, with [their] hymns (broken) the firm foundations, the Aṅgirases have broken the rock with [their] call.

77. See Bloomfield, *RV Rep.*, 88, for the emendation *muṣṇán.*

For us they have prepared great heaven's path; they have found the day, the sunlight, the light of the cows.

Vīḷú...dṛḷhá—belong to Vala; cf. 6.17.6; 7.75.7; 6.18.5.
Ádrim refers to *valá* see p. 101. It is in accordance with the *ṛtá* that the Aṅgirases open up the rock (see 4.3.11).
The meaning of pāda c is: they opened up the path along which light (see pāda d) could traverse the sky.
Ketúm usrā́ḥ: as *ketúr uṣásaḥ* 7.67.2; 76.2; 10.89.12 (Geldner, *HOS* 33, 92). Bergaigne (*Rel. Véd.* I, 134): *ketú* is 'banner' of day.

6.65.5 (To Uṣas)

idā́ hí ta uṣo adrisāno gotrā́ gávām áṅgiraso gṛṇánti
vy àrkeṇa bibhidur bráhmaṇā ca satyā́ nṛṇā́m abhavad deváhūtiḥ

For now, O Uṣas, resting on the ridge of the mountain, the Aṅgirases sing to your herds of cows.
They have split [the rock] with [their] chant and *bráhman*; the men's invocation to the gods was effective.

On this verse see Renou, *EVP* 3, 88; Lüders, *Varuṇa* I, 91, fn. 5.

Gotrā́ gávām: translation follows Renou (ibid.) in assuming 'herds' for *gotrā́* with *gṛṇanti*, and 'stalls' for *gotrā́* with $\sqrt{}$*bhid* (cf. *girím* $\sqrt{}$*bhid* 10.89.7; *ádriṃ* $\sqrt{}$*bhid* 1.62.3; 10.68.11; *valám* $\sqrt{}$*bhid* 2.24.3).

Arká (see p. 114). Renou (ibid.): the meaning 'with light' is possible here.

The Aṅgirases' eagerness to subdue the Paṇis is easily explained. These divine priests receive a part of the demons' treasure.[78] Indra opened the stall (*gotrá* 1.51.3; *vrajá* 1.132.4) for them;[79] he disclosed the cows for them.[80] He drove the cows out for the Aṅgirases and thrust Vala down (8.14.8). As the wealth

78. The priests receive that 'cow' which is essential to the ritual; this is the oblation-giving cow and the *dákṣiṇā* cow (see below). Schmidt's study (*Bṛhaspati und Indra*, p. 238) concludes that the Aṅgirases receive as *dakṣiṇā*, the released treasure.

79. Soma does the same 9.86.23 (*sóma gotrám áṅgirobhyo 'vṛṇor ápa*).

80. Note also 8.63.3 *áṅgirobhya índro gā́ avṛṇod ápa*.

was released, the Aṅgirases shouted, most probably for joy, with the cows (see 5.45.8; 4.3.11; 1.62.3). Their rejoicing took place at the time of dawn's appearance (cf. 5.45.8a). Then these priests appointed protectors among the cows (cf. 3.31.10d).

6. *The Navagvas and Daśagvas*: Besides the Aṅgirases, another group of priests to appear in this myth is mentioned in 10.108.8: the Navagvas.[81] 5.45.7 and 10.61.10[82] also cite them in connection with this myth. 10.61.10 indicates that they became involved in the struggle against the Paṇis because they were lacking in *dákṣiṇā*. Closely allied in this context with the Navagvas are the Daśagvas. Together they opened the stall containing cows (5.29.12); in their presence Indra split Vala open (cf. 1.62.4). With the Navagvas, Indra pursued the cows; with the Daśagvas, Indra found Sūrya (3.39.5).

7. *Other Priests:* The final verse of 10.108 states that priests in general (*ṛ́ṣayaś ca víprāḥ*) helped in the search for the cows. The passages listed below refer to the priests who assist or are assisted by a god in this myth:

6.32.2:[83] *svādhī́bhir ṛ́kvabhir vāvaśānā́ úd usríyāṇām asṛjan nidānam*

6.32.3[84] *sá váhnibhir ṛ́kvabhir góṣu śáśvan mitájñubhiḥ purukṛ́tvā jigāya/púraḥ purohā́ sákhibhiḥ sakhīyán dṛḷhā́ ruroja kavíbhiḥ kavíḥ sán*

1.6.5:[85] *vīḷú cid ārujatnúbhir gúhā cid indra váhnibhiḥ; ávinda usríyā ánu*

81. For a study on Vedic —*gva* terms and their meaning see Bloomfield, "Contributions", *Amer. Journ. of Philology* 17 (1896), 422ff.

82. *Gopá* in pāda c refers to Vala; cf. 10.67.6 where Vala is *rakṣitā́raṃ dúghānāṃ*.

83. Schmidt (*Bṛhaspati und Indra*, p. 151) and Geldner take this verse to describe Indra's freeing the rays of dawn with the assistance of the Aṅgirases.

84. The priests are, according to Schmidt (ibid.) the Aṅgirases. Cf. 3.39.5; 1.100.4. *Dṛḷhá* $\sqrt{}$*ruj* cf. 3.32.16; 7.75.7. *Vahní* cf. 10.138.1. *Vahní* occurs frequently in connection with Uṣas (e.g. 1.48.11; 5.79.4; 7.75.5) and may, in those verses, as well as the mythic contexts, refer to priests associated with the early morning ritual (cf. 3.20.1).

85. See Geldner *HOS* 33, p. 7 on *vahní*. Schmidt (ibid., p. 154): *vahní*=the Aṅgirases.

6.39.2:[86] *ayám uśānáḥ páry ádrim usrā́ ṛtádhītibhir ṛtayug yujānáḥ*

3.31.11:[87] *sá jātébhir vṛtrahā́ séd u havyaír úd usríyā asṛjad índro arkaíḥ*

4.16.6d:[88] *vrajáṃ gómantam uśíjo ví vavruḥ*

8. *Soma*: The inclusion of Soma (10.108.11) in the myth may be attributed to his being a ritual deity.[89] Soma in 9.86.23 opened the stall for the Aṅgirases; the soma juice found the cows in the stall (9.87.8—the cows found by Soma could be the oblation-giving cows). He took the wealth in cows from the Paṇis (see 9.22.7).[90]

b. The Weapon of Victory

The characteristics of the gods and demons demonstrate the fine balance of tension between these two opposing groups. As enemies, they are extremely well matched, representing as they do antithetical points of view regarding the Vedic sacrifice. The anti-sacerdotal forces placed in jeopardy their opponents by detaining items the sacerdotal forces needed in order to continue their functions. The latter however, and not the Paṇis, possess the decisive weapon. Appropriately, the weapon of victory is derived from their priestly function: it is primarily by means of the hymn and the *bráhman* which it activates that the opponents of the Vedic ritual are defeated.

86. *Ṛtádhītibhiḥ*: cf. *váhnaya ṛtám manvānā́ḥ* 10.138.1. Geldner and Schmidt identify the priests as Aṅgirases.

87. *Jātébhiḥ*: clearly indicates that besides mythic priests such as the Aṅgirases, mortal priests partake in the freeing of the 'cows'. This would be possible if priests (perhaps early morning priests—see fn. 83—performed in a ritual certain activity which the myth stipulates would free 'cows'. One such act easily suggests itself; it is the stimulation of the *bráhman* power through Vedic chanting (i.e. *arkaíḥ* 3.31.11 and see next page). These mortal participants may be the *vīrá* in 3.31.10d. *Úd* √*sṛj* in this myth: 2.23.18; 6.32.2; 10.67.8. On the emendation (*sajā́tebhiḥ* and *svéduhavyaiḥ*) suggested by Alsdorf (Lüders, *Varuṇa* II, 517, fn. 5) see also Schmidt (*Bṛhaspati und Indra*, p. 169). It is preferable to avoid emendations as do the transl. of Renou (*EVP* 17, 72) and Geldner (*HOS* 33, 368).

88. 6d=4.1.15d=10.45.11d. *Uśíj*: cf. 2.21.5; *vrājám ví* √*vṛ* cf. 1.132.4.

89. So also the Press Stones (10.108.11) are drawn into the myth because of their essential role in the sacrifice.

90. The only mention of the Paṇis in Book 9 is here and in 9.111.2.

Some indication that the outcome of the struggle will depend upon which side possesses the more effective words is given in 10.108. Verse 6 states that the words (*vácāṅsi*) of the Paṇis are not weapons, that is, they are weak and powerless. However the words of the gods have great potency. Indra vanquished the Paṇis with spells (*vácas* 6.39.2); the priests, with *vácas daívya* opened the firm pen (4.1.15).[91] *Vácas*, used by Indra's helpers split open the mountain (4.16.6). Clearly, the words (i.e. holy utterances) of the gods are the superior force and the weakness of the Paṇis lies in their ineffectual words, words which cannot evoke the *bráhman*. Of this weakness, the opposition takes full advantage. Brahmaṇaspati splits Vala with *bráhman* (2.24.3). The Aṅgirases used both *bráhman* and *arká* to split open the rock (6.65.5). The usage of *arká* is quite prevalent in this myth. Indra and his helpers released the *usríyāḥ* with *arká* (3.31.11). Bṛhaspati split the *jásu* of Vala with *arká* (10.68.6); with it he also drove asunder darkness (10.68.9). *Arká* fluctuates in meaning between 'hymn' and 'light' (Renou, *EVP* I, 6; see *EVP* 3, 69 and *EVP* 13, 125 for discussions on *arká*). When *arká* 'hymn' occurs in this myth, it signifies a magical spell.

The terms *ráva* and *ukthá* are used with the same meaning (e.g. 10.67.6; 1.71.2). Uṣas uses *dhī́* ('poetic vision' converted into hymns having magical powers; cf. J. Gonda, *The Vision of the Vedic Poets* [The Hague, 1963], p. 123), to open the stall (5.45.6). The efficacy of priestly utterances is also demonstrated through the use of *√gṝ* (2.15.8; 4.16.8; 1.62.5), *abhí √krand*, *prá √stu*, *úd √gā* (10.67.3), *√stan* (10.67.5).

The *ṛtá* is also connected with the opening of Vala and the freeing of the cows (cf. 10.108.11; 6.39.2; 1.121.4). Used in this context, Lüders considers *ṛtá* (or *ṛtásya rátha*, *ṛtásya dī́dhiti* etc.) as a synonym for *dhī́*, *matí arká*, *ukthá bráhman*, *vácas*[92] etc. He too is of the opinion that the hymn is a weapon used against Vala; its effectiveness, he believes, results from the 'truth' (*ṛtá*) which the hymns possess.[93] 'Truth', states Lüders, is the fundamental

91. Is *vácas daívya* the force (i.e. *sáhas daívya*) which has driven Saramā to the Paṇis place (10.108.9) ?

92. Lüders, *Varuṇa* II, 516.

93. Lüders, ibid. 515, fn. 4; 519.

meaning of *ṛtá*.[94] 'Truth' may be said to reside in the hymns in that they are thought to describe the correct nature of something; verbalizing such truths evokes magical power.[95] The role of *ṛtá* (which Lüders considers as 'Kultlied, Zauberspruch' in this context)[96] emphasizes, according to Lüders the point that the hymns chanted by the priests are possessed of truth and can thus work magic. (This position is followed quite closely by Schmidt, *Bṛhaspati und Indra*, pp. 238-240). My own understanding of the role of *ṛtá* in this myth is somewhat different. The concept *ṛtá* represents in this myth, as well as throughout the RV, is that of an independent cosmic force which establishes, governs and directs physical and psychical norms in worldly, human and ritual affairs, causing these to appear as right and true. Therefore, doing something in accordance with *ṛtá* consists of observing one's own function (see 3.4.7). In the myth of the Paṇis, when 'cows' are released by or according to the *ṛtá* (see 10.108.11;4. 23.9), the meaning is that 'cows' are freed to assume their natural function. In this way, the force of *ṛtá* is upheld and supported. However, the power which in this myth releases the 'cows' and the other phenomena is distinctly different. It is the esoteric

94. Lüders, ibid. I, 14. Renou states that *ṛtá* encompasses 'truth' and 'order' in meaning (*EVP* 7, 16; 9, 11).

95. Lüders (ibid. II, 509): the belief in the magic power of the correctly spoken word (i.e. satyakriyā stories of the Indian Middle Ages) was already in evidence in the Vedic period. Lüders suggests that in the myth of the Paṇis the hymns have magical power because they contain a 'truth' appropriate in the context. The 'truth' contained in the hymns, which frees the cows, is the enunciation of their secret name (521ff) which is 'dawns' (p. 528). This position raises several questions hard to answer. Since 'cows' other than 'dawns' are released from the Paṇis (see below) how could these be freed according to the 'truth statement' that cows are dawns (i.e. *usrā́*, *usríyā*) ? And why are 'cows' not then exclusively called *usrā́*, *usríyā* in this myth ? Further, how could all the other items having nothing to do with 'cows' or 'dawns' be released by the same truth ?

In a long article by A. Venkatasubbiah entitled "The Act of Truth in the Ṛgveda" (*Journ. of Oriental Research*, Madras Vol. 14 [1940] 133-165; 210-236; 274-285), a position similar to Lüders' is advanced, namely that 'the spell of truth' (expressed, according to the author, by *ṛtá*, *ukthá*, *dhī́*, *satyá*, *vácas* etc.) is the weapon of victory. The belief is that all those divinities who conquer the Paṇis do so through effective use of 'spells of truth' which work much the same way as the later satyakriyā stories. However the author cannot identify any verses formulated as statements of truth in the myth of the Paṇis, and this weakens the argument considerably.

96. Lüders (ibid.) 519.

power of *bráhman*, evoked by sacred speech and imbuing the hymns with magical properties. *Ṛtá*, thus, is not so much the force which conquers the Paṇis as it is the cosmic force which is upheld as a result of the conquest.

c. The Treasure of the Paṇis

What is the significance of the Paṇis' treasure ? Why would they want to withhold cows, horses, riches (10.108.7), the dawn, the sun, the fire, the path and the day ? Do these items have anything in common ? What do the cows, a significant aspect of the treasure symbolize ? Could they represent more than one concept (note *góvapus* 10.68.9) ?

In order to answer these questions let us turn once more to the evidence found in 10.108. Verse 7 identifies the Paṇis' *nidhí* as consisting of *gó*, *áśva*, *vásu*. This enumeration reoccurs in 7.90.6 where it figures together with *híraṇya* in a list of items the priests desire as *dákṣiṇā* (see p. 73). According to 10.107.7ab[97] these are precisely the sort of gifts that *dákṣiṇā* may consist of (*dákṣiṇā́śvám dákṣiṇā gā́m dadāti dákṣiṇā candrám utá yád dhíraṇyam*).

It seems very possible that *gó*, *áśva*, *vásu* in 10.108.7 are likewise *dákṣiṇā* items, *gó*,[98] being the cow so frequently presented for this purpose. It should be noted that in a ritual context, *gó* and *áśva* frequently occur together as the *dákṣiṇā* animals (10.97.4; 8.78.2; 6.46.2; 9.94.5; 8.4.21; 10.7.2; 8.46.22; 1.126.2). I have, on the basis of the above evidence, identified similar *gó*, *áśva* series occurring in the context of this myth, as *dákṣiṇā* animals which the priests desire to release from the Paṇis' hold[99] (1.83.4; 9.108.6; 10.25.5; 10.62.7; possibly 4.28.5).

If the Paṇis' *nidhí* consists of *dákṣiṇā* it would explain why the Navagvas, being *adakṣiṇá* (10.61.10) approached the cow-herder

97. Dákṣiṇā in verse 7 is the female deity personifying the ritual gift. *Gā́m* is used in the collective sense.

98. This meaning applies only to *gó* in v. 7. Since *gó* represents more than one concept in this myth, it is not always possible to determine its symbolic meaning when the term occurs alone and without qualifiers. Being so used in the rest of 10.108, it is not possible to be more specific as to its meaning in the hymn.

99. See Renou on *dákṣiṇā* in this myth (*EVP* 3, 7).

(*gopá* i.e. Vala; cf. 10.108.7 where the Paṇis are *sugopā́ḥ*) and desired to milk the solid rock. It would provide further insight into why the priests are so closely associated with this myth. They are striving to free that which ought to be bestowed upon them. This aspect of the myth simulates the actual relationship that may have existed between a Vedic priest and a *paṇí.*

The treasure of 'cows and horses' has additional significance. Since 'cows and horses' are symbols for 'rays of light' (for cows—see below; for horses—see Macdonell, *Ved. Myth.* pp. 31; 47) 10.108.7 could also refer to these celestial lights. This meaning for both *gó* and *áśva* by no means excludes their referring to the *dákṣiṇā* as well. To play upon words and allow them to yield as many desirable allusions as possible is an important feature of RV hymns. There is potency in establishing conceptual relationships since in effect such relationships seek to identify or clarify the more illusive concept by means of the more concrete one. The intended result gained from establishing conceptual relationships is that a magical potency is set into operation when the true nature of something is revealed. *Gó* and *áśva* in 10.108.7 are examples of terms capable of conveying multiple allusions. If these two terms are used to connote 'rays of light' then *gó* = the rays of Uṣas; if the terms are taken as connoting the *dákṣiṇā*, then *gó* would adopt another significant relationship with Uṣas. As *dákṣiṇā* cows, they become the imprisoned wealth of the goddess Dakṣiṇā with whom Uṣas is identified. Both meanings assigned to *gó* are relevant to the myth. The priests await the rays of dawn in order to launch the sacrifice, as well as the *dákṣiṇā* cows as recompense for their ritual efforts.

The Paṇis withhold not only the *dákṣiṇā* cow but also the milk cow used to provide the ritual oblation (4.50.5 *bṛ́haspátir usríyā havyasū́daḥ...úd ājat*). This is the second concept which 'cow' represents in the myth of the Paṇis. This identification explains why Indra is described as *āśíram ichámānaḥ* at the time he fights the Paṇi (10.67.6). Probably in this instance Indra is fighting to acquire the milk which the priests need for his offering; indeed it is said that one of the cows which was released, milked forth a sweet drink for him (3.31.11).[100] Note also that

100. Cf. 10.61.11cd; *te*=Indra see 1.121.5cd. 8.69.6 also says that the cows which Indra found in confinement gave forth their milk for Indra.

in 10.67.6 Vala is called *rakṣitā́ram dúghānām*. His food (*avasā́*) consists of cows (1.93.4); he is nourished by them (*gódhāyas*- 10.67.7). These must be the milk cows who would normally provide for the oblation.[101]

The significance of the retained 'cow' wealth discussed so far may be evaluated if we translate the mythic situation into its corresponding actual situation. The *dákṣiṇā* cow and the oblation-giving cow are two important functions an actual cow serves in the Vedic ritual. Lack of cows for these two uses would seriously hamper the performance of the rite. The Paṇis, in withholding these cows, are making an earnest attempt to prevent the sacrifice from operating smoothly. The scope of the priests' involvement thus broadens to include their desire to safeguard the sacrifice itself.

The treasure of the Paṇis swells with yet one more 'cow'. This 'cow', unlike the preceding ones, does not have an earthly prototype. However, it relates to the other two in that it represents an equally essential prerequisite for the performance of the sacrifice. The third 'cow' is 'light', in particular 'the rays of dawn'.

It is well known that terms meaning 'cow' may be used metaphorically for 'rays of light, rays of dawn, dawns'. The Indian lexical material is the earliest source to direct our attention to this figure of speech. Naighaṇṭuka 1.5 lists *gāvaḥ* and *usrāḥ* as *raśmi* terms, and Nirukta 2.6 reiterates this: *sarve 'pi raśmayo gāva ucyante*. In a list of animals associated with different gods in the capacity of vāhanas, Naighaṇṭuka 1.15 mentions *aruṇyo gāva uṣasām*. However, the reason underlying the correlation between *gó* etc. and 'light' is not so clear. Several suggestions are offered below:

The similes discussed in Chap. II contribute significantly towards understanding the correlation between 'cows' and 'rays of light', in particular 'rays of dawn'. The similes indicate that the association stems from a particular conceptualization of the

101. Cf. 6.17.1, *yám* refers to *sómān*. Here Indra burst open the Paṇis' stall to obtain the cows which give milk for the soma oblation.

nature of the cow's milk in daily life. This conceptualization considers the milk as a bright or heated substance (see under 1.66.2); it is believed that the milk undergoes 'cooking' (i.e. preparation) inside the cow. The 'cooking' process is the mythopoeic explanation for the remarkable fact that a food, ready for consumption, flows out of the 'raw' (i.e. unprepared) cow. The raw cow, conceived as carrier of the cooked, radiant milk, may by extension be considered likewise as bright and radiant.

This particular set of associations is translated into the mythic imagery concerned with Uṣas, goddess of the dawn. Uṣas is considered to be 'a cow' (see Chap. V) because she carries the bright rays of light in her breasts as a cow carries bright milk in her udder. Indeed this analogy underlies the image in 3.30.14: 'a great light has been placed in her udders; the raw cow wanders carrying the cooked milk'. The raw cow is Uṣas (see 1.92.4); the cooked milk is the great light of dawn. 3.30.14[102] is thus stating that the light of Uṣas, that is the rays of Dawn, is the equivalent of goddess' milk. The image is extended further; Uṣas as originator of the rays of dawn may be described as the mother of the rays (5.45.6; 4.52.2,3). These rays are metaphorically named 'cows' just as Uṣas is a 'cow'. In this sense (i.e. 'cows' = 'dawns') we find *gó* in the plural occurring appositionally with 'dawns' (pl. *uṣásaḥ* 1.92.1; 3.31.4 *uṣā́saḥ*). In that these 'cows' are the rays of dawn (they are called 'red cows' in 1.92.1.2; 1.124.11; 10.61.4) they turn back the darkness and extend light (7.79.2).

One explanation therefore for conceiving 'rays of dawn' as 'cows' could be that the conceptualization represents the mythic intensification of the Vedic belief that cows are radiant etc. creatures due to their carrying radiant milk. From this arises the image that the goddess of Dawn is a cow because she carries light as milk in her breasts. Further, the rays of dawn to which she gives birth are the herd of rosy cows which follow her.

Another conceptual correlation between Uṣas and 'cows'

102. For 3.30.14, cf. H. -P. Schmidt, *Bṛhaspati und Indra*, pp. 141, 143, 145, See also Janert, *Dhāsi*, pp. 27-28.

exists. Uṣas is both maternal and bountiful and as such displays qualities exemplified by the cow. Besides being the mother of the cows, her maternal aspect is stressed also in connection with Sūrya and Agni. Uṣas introduces the physical and ritual conditions which give rise to the sun and the sacrificial fire. The breaking of dawn announces the beginning of a new day as well as a new round of sacrifices. Needed for the rites to commence are light and fire; dawn heralds in both. She is the physical harbinger of the sun, the ritual harbinger of the sacrificial fire. Uṣas therefore is considered to be the 'mother' of both Sūrya and Agni (see Macdonell, *Ved. Myth.* p. 48).

The bountiful nature of Uṣas is emphasized by the epithet *maghónī*, 'the liberal goddess' applied almost exclusively to Uṣas (see M. Bloomfield, *Rel. of the Veda*, p. 69). Other epithets too stress the liberality of the goddess.[103] Therefore, since the goddess exemplifies. as does a cow, feminine abundance, this may also contribute to her being 'a cow' and to her rays being 'herd of kine'.

How do we know that the third type of 'cow' withheld by the Paṇis represents the rays of Dawn ? The frequent use of *usrā́* and *usríyā* in this context is the first indication. Both terms are derivatives from √*vas* 'to shine'. Renou (*EVP* 3. 4, fn. 2) defines *usrā́, úsri, usríya* as 'being of Uṣas' nature', with the specialized meaning of 'cow' (secondarily 'bull'). Of the 21 fem. occurrences of *usrā́*, the majority are in a mythic context. In that context, *usrā́* means 'morning light, cow'. *Usríya* has 33 fem. occurrences. Used literally in an economic or ritual context, *usríyā* means 'milk cow' (10.87.17; 9.68.1; 9.96.14; 9.93.2; 1.93.12; 10.61.26). In the myth of the Paṇis, *usríyā* is the cow as 'light' (7.75.7), as well as the oblation-giving cow (4.50.5).

Further proof that 'cow' is 'rays of Dawn' comes from passages

103. Other epithets of Uṣas emphasizing her liberality are: *citrāmaghā* 'granting wonderful gifts'; *sumnāvarī* 'bringing favor, kind, benevolent'; *sūnṛtā* 'youthfully vital' (Renou, *Étude Voc. RV*, p. 8, fn. 2: 'the generous one'); *sūnṛtāvatī* 'rich in youthful vitality suggests prosperity, ability to help and bestow gifts and advantages'; *sūnṛtāvarī* "id."; *vājinīvatī* 'possessing the generative power by which new food and new life is obtained'; *dāsvatī* 'disposed to give' (words and meanings from J. Gonda, *Epithets in the Ṛgveda*, Disputationes Rheno-Trajectinae IV (The Hague .1959), 96ff.

dealing with the Uṣas theme in the context of the myth of the Paṇis. These passages show that the image of Uṣas and her cows is not merely a descriptive convention but a symbolic expression which fits into the framework of this myth.[104] 5.45.6 states that the mother (i.e. Uṣas) opened the stall of cow(s) with *dhī́*[105] (*étā dhíyaṃ kṛṇávāmā sakhāyó 'pa yā́ mātā́m̐ ṛṇutá vrajáṃ góḥ*); Vala is *vrajá* of *gó* (3.30.10). 7.75.7cd connects this event (expressed as *rujád dṛḷhā́ni*[106] with the release of the cows (*dádad usríyāṇām práti gā́va uṣásaṃ vāvaśanta*). To aid the goddess, the Añgirases with their *arká* and *bráhman* split the stall containing her herd of cows (6.65.5). Again in 4.1.13; calling to the dawns, they (i.e. the Añgirases) drove out the cows, the milk cows from within the cave, [the cows] whose stall is a rock.[107] These verses indicate that Uṣas is drawn into the myth because her rays, as well as she herself (e.g. 10.67.5) have been captured by the Paṇis.

We may now identify the Paṇis' treasure: dawn's light, the *dákṣiṇā* animals, the oblation-giving cows, as well as the sun, the path of light, the day and the ritual fire. In consequent, the chances for performing a sacrifice are virtually nil. That, of course, is the aim of the Paṇis. But due to the mystic power evoked by the priests' hymns, the Paṇis' scheme is thwarted and their treasure is released.

When Uṣas and her cows shine forth, Agni will likewise be present in each house (see 1.124.11), and the sun manifests itself (4.3.11).[108] Thus a new day is born; that is why *áhar* (1.71.2) was found by the Añgirases.

d. Further discussion on the meaning of 'cows' in the Myth of the Paṇis

104. Cf. H. Oldenberg, *Die Religion des Veda* (Stuttgart and Berlin, 1923), p. 147.

105. See J. Gonda, *The Vison of the Vedic Poets*, Disputationes Rheno-Trajectinae VIII (The Hague, 1963), p. 123-4 for *dhíyam*.

106. Uṣas is subj. of $\sqrt{}$*ruj*.

107. Note that two 'cow' concepts appear in this verse: 'the rays of dawn' (*usrā́ḥ uṣásaḥ*) and 'the oblation-giving cows' (*sudúghāḥ*). The 'cows' are *áśmavrajāḥ* because Vala acts as their enclosure.

108. Pāda b shows that the context of the verse is the myth of the Paṇis. Pāda d also occurs in 10.88.2b, a verse Renou (*EVP* 14, 91) considers to display a cosmogonic theme.

It has been shown above that the Paṇis' treasure consists of Uṣas, Agni, Sūrya, *svàr*, the path along which light travels, the day, and cows, horses and riches. The cows, as we have seen, represent three concepts: the *dákṣiṇā* cow, the oblation-giving cow and rays of dawn. The question now remains whether it is possible to determine which concept is meant when a 'cow' term occurs. Does a 'cow' term have a different meaning if it appears in the singular or in the plural ? Does a particular 'cow' term refer to one of the three concepts, or is there overlapping ?

It should be stated at the outset that in the majority of cases it is not possible to assign a particular meaning to a particular 'cow' term. It does not seem possible to restrict the meaning of *gó* to the *dákṣiṇā* cows or the oblation-giving cows, and *usrā́*, *usríyā* to 'light cows'. We can be quite sure, for example, that *gó* in 3.31.4 represents 'the rays of dawn' (and outside of the myth of the Paṇis, *gó* in 1.92.1,2; 7.79.2 has this meaning). And we know that *usríyā* can also refer to the oblation-giving cow: 4.50.5 (cf. 1.21.5 = 10.61.11 for the same meaning of *usríyā* outside of the myth).

Usrā́, it is true, is used in the myth mainly to symbolize the light of dawn (4.1.13; 1.71.2; 10.67.4; 6.39.2 [based on the contents of verse 3]); but this meaning is not restricted to *usrā́*. As stated above, *gó* also can symbolize dawn's light (1.124.11; 7.36.1), and so may *usríyā*.

The oblation-giving cow is designated as *gó* (10.67.6; 1.93.4; cf. 10.67.7; 3.31.11), in addition to *usríyā* (see above).

Only the *dákṣiṇā* cow is consistently called *gó* (see p. 116 above). But since *gó* can equally well connote the other two concepts, the meaning of 'dakṣiṇā' cow is assigned to *gó* only when the term occurs together with *áśvan*, *átya* etc.

The sort of overlapping demonstrated above shows that unless the context offers some aid, it is not possible to associate one of the particular 'cow' concepts with either *gó* or *usríyā*. In fact there are several instances where *gó* and *usríyā* occur together as if they were synonyms (7.75.7; 1.62.3; 10.67.8; 6.17.6). In

5.30.4, *usríya* modifies *gó* and the meaning could be either 'milk cows' or 'light cows'. Probably the lack of sharp distinction between *gó* and *usríyā* is due to *gó* being the most general 'cow' term and therefore the most varied in meaning.

The foregoing (observations) have been restricted mainly to the plural of *gó*, *usríyā*, *usrá*. Do they also apply to the singular use of *gó* etc., or does the singular have a more consistent meaning ? Could the singular refer to one of the deities released from the Paṇis ?

There is a set of phrases where the sing. of *gó* is to be understood in the collective sense. The phrase *vrajá góḥ* 'stall of cow (s)' (3.30.10; 5.45.6) defines Vala as an enclosure full of cows. *Gór áśvasya...vrajám* (8.32.5) and *ūrvám áśvyam góḥ* (4.28.5) could designate the *dákṣiṇā* portion of the treasure enclosed within Vala.

4.58.4 uses the loc. s. of *gó* to designate the cow in which the gods found the *ghṛtá*[109] hidden by the Paṇis and consisting of three forms. The verse goes on to state that Indra produced one, Sūrya another and through their own innate aptitude, they produced one from the seer.[110] In keeping with the rest of the hymn, the focus is on the *ghṛtá*, and verse four seems to consider the origin of the triple *ghṛtá* that is the triple elements which further the sacrifice. The elements spoken of here are identified as being those which the Paṇis withheld, presumably at a later time. Accordingly, the *ghṛtá* would constitute the milk cow, the rays of dawn, and the dakṣiṇā cow; it is to these three elements respectively which pādas cd refer. The initial creation of these elements is taken up in pādas ab. These elements were 'found' by the gods in the 'cow'; that is, creation of these elements occurred as the cow, assisted by the gods, brought forth the triple *ghṛtá*. Who is the Cow emitting these sacrificial elements ? It could be Vāc (called *gaurī́* in 1.164.41) whose role is prefigured

109. *Ghṛtá* (the sacrificial oblation; ghee) is to be taken in the sense of 'fructifying sacrificial element, an element advancing the cause of the sacrifice.'

110. *Trídhā hitám paṇíbhir guhyámānam gávi devā́so ghṛtám ánv avindan índra ékaṃ sū́rya ékaṃ jajāna venā́d ékaṃ svadháyā niṣ ṭatakṣuḥ*. Svadhā́: see Renou (*EVP* 1, 24): "dispositions-innées". On venā́t see Gonda, *Visions*, p. 356.

in the preceding verses which mention Soma (lord of Vāc) as *gaurá*.[111]

Other opinions on 4.58.4: Sāy. understands ***trídhā hitám... ghṛtám*** as the three types of offering derived from the cow: milk, curds, ghee; he takes *gávi* in the sense of *goṣu*. Other interpretations for *ghṛtá*: Renou (*EVP* I, 24) follows K. Geldner ("Zur Erklärung des Rigveda," *ZDMG* 71 [1917] 340ff) in considering the triple *ghṛtá* as the actual *ghṛtá* (i.e. the milk) of the cow; the *ghṛtá* of Soma; the *ghṛtá* of Speech (cf. Geldner *HOS* 33, v. cit.). *Gávi* according to Geldner is "der Urherde" (p. 342). On pāda d: Geldner (*HOS* 33), 'the poetry which the gods brought from the seer, cf.1.163.2d; Renou (*EVP* I, 24): oratorial or spiritual aspect of poetic imagination; Bergaigne (*Rel. Véd.* I, p. 24 fn. 1 and p. 264): Vena = Soma; Soma may stand for Agni.

e. Conclusion

The conclusion arrived at in this study is that the myth of the Paṇis illustrates the belief that the *bráhman*, activated by Vedic chants, safeguards the sacrifice against forces wishing to undermine it. The struggle, waged and won primarily by the mythic priests, secondarily by Indra, in essence, releases conditions needed for the sacrifice, assures its performance, defends the *ṛtá* and works to uphold ordered existence. In this sense, the myth of the Paṇis does not give an account of the origin of existence, but rather of its safe maintenance.

This conclusion is based on two factors:
(1) The internal evidence of the myth of the Paṇis, as given above, and (2) a comparison between the myth of the Paṇis and the well recognized creation myth, namely the Indra-Vṛtra myth. A comparison between these myths may be fruitfully attempted since both the Indra-Vṛtra myth and the myth of the Paṇis are on the same level of conceptualization with regard to the statement of the problem and its solution: aspects of the problem are represented by metaphorical equivalents and the explanation is worked out

111. See D. Srinivasan, "The Religious Significance of Multiple Bodily Parts to denote the Divine: Findings from the Rig Veda", *Asiatische Studien* XXIX (1975), fn. 64.

within the framework of a story. It is thus possible to construct a list of corresponding features and compare them. This is done directly below. In so doing, the aim is to see how the features of the myth of the Paṇis relate to the features of the creation myth.

Indra-Vṛtra Myth	Myth of the Paṇis
(1) Personages: Ādityas, Dānavas (Vṛtra), Indra	Priests, Paṇis (Vala), Indra

There is no mythic correspondence between the Ādityas and the priests, the Dānavas and the Paṇis. One can only say that both parties in the first group are attempting to release something which the latter parties are restraining. Vala and Vṛtra are derivatives of $\sqrt{}$*vṛ*. I interpret this as being due to their analogous positions in their respective myths, rather than due to a generic connection.

Indra plays a primary role in the fight against Vṛtra, a secondary role with regard to the Paṇis.

(2) Helpers: Maruts, Rudra, Viṣṇu, Soma, Agni	Soma, Agnī-Somā, Press Stones

The helpers of the P myth are ritual godheads; this is not entirely the case in the Indra-Vṛtra myth. The Maruts and Rudra as well as the *vájra*, signify the power in the atmosphere which comes to the aid of Indra. This is not the main power to defeat the Paṇis.

(3) Major Weapons: *vájra*, Soma i.e. force	*bráhman* i.e. magic
(4) 'Cow' symbolism: Cosmic Waters	*dákṣiṇā*, oblation-giving cow, rays of dawn

The release of cows is common to both myths, however the symbolic equivalent for 'cow' is different. Since symbols are employed with general consistency in a myth, this change is significant. It poses the following two questions: if the P myth were to be viewed as a creation myth, then what significance may be attributed to the *dákṣiṇā* and the oblation-giving 'cow' in the creation scheme; and, why do the 'cows' not represent 'water', which is so important to the creation myth ? A quick look at the creation theories described by W. Norman Brown[112] shows how closely the concept of water and moisture is associated even with theories subsequent to the Indra-Vṛtra myth: 10.72.6 (*salilá*); 10.72.7 (*samudrá*); 10.82.5, 6 (*áp*); 10.121.7,8,9 (*áp*); 10.129.3 (*salilá*).

According to Lüders and Janert, the concept of Water is not absent in the P myth. Lüders is of the opinion that not only light, but also water was released when Vala was broken.[113] He cites the following verses to support his idea: 4.3.12; 7.90.4; 9.108.6; 2.24.4; 10.138.1; 4.19.7; 1.62.5. Janert, in his discussion on the *dhāsí* found by Saramā in 1.62.3, offers his interpretation for the meaning of 'cows' in the P myth; he considers both water and light to be released from the rock, and, 'cows' to signify either or both of these concepts.[114] Thus he makes the following identifications: 10.108.5 *gó*=waters; 5.30.4 *gó... usríyā*=dawns; 7.90.4 waters; 5.45.8 *gó*=waters; 4.16.8 waters/light.

The opposite view supported by my own findings, namely that the release of water and the release of light represent the results of two separate myths, is held by Strauss, Hillebrandt and Geldner. Geldner in his exegesis of 6.13.3[115] outlines other basic differences between the two myths.[116] However, Strauss[117] cites 2.23.18; 2.26.2 and 10.65.10 as exceptions to the separate nature of each myth, and Hillebrandt[118] considers 7.90.4 and 9.108.6 as the only examples where 'cows' in the enclosure are 'waters'.

Clearly what is needed is a closer look at some of the controversial passages cited by Lüders, Strauss and Hillebrandt.[119] It will be noticed that a number of these verses are included in

112. W. Norman Brown, "Theories," 23ff.
113. Lüders, *Varuṇa* II, 533ff.
114. Janert, "*Dhāsi*," p. 11.
115. *HOS* 34, v. cit.
116. See also Geldner, *Ved. Stud.* II, 277.
117. *Bṛhaspati*, 33ff.
118. *Ved. Myth.* III, 261.
119. 4.3.12; 4.19.7; 10.65.10; 2.26.2 are not reviewed here since they do not bear directly upon the problem of 'cow' and 'water' symbolism.

hymns to Indra (1.62.5; 10.138.1; also 4.16.8). I consider this a rather important point, for, as has been observed above, the great deed performed in the P myth belongs originally to the priests; it is Indra who is drawn into the myth. To be sure, he relinquishes none of his Vṛtra-killing fame in doing so;[120] he but extends his glory, for the defeat of the Paṇis and Vṛtra are two major deeds in Rig Vedic mythology. It therefore seems extremely appropriate to mention both deeds side by side when praising Indra. It is not at all uncommon to honor the god's might by enumerating his various feats. One need only look at 2.12.3ab and 2.14.3ab to find examples of Indra's other deeds mentioned together with the defeat of Vala in the same hemistich; indeed RV 1.62.5 illustrates this point well. The first hemistich pertains to the P myth; the second describes Indra's deeds of creation. In 8.14.7 Indra's two deeds are not described in two separate lines but are mingled in such a way that the creation deed is seen as the result of Indra' splitting Vala. Verse 7 no longer expresses the primary features of the P myth, but a secondary mythic stratum combining the various deeds of Indra. This secondary stratum is also evident in 10.138.1 (likewise a hymn to Indra) where the appearance of *uṣás* and *áp*[121] occur as Vala is burst open. A blending of themes may also be seen in 4.16.6.[122] Pādas cd of verse 6 use terms closely associated with the P myth; Pāda d in fact reoccurs in 4.1.15d, a verse describing the P myth. Pāda b however appears to refer to the Indra-Vṛtra myth (cf. Geldner, *HOS* 34, 435). RV 6.17.1 is another example wherein the Vala/Vṛtra themes are combined in praise addressed to Indra. The first hemistich cites the P myth;[123] the second is in the language of the Vṛtra myth. Similarly, both themes occur in 2.23.18, a hymn to Brahmaṇaspati. The P myth is described in the first half, the Vṛtra myth in the second half of the verse which may be compared to 1.56.5; 1.85.9. Here is an instance where the language of the Vṛtra myth is associated with Brahmaṇaspati, apparently drawn into the Indra mythology in 2.23.18.

120. E.g. 3.31.11 Indra, in the context of the P myth is called *vṛtrahán*.

121. The characteristic term for the Cosmic Waters.

122. In 4.16.8 occur the words *gotrā́* and *apó* in an apparent reference to the Vala and Vṛtra myths, respectively. Oldenberg's suggestion (*Noten*, v. cit.) is better; he takes *apó* from *ápo* (*ápa u*) changing under the influence of *apó* in verse 7.

123. For *ūrváṃ gávyam*, cf. 10.108.8.

How is *usríyā ápyā* in 9.108.6a to be understood ? *Usríyā* is not used in the Vṛtra myth. The phrase ought to belong within the P context since other terms in the verse (*áśmanaḥ*, *vrajáṃ* and *gávyam áśvyam*) point in that direction; however there is no other passage in the P myth where 'cows' are described as *ápya* ('watery'). Perhaps the best one can do is to note that pāda a is repeated in SV 1.585a where it reads: *ya usriyā api yā antar aśmani.*[124] There would be no difficulty in accepting this reading as belonging to the P myth. RV 7.90.4cd should be considered next. The pādas read *gávyam cid ūrvám uśíjo ví vavrus téṣām ánu pradívaḥ sasrur ā́paḥ*: 'The Uśíj have opened the stall filled with cows; their waters flowed after a long time.' *Gávya* — probably connotes 'light' (see pāda b). For Geldner (*Ved. Stud.* II, 277) pāda d refers to the Vṛtra myth (but cf. his position in *HOS* 34, 261). Another interpretation is possible; *áp* could indicate the manner in which light (*gávya-*) spreads. Note the simile in 1.92.12b which compares the spread of light to the flow of a river. This imagery is found within the P myth context as well; see 2.24.14cd.

(5) Results of the Battle:	Release of the Cosmic Waters; emergence of the Sun	Release of *dákṣiṇā* (cows, horses, wealth), oblation-giving cows, dawn (Uṣas, rays of Uṣas), sunlight (Sūrya, *svàr*), Agni, path, the day.

The narrative and symbolic divergencies enumerated above have been interpreted by some scholars as a shift of emphasis in the force used to effectuate creation. It is explained that physical energy is supplanted first by the sacrifice, then by the sacrifice and Vāc (in 1.164), the latter being author of the sacrifice and the material universe. Further it is explained that whereas the Indra-Vṛtra myth represents the primary and more folkloric version, the P myth offers a subsequent priestly solution to the problem of creation.[125] This solution is viewed as a development

124. *Apyā* resulting from *api yā*; cf. Whitney, *Sanskrit Grammar* (Leipzig, Boston, 1891), 233a. Bloomfield (*Ved. Concordance*, p. 726) who used T. Benfey's *Sāmavedārikam* (Leipzig, 1848).

125. Lüders, *Varuṇa* II, 537; cf. W. Norman Brown's remark ("Creation Myth," p. 96, fn. 64) that the myth of Saramā and the Paṇis may possibly be associated with the events leading up to the Indra-Vṛtra battle.

within the creation mythology which reflects the gradually increasing importance of the Vedic sacrifice.

The difficulty with this point of view is that it raises more questions than answers. In the first place, subsequent theories of creation, whether they proceed from the Indra-Vṛtra myth, or refute it, rectify it or alter it, they continue in some manner to relate to it.[126] A continuity is apparent because subsequent theories assume a position on some or all of the following questions: what is the origin of matter; how did the differentiation of matter take place; how did the elements of nature come into being; what is the origin of beings; how did it come to pass that all that was created functions in an orderly fashion. However these questions are not raised by the P myth.

Secondly, in scanning the creation theories described by Brown, one is impressed by the fact that theories subsequent to the Indra-Vṛtra myth manifest an ever increasing attempt towards abstract conceptualizations. However, were the P myth considered as a creation myth, we would have to conclude that at a time when other theories were expressed through abstract ideations, the more concrete allegorical approach still had currency. This conclusion has little appeal since theories which do consider the sacrifice as the cause of creation have abandoned the narrative in presenting their view.[127] It would be even more difficult to consider the P myth (if taken as a creation myth) as contemporaneous with the Indra-Vṛtra myth because of the difficulty in understanding why two different narratives are needed to explain the same problem.

At present, it is my belief that the myth of the Paṇis is not so much concerned with the mystery of creation as with the problem of maintaining that which has already been created. It is worthwhile to remember that according to the Indra-Vṛtra myth, the creation of the universe was only won through the utmost exertion of the mightiest of gods. Moreover, forces of evil were not eliminated when the universe was created; they were relegated to a specific area below the Vedic world and ruled there by *ánṛta*.

126. See W. Norman Brown, "Theories".
127. Brown, "Theories"; e.g. 10.72; 10.90.

In this way, the orderly world inhabited by Vedic man was dearly won, precariously maintained and constantly threatened. The chief security against those forces desirous of upsetting order is the sacrifice. It is against this general background that the myth of the Paṇis assumes its meaning.

C. 'COW' IN OTHER MYTHOLOGICAL CONTEXTS

1. *dhenú* as 'rivers'

5.69.2ab

írāvatīr varuṇa dhenávo vāṃ mádhumad vāṃ síndhavo mitra duhre

Your cows O Varuṇa are rich in food; your rivers O Mitra milk forth the sweet liquid.

Lüders (*Varuṇa* I, 147): the heavenly waters are called milk cows. See Section D, Chap. II for cows compared to real bodies of water.

2. The Race of Mudgalānī

10.102.5,7,8,9

vss. 5 and 9: *śatávat sahásraṃ gávām*[128]—1100 cows, the prize in the race won by the Mudgalānī; these cows are also mentioned in verse 8.

v. 7: *pátim aghnyānām*—(lord of the cows); the steer pulling Mudgala's cart (cf. Schmidt, "*aghnya-*", 24).

3. *gó* and Śvitrya, a Protégé of Indra

1.33.15ab

ā́vaḥ śámaṃ vṛṣabháṃ túgryāsu kṣetrajeṣé maghavañ chvítryaṃ gā́m

Among the Tugrya you helped the gentle bull O Maghavan, the Śvitrya bull in gaining land.

Gā́m: masc. s. 'bull' describing Indra's protégé.

The Śvitrya bull prob. = *śármaṃ vṛṣabhaṃ*=*śvaitreyaḥ* (1.33. 14d).

128. Schmidt ("*aghnya-*", 24): 1000 cows and 100 steers.

Śvitrya seems to have the same sense as *śvaitreya* (Macdonell, Keith, *Ved. Index* ad Śvaitreya).
Cf. Oldenberg, *Noten* v. cit.
For attempts to identify *śvítryaṃ gắm* see Geldner, *Auswahl,* II, v. cit.

4. *dhenú* as 'rainclouds'

5.55.5c

ná vo dasrā̃ úpa dasyanti dhenávaḥ

Your milk cows O Wonder Workers do not become dry.

Note that the rain the Maruts shed is called 'milk' (1.166.3).
Sāy. *dhenavaḥ: prīṇayitāro meghāḥ*
TS 2.4.8c (= RV 5.55.5c) forms part of a request for rain.

3.55.16ab

ắ dhenávo dhunayantām áśiśvīḥ sabardúghāḥ śaśayắ ápradugdhāḥ

Let the milk cows who have no calf flow noisily, yielding milk, productive, unexhausted.

Aśiśvīḥ: Geldner (*Auswahl*, II, v. cit): even though they (i.e. cows as 'rainclouds') have no calf, they let their milk (i.e. rain) flow.

Dhunay-: Renou (*EVP* 4, 53): said of the noise of a river; image of milk (or water) which flows.

5. The Cows and Namī Sāpya

10.48.9b

gávām éṣe sakhyắ kṛṇuta dvitắ

"Auf der Suche nach Rindern schloss er abermals Freundschaft (mit mir)." (Geldner, *HOS* 35, 207).

Namī Sāpya is with Indra when the latter fights Namuci. With the defeat of Namuci soma is released (Bloomfield, "Contributions," *JAOS* 15 [1893], 158). *Gó* are the cattle Indra wins for his helper.

6. *gó* and Viṣṇu

1.154.6ab

tā́ vām vā́stūny uśmasi gámadhyai yátra gā́vo bhū́riśr̥ṅgā ayā́saḥ
We wish to go to these your dwellings, where there are bulls, many-horned and agile.

Gā́vaḥ: Note that *ayā́s* is associated with the soma juices in 9.41.1 (which see), and these are compared to *gā́vaḥ* i.e. 'bulls'. Most scholars take *gó* in 6b as 'stars': Grassmann, *Wö* (under *gó*); Geldner, *HOS* 33, 213; Ludwig, *RV*, IV, 150; *PW*. Macdonell (*Ved. Myth.*, 38) suggests 'clouds'.

7. *gó* and Triśoka
8.45.30

yáḥ kr̥ntád íd ví yonyáṃ triśókāya giríṃ pr̥thúm/góbhyo gātúṃ níretave
Who cut through the enclosing, the large mountain for Triśoka, [he made] a path for the cows to come out.

Góbhyaḥ gātúm is reminiscent of the language of the P myth. *Gatū* is one of the things released from the Paṇis' hold (3.31.15). Cf. 3.30.10.
Gātú is the path out of darkness, therefore a path light travels. *Gó* signifies the light of dawn.
Triśoka is a mythical seer (see Macdonell and Keith, *Ved. Index* I, 331).

1.112.12c
yā́bhis triśóka usríyā udā́jata
With which [i.e. aids of the Aśvins] Triśoka drove out the cows.

As above, language of pāda c recalls P myth. On mythic contexts of *usríyā* see p. 120. *Ud* $\sqrt{}$*aj* frequently occurs in the P myth: 10.68.7; 2.24.3; 2.14.3; 8.14.8.

8. *gó* and Arbuda

8.3.19cd
nír árbudasya mŕ̥gayasya māyíno níḥ párvatasya gā́ ājaḥ
You drove the cows out of the mountain, out of Arbuda, the skillful beast.

Not enough is known about Arbuda to determine what the cows symbolize. Mayrhofer (s. v.) states that Arbuda is perhaps of autochthon origin; so also Wackernagel (Intro. to *AiG*. 9; *AiG* III, 376). The terminology in this verse is not distinctive of a particular myth.

Macdonell (*Ved. Myth.*, 160) notes that Arbuda is mentioned together with Vṛtra; perhaps he is a similar type of demon. Sāyaṇa associates *gā́ḥ* with Vala.

9. *gó* and Śuṣṇa

8.96.17cd

tvám̐ śúṣṇasyā́vātiro vádhatrais tvám̐ gā indra śácyéd avindaḥ

With weapons you overcame [those] of Śuṣṇa; through your power O Indra, you found the cows.

Gā́ḥ—probably metaphor for Waters; Bergaigne (*Rel. Véd.* II, 334), considers the action against Śuṣṇa to be associated with the action against Vṛtra. Grassmann (*Wö* s.v.) also interprets the 'cows' here as those occurring in the Vṛtra legend (i.e., 'rainclouds'). Cf. Macdonell, *Ved. Myth.* par. 69.

10. *gó* associated with Trita and Viśvarūpa

10.48.2b

tritā́ya gā́ ajanayam áher ádhi

I produced the cows from the dragon for Trita

Gā́ḥ could symbolize 'Waters'. *Áhi* commonly designates Vṛtra; Trita is said to slay Vṛtra (1.187.1; 8.7.24). Geldner sees the dragon as Viśvarūpa. Cf. 10.8.8,9; (for the meaning of *gó* associated with Viśvarūpa, see Hillebrandt, *Ved. Myth.* I, 519-520). However, *áhi* is not said of Viśvarūpa (see Grassmann, *Wö*). For a recent discussion of the Trita myth and its Indo-European parallels, see Bruce Lincoln, "The Indo-European Cattle Raiding Myth", *Hist. of Religions* 16 (1976), 42-65. He considers this myth to deal primarily with the nature of the warrior function in I-E society.

10.46.3ab

imám̐ tritó bhū́ry avindad ichán vaibhūvasó mūrdhány aghnyā́yāḥ

Trita found him seeking often, the son of Vaibhūvas, on the head of the cow.

Ághnyāyāḥ—Brown ("Sanctity," 33): epithet of Cosmic Waters; "possibly the reference is to the Cloud as the mother of Agni = the lightning." Renou (*EVP* 14, 77): analogous to 1.30.19 where *aghnyá* is masc. Schmidt ("*aghnya-*," 23): *aghnyāyāḥ* = Waters; *mūrdhány ághnyāyāḥ* = abodes of the Waters, which in turn Schmidt identifies with the abodes of Truth situated in the highest heaven (cf. Bergaigne, *Rel. Véd.* II, 82, 328). For Ludwig (*RV*, IV, 409) *ághnyāyāḥ* = rubbing sticks; Sāy. 'the earth'; Macdonell ("Mythological Studies in the Rigveda," *Jour. of the Royal Asiatic Society* [1893] p. 450) ventures 'clouds'; Vaibhūvasa is twice an epithet of Soma.

11. The Cow and the Ṛbhus

The amazing feat performed by the Ṛbhus is that they formed a lame cow (1.161.7) out of a skin (1.110.8; 3.60.2). This they did with the power of their 'vision' (*dhītí*).[129] For one year they guarded and formed the cow (4.33.4). The cow they fashioned is a milk cow (*dhenú* 1.161.3; 4.34.9). She is all-impelling and omniform (4.33.8), made for Bṛhaspati (cf. 1.161.6) and called the Sabardúghā cow (1.20.3).[130]

12. Śayu's Cow

The Aśvins, noted for rescuing worshippers out of all sorts of dire predicaments, perform the miracle of making Śayu's barren cow yield milk. The designation of Śayu's cow is as follows:

1.117.20 *ádhenu...starí*; *gó*
1.116.22 *starí...gó*
10.39.13 *dhenú*
1.118.8 *dhenú*

129. 1.161.7a = 4.36.4b. *Dhītí*— (Gonda, *Vision*, 200): "higher insight, extraordinary intuition, imagination". *Dhītíḥ* is "the mental quality enabling the Ṛbhus to fashion a cow"...(ibid.).

130. Another possibility is that the Sabardúghā cow was made for the All-gods (see Bṛhad Devatā 3.85). Note that a heavenly milk cow in AVŚ 9.5.10 is called viśvarūpá and kāmadughā; see D. Srinivasan, "The Religious Significance of Divine Multiple Body Parts in the Atharva Veda." *Numen* Vol. 25, fasc. 3 (1979).

1.112.3 (which Sāy. places in this context) *dhenú asvà*
1.119.6 *gó*
6.62.7 *gó*
7.68.8 *aghnyā́...starī́*

Because of this marvelous deed, the Aśvins are asked to swell the milk cow, the nourishment of the RVedic man (6.63.8).

13. The Cooked Milk in the Raw Cow

The mythic theme of the 'cooked' milk in the 'raw' cow relates to a question which intrigues Vedic man: how did the milk get into the cow ? Who put it there ? The manner in which this question is explored shows that the milk cow is viewed as something of a paradox: the cow is 'raw' (which could mean that she needs further preparation to be converted into food) and yet she carries within her milk which is already cooked (i.e. needs no further preparation). The question crops up frequently in the hymns and employs a set of recurring terms: √*dhā* 'to put' etc.; *pakvá*[131] 'cooked'; *āmá*[131] 'raw'.

Āmá is associated with *gó* and *usríyā*. In 1.180.3 *usríyā* (s.) is referred to as *āmā́*; in 2.40.2 *usríyā* (pl.). 6.72.4 speaks of *āmā́sv...gávām...vakṣáṇāsu.*

8.32.25c refers concisely to the theme with: *yó góṣu pakvám̐ dhāráyat* (cf. 6.44.24; 10.73.9).

The answer most often given is that Indra put the cooked milk in the raw cow. The feat seems primarily to belong to him; indeed in 10.49.10 he boasts that not even Tvaṣṭṛ could perform this deed.[132] Precisely when he did this is uncertain, but it may be surmised that the miracle was accomplished when the universe was created since the theme is mentioned together with other creation feats (e.g., 6.44.24; 8.32.25 ?[133] 5.85.2 where the feat is attributed to Varuṇa).

Several scholars have assumed a metaphorical significance for 'cow' in this context. Bergaigne (*Rel. Véd.* II, 476) considers the

131. See Blair (*Tapas*, p. 133) for these terms.
132. Note that *rúśat* denotes white [milk]; cf. 3.30.14.
133. *Phaligá* — Geldner (*HOS* 34, 345): Vṛtra; note however that the term is used with Vala in 4.50.5; 1.62.4.

cows in 6.72.4 to be 'celestial'. Brown ("Creation Myth," 97) believes that *gó* in 10.49.10c means 'Waters'. Janert (*Dhāsi*, 24) also considers this possibility. He wonders whether 'cows' could refer to *sravátaḥ* and *sīrā́ḥ* in v. 9. These are not, however, the usual terms for Cosmic Waters. I consider v. 10 to stand independent of v. 9. Each verse describes a different deed, and I can find no compelling reason to understand *gó* in v. 10 in a figurative sense. Apparently *gó* and *usríyā* are used literally in this mythic context.

In 1.180.3, the theme refers to one cow. It is problematic whether the singular of *gó* and *usríyā* refers to a special cow (as is possibly the case in 4.3.9) or whether the terms are used in the collective sense. The verse reads as follows:

1.180.3ab (To the Aśvins)
yuváṃ páya usríyāyām adhattaṃ pakvám āmā́yām áva pūrvyaṃ góḥ
You two put the milk in the cow, the cooked in the raw, the first [milk?] of the cow.

Geldner (*HOS* 33, 258): the same deed is associated with Indra in 1.62.9; 2.40.2; 3.30.14; 6.17.6[134]; 6.44.24; 6.72.4.
Note that *gó* and *usríyā* refer to the same 'cow'.

14. The Secret Name(s) of the Cow(s)
The following verses refer to this theme:

1.84.15: *átrā́ha gór amanvata nā́ma tváṣṭur apīcyàm/ itthā́ candrámaso gṛhé*

4.1.16: *té manvata prathamáṃ nā́ma dhenós tríḥ saptá mātúḥ paramā́ṇi vindan/ táj jānatī́r abhy ànūṣata vrā́ āvír bhuvad aruṇī́r yaśásā góḥ*

5.3.3cd: *padáṃ yád víṣṇor upamáṃ nidhā́yi téna pāsi gúhyaṃ nā́ma gónām*

134. Janert (*Dhāsi*, 27) associates the first hemistich with the second, thus assuming that the placing of the milk in the cow occurred when the cows were released from the Paṇis (i.e. at daybreak). I would interpret these as two different deeds, separated by time and mythic content, but mentioned in the same verse because Indra accomplished each feat (so also 2.40.2, having Soma-Pūṣan as subject).

7.87.4[135] *tríḥ saptá nā́mā́ghnyā bibharti*
8.41.5: *yá usrā́ṇām apīcyā̀ véda nā́māni gúhyā*
9.87.3: *apīcyàṃ gúhyaṃ nā́ma gónām*
10.68.7: *nā́ma svarī́ṇāṃ sádane gúhā yát*

Gúhya (also *apīcyà*) *nā́man* plus the genitive of a 'cow' term (exception: 7.87.4) is the usual way this theme is expressed. The term may be in the sing. or pl.; 'cow' terms used in this context are: *gó, dhenú, usrā́, ághnyā* (*svarī́*[136] is in apposition with *usrī́yā* in 10.68.7).

What is the significance of the expression ? Lüders (*Varuṇa* II, 528) proposed 'Dawn' as the true and secret name of the cow. While 'dawn' or 'dawns' is suitable in 4.1.16[137]; 10.68.7[138]; and 8.41.5, this identification is questionable in the other verses. For example, the cows, whose secret name Soma discovered (9.87.3) could well be the milk cows.[139] 'Dawn(s)' also does not seem appropriate in 1.84.15[140] or 5.3.3.

The diversity of the contexts containing the expression may be a good indication that we ought not to look for a single 'name' as the key to understanding the expression. The text itself tells us that cows may have many hidden names (i.e. 8.41.5 *nā́māni*), that they may have 3 times 7 names (7.87.4; cf. 1.164.3 seven names of the cows).[141] Geldner, commenting upon 7.87.4 states

135. Cf. Renou' *Études Voc. RV*, 22.

136. Bergaigne (*Rel. Véd.* I, 317, fn.1): *svarī́nāṃ* could be fem. of *svarya* 'brilliant or heavenly'.

137. *Vrā́h*, the troop, is the herd of cattle as Uṣas' rays, which bellow to her (7.75.7); cf. Geldner (*HOS* 33, v. cit.). *Gó* in 'd' is also Uṣas; see exegesis under 10.106.11. Renou (*EVP* 13,3): "le (don) distinctif (émanant) de la vache."

138. 10.68 relates the P myth. Since *svarī́* is in apposition with *usriyā*, we may conclude that these are dawn's rays.

139. Both Geldner (*HOS* 35,85) and Bergaigne (*Rel. Véd.* I, 218) consider the verse a play on the myth of the Paṇis; even so, 'milk cow' would still be suitable.

140. Geldner (*HOS* 33, 108) connects this verse with the Dadhyañc legend. Sāy. *góḥ*=sun; Nir. 2.6; 4.25 — 'ray'.

141. *Gávām*: Grassmann (*Wö*,): stars; *Sāy.*: seven notes of music; Geldner (*HOS* 33, 228): seven names of cow are 3 times 7 names (7.87.4); the lan-

that the 3 times 7 names of the cow could signify either that "the cow has 21 names or that the word 'cow' has 21 meanings". Note that Naighaṇṭu begins with 21 names for 'earth' and the first entry is *gaúḥ*. In any case, 7.87.4 refers to poetic speech, rich in symbols and metaphors. I agree with Geldner's proposals but do not believe that we ought to take 3 times 7 literally (so also Hillebrandt, *Lieder*, 78: "Zahlreich;" not so Ludwig, *RV* IV, 89). It is my belief that the 'secret name(s) of the cow(s)' is an expression allied to Vedic notions on the potency in establishing correct associations (i.e. naming correct names). Knowing the secret name is equivalent to knowing the appropriate term needed to affirm a correct association. The use of *gó* etc. in the economic, ritual and mythological contexts demonstrates the many figurative uses of 'cow' terms. From this wide variety of meanings, the appropriate 'cow' word or name is sought in order to make the correct identification between 'cow' and another concept. Speaking the right name of the cows is known through the rite (10.169.2). The importance of correctly identifying something is essentially magical; one controls that which one names correctly.

15. *Padá gó*

The phrase *padá gó* is a figurative expression; the phrase usually has *padá* in the loc. s.; *gó* is always in the gen. s.

The first meaning of *padá* is 'footprint, trail' sometimes 'foot'.[142] Renou traces the development of *padá* and demonstrates how it can mean 'place' and 'word' in the RV.[142]

In 1.158.2 *padé góḥ* could designate the area of the sacrifice, probably the altar: 'Who would honor you for your favor O Vasus when you would give, due to the homage [paid you] at the place of the cow.'[143] Geldner (*HOS* 33, 216) interprets *padé góḥ* as the offering place, the stations of Dakṣiṇā. Ludwig (*RV*, IV, 43): the cow's place is her udder.

guage of the poet, rich in metaphors, is alluded to here. W. Norman Brown, "Agni, Sun, Sacrifice and Vāc: A Sacerdotal Ode by Dīrghatamas (Rig Veda 1.164)", *JAOS* 88 (1968), 213, considers the 7 names of the cows to be a reference by metonomy to the 7 Waters. Note: 9.70.1: 3 times 7 milk cows gave soma milk; 9.86.25: 7 soma milk cows.

142. See Renou, *Études Voc. RV*, p. 21.

143. *kó vāṃ dāśat sumatáye cid asyaí vásū yád dhéthe námasā padé góḥ.*

Padé góḥ in 1.163.7 may also allude to the fire altar; but cf. Geldner, *Auswahl* v. cit. and *HOS* 33 v. cit.; also D. P. Patanjal, *A Critical Study of Ṛgveda* (New Delhi, 1963), p. 415. This verse is included in the section on the horse sacrifice in TS 4.6.7.3.

The image in 4.5.10cd appears to refer to the same sacrificial area: In the mother's highest place, before the cow's place, the bull's[144] tongue of soaring flame.[145] Ludwig (*RV*, IV, 316) identifies the cow as Pṛśni. Cf. Geldner, *HOS* 33, 425. If Agni's flame is before the cow's place, then the latter must be associated with the sacrificial area.

Renou's interpretation of *padé góḥ* in 3.55.1 (*EVP*, 4, 51) is: the great syllable is born in the house of transcendent language. Cf. J. A. B. van Buitenen, "*akṣara*," *JAOS* 79 (1959), p. 178. Geldner (*HOS*, 33, 399) considers the phrase to have more than one meaning: it can refer to the offering places and also to the Aṅgirases' campaign against the Paṇis. Ludwig (*RV*, IV, 200) follows Sāy., namely that *padé góḥ* = heaven.

In 4.5.3 *padáṃ ná góḥ*[146] refers to poetic thought according to Renou (*Études Voc. RV*, 21); Gonda (*Vision*, 51): Agni has "proclaimed . . 'emotional thought' or 'wisdom' . . in connection with the hidden footprint of the cow." Geldner (*HOS*, 33, v. cit.) and Renou (*Études Voc. RV*, 22) interpret *padám* as 'word', i.e. poetic thought.

9.71.5cd reads: He should come; he goes up to the secret of the cow, the word which his wise ones (?) have produced.[147] The caesura comes after *apīcyam*; I would take *gór apīcyàm* to be in apposition with *padám*. The translations of Ludwig, Lüders, and Grassmann disregard the place of the caesura. Lüders (*Varuṇa* I, 252) understands *apīcyàm padám* to signify the flood of milk in heaven towards which Soma climbs; for Ludwig (*RV*, V, 360) it is the udder of heaven. Geldner keeps the caesura; he

144. Agni.

145. *mātúṣ padé paramé ánti ṣád gór vṛ́ṣṇaḥ śociṣaḥ práyatasya jihvā́*

146. Pischel (*Ved. Stud.* II, 211): *pastyàm gór* (10.96.11) is usually expressed by *padám góḥ*, which he identifies as 'heaven'. Sāy. for 10.96.11: *góḥ*: *jātyekavacanam gavām*. Geldner (*HOS* 35) connects 10.96.11 pādas cd with the myth of the Paṇis.

147. *jígād úpa jrayati gór apīcyàṃ padáṃ yád asya matúthā ájījanan.*

understands *gór apīcyàm* to be the milk and takes *padám* as the obj. of √*jan*. *Gór apīcyàm* seems to me to be reminiscent of *nā́ma...apīcyàm* of the cow (1.84.15) and cows (8.41.5; 9.87.3). Perhaps *nā́man* is to be understood after *gór apīcyàm*, in which case 'the secret name of the cow' = *padá*.[148] The image of 9.71.5cd is that of Soma at the altar, from where prayer is generated by the priests.

148. See Renou (*Études Voc. RV*, 22) for vss. associating *padá* and *nā́man*.

CHAPTER V

EPITHETS

A. *GODS*

1. Indra

term	*verse*	*translation/notes*
gó	6.45.26	*cow*
dhenú sudúghā	8.1.10	bountiful milk cow; see fn. 1.
gojít	2.21.1	conquering cattle
gojít bāhú	1.102.6	whose arms win cattle
gotrabhíd	6.17.2; 10.103.6	splitter of cow stalls (said of Bṛhaspati's car 2.23.3)
godari	8.92.11	splitting cow stalls; see fn. 2.
godatra	8.21.16	giver of cattle
godá	3.30.21	giver of cattle
	4.22.10 (cf.1.4.2)	
	8.45.19	
gópati		lord of cattle; see fn. 3.
gávām gópati[4]	1.101.4; 7.98.6[5]	lord of cattle
gópati gónām	10.47.1	lord of cattle
janitṛ́ gávām	8.36.5	creator of cattle
purukṛ́t gávām	8.61.6	increaser of cattle

1. Cf. pp. 46-47.
2. So *PW*. In defense of this meaning can be cited √*dṝ* referring to the action involved in opening a place which holds cows (*gotrá* 3.30.21; *vrajá* 8.32.5; 6.66.8; *gódhāyas* 10.67.7). However, note *durá...gór* (1.53.2) said of Indra; here *góḥ* is used in the collective sense.
3. See Gonda, *Epithets*, 74ff.
4. Note the redundancy illustrating instances where *gópati* should have lost its specific reference to cows and should have come to mean 'keeper, protector' in general (see Lanman, 'Diction,' *JAOS* 20, p. 16). The same meaning may be applied to *gopá* (e.g. 6.51.3 where Aditi, Mitra, Varuṇa and the Nobles are described as *ṛtásya gopá́n*).
5. 6c is simlar to 3.31.4d; but *gó* in 4d represents 'rays of dawn'. Therefore in this verse Indra is lord of the 'light-cows'.

term	verse	translation/notes
2. Agni		
dhenú	10.5.7	Agni as a cosmic principle is both a milk cow and a bull. Cf. 3.38.7 and see discussion in Srinivasan, "RV Multiplicity", 148.
gó	8.74.10	'cow' or 'bull'; see fn. 6.
gó	10.31.10	see p. 80.
gó	1.173.3	bull; see fn. 7.
gó	1.121.2[8]	bull
gojá́	4.40.5	born of cows (i.e. dawn's rays); see fn 9.
3. Soma		
páti gávām	9.72.4	lord of cows
gópati	9.97.34	lord of cows
gómat	9.107.9	possessor of cows
gojít	9.78.4	winner of cows
4. Sūrya		
gó[10]	10.189.1	bull
gó	10.111.3	bull; see fn. 11.

6. See Oldenberg, *Noten* v. cit.; cf. Geldner, *HOS* 34 v. cit.

7. We can take cd as referring to Agni. Agni is a steed (see Macdonell, *Vedic Myth.*, p. 89). Agni as a bull bellows to heaven and earth (10.8.1b= 6.73.1d said of Bṛhaspáti). If however *vāc* in d is understood as the goddess, then *gó* in c could refer to her.

8. 2c: *ánu svajām mahiṣáś cakṣata vrāṃ ménām áśvasya pári mātáraṃ góḥ*. *Vrā́m* 'female' (Pischel, *Ved. Studies* II pp. 121; 313). Conceptually, *vrā́*=*ménā áśvasya*=*mātṛ góḥ*. The problem is to identify the female who is generated by Indra (*svajāṃ*: Pischel, p. 316 'generated by him'; *mahiṣá*= Indra), and, who is the wife of the horse, mother of *gó*. If *gó* is taken as m. 'bull' (symbolizing Agni), the female is easily identified. Uṣas is generated by Indra (2.12.7); she is the wife of Sūrya (7.75.5) who is pictured as a steed (7.77.3) and she is the mother of Agni (cf. 3.58.1 where Uṣas is spoken of as Dakṣiṇā).

9. This verse is attributed to the Sun by the commentaries and the Anukramaṇī. More exact, the subject is Agni's various forms (Geldner, *HOS* ad 4.40.5; so also Lüders, *Varuṇa* I, 301; II, 622). Agni as the Sun is born of dawn's rays; Sāyaṇa offers the same meaning for *gójā́*.

10. *Gó* could also refer to Agni; see Geldner, *HOS* 35 ad 10.189.

11. This identification is uncertain. *Ménā* 'female' (see M. Mayrhofer,

	term	verse	translation/notes
5.	Maruts		
	góbandhu	8.20.8	having the cow as relative
	gómātṛ	1.85.3	having a cow as mother
6.	Bṛ́haspátí		
	gópati	10.67.8	lord of cows
7.	Parjanya		
	starī́	7.101.3	barren cow
8.	Dyaus		
	usríya vṛṣabhá	5.58.6	reddish (or bright) bull; see fn. 12.
9.	Viśvedevas		
	gójāta	6.50.11 7.35.14 10.53.5 (To Agni Sauchīka, Gods)	born of the cow; see fn. 13.
10.	Priests		
	gó (m. pl.)[14]	1.84.16	bulls

"Das Bemühen um die Surkh-Kotal-Inschrift," *ZDMG*, 112 [1962], 336b) in 1.121.2 is taken to be Uṣas, *ménām áśvasya* referring to Uṣas as wife of the horse, Sūrya. Either *gó* in 10.111.3 refers to Sūrya, thus keeping the same relationship established in 1.121.2 or *gó* is Agni as in 1.121.2 in the phrase *mātáram góḥ*. For Agni as Uṣas' lover, see Macdonell, *Ved. Myth.* p. 48.

12. Similarly said of Soma: 9.74.3 *usríyo vṛ́ṣā*; cf. 9.70.6.

13. The cow could be Pṛśni (so also Renou, *EVP* 14 ad 10.53.5: *gójāta*—a generalization of *gómātṛ*, *pṛ́śnimātṛ* as epithets of the Maruts). However, Renou, *EVP* 4 ad 7.35.14: *gójāta* replaces the Waters. Bloomfield has shown that *gó* cannot be Aditi (*RV Rep.*, 316); he takes *gójāta* as born of the atmosphere, epithet of the atmospheric gods. Geldner (*HOS* 34, ad 7.35.14): born of Aditi or Pṛśni (so also Sāyaṇa). *PW*: born in the starry heaven.

14. Geldner, (*HOS* 33, 108) Ludwig (*RV* V, 27) and T. Aufrecht *Die Hymnen des Rigveda* (Bonn, 1877), xliv, identify *gā́ḥ* as the priests. According to Lüders (*Varuṇa* II, 455) the Maruts are meant. I prefer 'priests' for the following reasons: pāda a: cf. 10.61.10 *ṛtáyukti* — said of the Navagvas who are mythic priests; *ṛtayúj*, *ṛtadhīti* said of Indra and mythic priests respectively, in 6.39.2. Pāda b: *śímīvataḥ*, as Lüders points out, is used in

	term	verse	translation/notes
11.	Vala		
	gódhāyas	10.67.7	he whose nourishment is cows
B.	*GODDESSES*		
1.	Uṣas		
	aghnyá	1.164.27	cow; see fn. 15.
	usrá[16]... *devi*	9.58.2	the goddess Dawn
	usrá	10.35.4	bright cow
	usríyā gó	4.5.9	bright or ruddy cow
	gó	1.164.9[17]	cow
	gó	1.164.17[18]	cow
	gó	1.164.28[15]	cow
	gó	3.30.14[19]	cow
	gó	4.1.16[20]	cow
	gó	4.44.1	cow; see fn. 21.
	gávām jánitrī	1.124.5	mother of the cows (i.e. light)
	gávām mātṛ́	7.77.2	mother of the cows[22] (which are her rays).
		5.45.2	,,
	mātṛ gávām	4.52.3	,,
	gávām netrī́	7.76.6	leader of the cows (i.e. rays); see fn. 23.

connection with the Maruts. It is also said of the hymns (*arká* 1.141.13). Pāda c: *āsánniṣūn: íṣu*=priests' words; cf. 9.69.1; 2.24.8; 10.42.1. See Geldner, *HOS* 33 ad 1.84.16. Pāda d: *eṣām* (i.e. *gā́ḥ*) *bhṛtyā́m*: associated with the hymn in 8.66.11; 9.103.1.

15. 'Cow' terms in 1.164.26-28 assume a double meaning. They not only function as epithets of Uṣas but also refer to the role of the cow in the Pravargya ceremony; see Chap. III. Cf. Brown, "...(Rig Veda 1.164)", 214.

16. Only use of *usrā* in Book IX.

17. *Mātā́, Dákṣiṇā=Uṣas.* See Brown, "..(Rig Veda 1.164)", 214.

18. 17 b: ***Padā́ vatsám bíbhratī gaúr úd asthāt.*** *Bíbhrat gaúr* said of Uṣas in 3.30.14: *bíbhratī* and *úd asthāt* said of Uṣas in 7.77.2. Padā́ may refer to her ray of light (cf. *arcínā padā́* 8.41.8).

19. See Verse Index for other discussions on this verse.

20. See Verse Index for other discussions on this verse.

21. Cf 7.69.5 and Lüders, *Varuṇa II*, 370 fn. 1.

22. These 'cows' delight in the brightly shining Uṣas 1.71.1.

23. Renou (*EVP* 3, 95) compares this epithet to *netrī́ sūnṛ́tānām* (1.92.7; 1.113.4) *netry áhnām* (7.77.2).

term	*verse*	*translation/notes*
dhenú	1.164.26[15]	milk cow
dhenú	3.58.1	milk cow; see fn. 24.
2. Sacred Speech[25]		
aghnyā́	1.164.40	inviolable cow; see fn. 26.
gaurī́	1.164.41	buffalo-cow; see fn. 27.
gó	4.58.4	buffalo-cow; see p. 123
gó prob. Vāc.	10.65.6	see fn. 28.
	3.7.2	cow; see fn. 29.

24. If Uṣas=*dhenú*, then pāda a refers to the Dawn emitting her rays. Note that Uṣas could be taken as the subject of the rest of the verse (Dakṣiṇā is identified with Uṣas). However, it is also possible for *dhenú* to=Vāc, see fn. 33, below.

25. In the following three categories (i.e. the cow as Sacred Speech, Aditi, Dakṣiṇā) there is a lack of consensus among Vedic scholars as to the identification of 'cow'. One reason for this is that the same image, namely the bountiful milk cow, is appropriate for each goddess. Motherhood is one of the main characteristics of Aditi (Macdonell, *Ved. Myth.*, 121) and generosity characterizes Vāc and Dakṣiṇā. It is possible that for the Vedic Aryans, the concepts personified by these goddesses may have had a symbolic interrelationship.

26. *Aghnyā́* probably=Vāc, the cow in the succeeding verse. See Brown, "...(Rig Veda 1.164)", 216. The image of Sacred Speech as a cow nourished in the pasture comes close to the simile in 9.94.2 which see.

27. *Gaurī́* is one of the names of *Vā́c* (Naig. 1.11). On this verse see: van Buitenen, "*akṣara*", 178 ff; Lüders, *Varuṇa* I, p. 252. Brown, "...(Rig Veda 1.164)", 216-217; Srinivasan, "RV Multiplicity", *Asiatische Studien XXIX*, 172-174.

28. Bṛhad-devatā 7.106 states that 10.65.6 is in praise of the Middle Vāc, that is the thunder (cf. Nir. 11,27; Macdonell, *Ved. Myth.*, p. 124) : *Páyaḥ dúhānā* in pāda b could allude to Vāc in her capacity to grant the sacrificer's wishes. The beneficent quality of 'visions' which are fashioned into sacred speech are several times presented in the guise of a cow overflowing with milk; note *dhī́* as *dhenú* in 2.2.9; see *dhī́* as *máhi gó* pp. 54-55. Cf. 3.57.1 (discussed by Schmidt, *Weide*, p. 3; Renou, *EVP* 4, 55). See also 8.100.11. In 8.100.10 it is said of Vāc: *ū́rjaṃ duduhe páyāṅsi*. Bergaigne (*Rel. Véd.* I, 310) also considers *gó* in 10.65.6 as 'prayer'; Geldner (*HOS*) identifies *gó* in 10.65.6 and 3.7.2 as 'Schmalzlöffel'. Lüders (*Varuṇa* II, 719) states that 10.65.6 speaks of the stream which dispenses rain. It should be pointed out that a number of terms in 10.65.6 are also associated with Uṣas. *Vartaní* in 10.172.1 is the path of Uṣas. *Niṣkṛtá* in 1.123.9 is the place where Uṣas appears. *Páyaḥ dúhānā* is equally suited to Uṣas (see p. 119).

29. Discussed by Lüders, *Varuṇa* II, p. 593.

term	*verse*	*translation/notes*
dhenú	8.100.11	milk cow; see fn. 30.
gó	5.41.18	cow; see fn. 10; Chap. III.
3. Aditi		
gó	8.105.15	cow
gó	8.101.16	cow; see fn.31.
dhenú	1.153.3	milk cow
4. Dakṣiṇā [32]		
dhenú	3.58.1	milk cow; see fns. 24 and 33.
5. Pṛśni		
gó	5.52.16	cow
gó	8.94.1	cow
6. Rātrī		
gó	4.3.9	cow; see fn. 34.

C. *DUAL DIVINITIES*

1. *Rodasī*		
dhenú (f. du.)	1.146.3	two milk cows; see fn. 35.
dhenú (f. du.)	3.6.4	two milk cows
dhenú (f. du.)	4.23.10[36]	two milk cows

30. Discussed by Gonda, *Visions*, 92 ff.

31. Cf. Gonda's discussions on 8.101.16 (*Visions* 91ff and 126). Note that Naig. 1.11 gives *áditi* as a synonym for *vāc*. In any case, vss. 15 and 16 seem to be about the same cow, who is identified as Aditi in vs. 15.

32. See also *gó* in 1.180.5.

33. Verse 1 speaks of the Goddess of dawn as Dakṣiṇā (ab) and Uṣas (cd). Bergaigne (*Rel. Véd.* I, 299): vache=prayer; so also Lüders (*Varuṇa* II, 621). Ludwig (*RV* IV, 50) *dhenú*: the earth or Uṣas. Geldner (*HOS* 33,405): 'cow' whose milk is used in the soma or gharma drink, or, perhaps the 'cow' is prayer.

34. This vs. is discussed by Janert, *Dhāsi*, Chap. III.

35. *Suméke* (adj.) modifies *dhenū́*. *Suméke* occurs seven other times in the du. f.; six times with *ródasī*, once with *náktoṣā́sā*. Geldner (*HOS*, 33,204) and Renou (*EVP*, 12, 37) *dhenū́*=Night and Dawn.

36. Geldner (*HOS*, 33, 451) *dhenū́*: Heaven and Earth; cf. 6.70.2.

BIBLIOGRAPHY

Aitareya Brāhmaṇa...Commentary of Sāyaṇa Acharya, 4 vols. S. Samasrami ed. in *Bibliotheca Indica*, Calcutta, 1894-1897.

Alsdorf, A., "Beiträge zur Geschichte von Vegetarismus und Rinderverehrung in Indien," No. 6 (1961) in *Abhandlungen der Geistes und sozialwissenschaftlichen Klasse* published by the Akademie der Wissenschaften und der Literatur, Mainz, 557-625.

Āśvalāyana Gṛhya Sūtra, editor R. N. Vidyaratna, Bibliotheca Indica, Calcutta, 1866.

Atkins, S. D., *Pūṣan in the Rig-Veda*, Ph.D. diss. Princeton, 1941.

—— "The Meaning of Vedic *aktú*, *JAOS*, 70 (1950), 24-40.

Atharvaveda (Śaunaka), editor V. Bandhu, Hoshiarpur, 1961.

Aufrecht, T., *Die Hymnen des Rigveda*, Bonn, 1877.

Bailey, H. W., "Analecta Indoscythica II," *Jour. of the Royal Asiatic Society* (1954), 26-34.

Bergaigne, Abel, *La Religion Védique* 3 vols. (36, 53, 54 in *Bibliothèque de l'École des Hautes Études*), París, 1878-1883.

—— "Quelques Observations sur Les Figures de Rhétorique dans le Ṛig-Veda, "*Mémoires de la Société de Linguistique de Paris* 4 (1881), 96-137.

—— "La Syntaxe des Comparisons Védiques" in *Mélanges Renier, Bibliothèque de l'École des Hautes Études*, 73 (Paris, 1887) 75-101.

Bhave, S. S., *The Soma-Hymns of the Ṛgveda* Pt. II, in *M. S. Univ. of Baroda Research Series* 5, Baroda, 1950.

Blair, C. J., *Heat in the Rig Veda and Atharva Veda* (vol. 45 in the *American Oriental Series*), New Haven, 1961.

Bloomfield, M., "Contributions to the interpretation of the Veda"; 6th series; *ZDMG* 48 (1894), 541-579.

—— "Contributions to the Interpretation of the Veda," *Amer. Journal of Philology*, 17 (1896), 399-437.

—— "American Oriental Society's Proceedings, March 1894, *JAOS*, 16 (1896), cxxiii-cxxvi.

—— *Hymns of the Atharva-Veda*, translated (vol. 42 in *SBE*), Oxford, 1897.

—— *A Vedic Concordance* (vol. 10 in *HOS*), Cambridge, 1906.

—— *The Religion of the Veda*, New York and London, 1908.

—— Rig-Veda Repetitions, (vols. 20, 24 in *HOS*), Cambridge, 1916.

—— "Some Cruces in Vedic Text, Grammar and Interpretation," *American Journal of Philology*, 38 (1917), 1-18.

Böhtlingk, O. and Roth, R., *Sanskrit-Wörterbuch* (herausgegeben von der Kaiserlichen Akademie der Wissenschaften), 7 vols. St. Petersburg, 1855-75.

Brown, W. Norman, "The Sources and Nature of *pūruṣa* in the Puruṣasūkta...," *JAOS*, 51 (1931), 108-118.

—— "Rig Vedic Equivalent for Hell," *Journal of the American Oriental Society* 61 (1941), 76-80.

—— "The Creation Myth of the Rig Veda," *JAOS*, 62 (1942), 85-98.

—— "The Sanctity of the Cow in Hinduism," *Journal of the Madras University* 28, No. 2 (1957), 29-49.

—— "La vache sacrée dans la religion hindoue," *Annales*, 4 (1964), 643-664.

—— "Theories of Creation in the Rig Veda," *JAOS*, 85 (1965), 23-34.

—— "Agni, Sun, Sacrifice and Vāc : A Sacerdotal Ode by Dīrghatamas (Rig Veda 1.164)," *JAOS* 88 (1968), 199-218.

van Buitenen, J. A. B., "*akṣara*," *JAOS*, 79 (1959), 176-187.

—— *The Pravargya*, Poona, 1968.

Burrows, T., *The Sanskrit Language*, London, 1955.

Caland, W., tr. *Pañcaviṃśa-brāhmaṇa* in *Bibliotheca Indica*, Calcutta, 1931.

—— tr. *Śāṅkhāyana-Śrautasūtra*, Nagpur, 1953.

Chattopadhyay, A., "A note on beef-eating in Mauryan times", *Indo-Asian Culture* 17 (1968), 49-51.

Dandekar, R. N., *Vedic Bibliography*, 2 vols. Bombay, 1946, Poona, 1961.

Debrunner, A., *Altindische Grammatik*, Band II_2, Göttingen, 1954.

Dikshitar, V. R. Ramachandra, "A Note on Cow Veneration in Ancient India," *Vol. of Eastern and Indian Studies* extra series I, presented to F. W. Thomas, (1939), 75-77.

Dumont, P. E., *l'Aśvamedha*, Paris, Louvain, 1927.

Geldner, K. and Kaegi, A., *Siebenzig Lieder des Rigveda*, übersetzt, Tübingen, 1875.

Geldner, K. F., *Der Rigveda in Auswahl*, 2 parts, Stuttgart, 1907-09.

—— "Zur Erklärung des Rigveda," *ZDMG*, 71 (1917), 315-346.

—— *Der Rig-Veda*, übersetzt, 4 vols. (33, 34, 35, 36 in *Harvard Oriental Series*) Cambridge, 1951-57.

Gonda, J., *Remarks on Similes in Sanskrit Literature*, Orientalia Rheno-Traiectina, Vol. 1, Leiden, 1949.

—— *Notes on Bráhman*, Utrecht, 1950.

—— *Epithets in the Ṛgveda*, Disputationes Rheno-Trajectinae IV, The Hague, 1959.

——*Stylistic Repetition in the Veda*, in *Verhandelingen der Koninklijke Nederlandse Akademie van Wetenschappen, afd. Letterkunde*, N. R. Deel 65, No. 3, Amsterdam, 1959.

Gonda, J., *Ellipsis, Brachylogy and Other Forms of Brevity in Speech in the Ṛgveda*, in *Verhandelingen der Koninklijke Nederlandse Akademie van Wetenschappen, afd. Letterkunde*, N. S. Vol. 67, No. 4, Amsterdam, 1960.

—— *The Vision of the Vedic Poets*, Disputationes Rheno-Trajectinae VIII, The Hague, 1963.

—— *The Savayajñas* in *Verhandelingen der Koninklijke Nederlandse Akademie van Wetenschappen, afd. Letterkunde* N. S. Vol. 71, no. 2, Amsterdam, 1965.

—— *The Meaning of the Sanskrit term dhāman*— in *Verhandelingen der Koninklijke Nederlandse Akademie van Wetenschappen, afd. Letterkunde*, N. S. Vol. 73, No. 2, Amsterdam, 1967.

—— *Aspects of Early Viṣṇuism*, 2nd ed. Delhi, 1969.

Grassmann, H., *Rig-Veda*, übersetzt, 2 parts, Leipzig, 1876-7.

—— *Wörterbuch zum Rig-Veda* (3rd ed.), Wiesbaden, 1955.

Griffith, R.T.H., *The White Yajurveda*, Benares, 1899.

— *Hymns of the Ṛgveda*, 2 vols. (vol. 35 in the *Chowkhamba Sanskrit Studies*) Varanasi, 1963.

Heesterman, J., "Reflections on the Significance of *dákṣiṇā*," *Indo-Iranian Journal,* III (1959), 241-258.

Heston, A., "An Approach to the Sacred Cow of India", *Current Anthropology* (April, 1971), 191-209.

Hillebrandt, A., *Ueber die Göttin Aditi*, Breslau, 1876.

—— *Vedische Mythologie*, 3 vols. Breslau, 1891-1902.

— *Lieder des Rigveda*, Göttingen, Leipzig, 1913.

— "Vedisch *dhắman*," *Indogermanische Forschungen*, 44 (1927), 139-150.

Janert, K. L., *Sinn und Bedeutung des Wortes "dhāsi"...*, Wiesbaden, 1956.

Kapadia, B. H., "The Paṇis in the Ṛg-Veda," *Poona Orientalist*, vol. 27, nos. 1 and 2 (1962), 50-60.

Keith, A. B., trans. *The Veda of the Black Yajus School entitled Tattiriya Sanhita*, (vol. 18 and 19 in *HOS*) Cambridge, 1914.

—— *The Religion and Philosophy of the Veda and Upanishads*, (vols. 31 and 32 in *HOS*), Cambridge, 1925.

Kirste, J., "Zum Citralakṣaṇa," *ZDMG*, 74 (1920), 270-273.

Kosambi, D. D., *Myth and Reality*, Bombay, 1962.

Kuiper, F. B. J., "The Ancient Aryan Verbal Contest", *IIJ* 4 (1960), 217-281.

—— "Rigvedic *pấrye diví*" *IIJ* 5 (1961-62), 169-183.

—— "Cosmogony and Conception : A Query", *IIJ* 10 (1970), 91-138.

Lanman, C. R., "Sanskrit Diction as Affected by the Interest of Herdsman, Priest and Gambler," *JAOS* 20 (1899), 12-17.

Lincoln, B., "The Indo-European Cattle Raiding Myth", *History of Religions* 16 (1976), 42-65.

Lüders, H., "Von indischen Tieren," *ZDMG*, 96 (1942), 23-81.

—— *Varuṇa*, 2 vols. Göttingen, 1951-1959.

Ludwig, A., *Der Rigveda*...übersetzt, 6 vols. Prag, 1876-88.

Macdonell, A. A., "Mythological Studies in the Rigveda," *Jour. of the Royal Asiatic Society* (1893), 419-496.

—— *Vedic Mythology* (III Band, 1. Heft A in *Grundriss der indo-arischen Philologie und Altertumskunde*), Strassburg, 1897.

—— *The Bṛhad-Devatā...*, (5 and 6 in *HOS*), Cambridge, 1904.

—— *Vedic Grammar* (I Band, 4 Heft in *Grundriss der indo-*

arischen Philologie und Altertumskunde), Strassburg, 1910.

—— *A Vedic Grammar for Students*, Oxford, 1916.

—— "The Uṣas Hymns of the Rigveda," *Jour. of the Royal Asiatic Society* (1932), 345-371.

Macdonell, A. A. and Keith, A. B., *Vedic Index*, 2 vols. London, 1912.

Margul, T., "Present day worship of the Cow in India", *Numen XV* (1968), 63—80.

Mayrhofer, M., *Kurzgefasstes etymologisches Wörterbuch des Altindischen*, Heidelberg, 1956.

—— "Das Bemühen um die Surkh-Kotal-Inschrift," *ZDMG*, 112 (1962), 325-344.

Mayrhofer-Passler, E., "Haustieropfer bei den Indoiraniern und den anderen Indogermanischen Völkern,' *Archiv Orientalni*, 21 (1953) 182-205.

Monier-Williams, M., *A Sanskrit-English Dictionary*, reprinted at Oxford, 1956, 1960.

Müller, Reinhold, F. G., "Zu dem Fremdling im Ṛgveda", *Weiner Zeitschrift für die Kunde Süd-und Ostasiens* X (1966), 1-5.

Muusses, M. A., *Koecultus bij de Hindoes*, Thesis, Utrecht, 1920.

Oertel, H., "Contributions from the Jāiminīya Brāhmaṇa to the History of Brāhmaṇa Literature," *JAOS*,19(1898),97-125.

Oldenberg, H., *The Gṛhya Sūtras* (vol. 29 in *SBE*), Oxford, 1886.

—— "Ṛgveda VI, 1-20," *ZDMG*, 55 (1901), 267-330.

—— *Ṛgveda*, Textkritische und exegetische Noten, 2 vols. in *Abhandlungen der königlichen Gesellschaft der Wissenschaften zu Göttingen*, Phil.-Hist. Kl., N.F., 11, nr. 5; N.F., 13, nr. 3, Berlin, 1909-12.

—— tr. *Vedic Hymns* Vols. 32 and 46 in *SBE*, Oxford, 1891, 1897.

—— *Die Religion des Veda*, Stuttgart, Berlin, 1923.

—— "Vedic Words for "Beautiful" and "Beauty"...trans. from the German in *Rupam* No. 32 (Oct. 1927)98-121.

Oliphant, S. G., "The Vedic Press-Stones," *Studies in Honor of Maurice Bloomfield*, New Haven, 1920, pages 225-250.

Patanjal, D. P., *A Critical Study of Ṛgveda*, New Delhi, 1963.

Patel, M., *The Dānastutis of the Rig-Veda*, trans. B. H. Kapadia, Vallabh Vidyanagar, 1961.

Pischel, R., "Miscellanea," *ZDMG*, 35 (1881), 711-724.

Pischel, R. and Geldner, K. F., *Vedische Studien*, 3 vols. Stuttgart, 1889-1901.

Prakash, O., *Food and Drinks in Ancient India*, Delhi, 1961.

Raj, K. N., "India's Sacred Cattle" *Economic and Political Weekly* Vol. 6 (Jan.-March, 1971), 717-722.

Renou, L., *Vedic India*, vol. 3 in *Classical India*, Delhi, Varanasi, 1971.

—— "Sur la notion de 'bráhman' " *JA*, 237 (1949), 7-46.

—— *Études Vediques et Pāṇinéennes*, Paris, 1955.

—— *Études sur le Vocabulaire du Ṛgveda* No. 5 in Publications de l'Institut Françáis D'Indologie, Pondichéry, 1958.

—— "Vedic svásara," *Vishveshvaranand Indological Journal*, vol. 1, pt. 1 (March, 1963), 37-39.

—— "Sur Quelques Mots du Ṛgveda," *JAOS*, 85 (1965), 79-85.

Ṛgveda-Samhitā with the commentary of Sāyaṇācharya, N. S. Sontakke ed., Tilak Maharashtra University, Vaidic Samshodhan Mandal, 4 vols. Poona.

Roth, R and Whitney, W. D., *Atharva-Veda Sanhita*, Berlin, 1924.

Saṇkalia, H. D., *Aspects of Indian History and Archaeology*, Delhi, 1977. Chap. 17 : "The Cow in History".

Śāṅkhāyana Śrautra Sūtra, edited by A. Hillebrandt, 3 vols, in Bibliotheca Indica, Calcutta, 1888-1897.

Sarup, L., *The Nighaṇṭu and the Nirukta*, edited and translated, reprint, Varanasi, 1967.

Schmid, W. P., "Die Kuh auf der Weide," *Indogermanische Forschungen*, 64 (1958), 1-12.

Schmidt, Hanns-Peter, "*aghnya-*", *Zeitschrift für vergleichende Sprachforschung auf dem Gebiet der Indogermanischen Sprachen* 78 (1963), 1-46.

—— *Bṛhaspati und Indra*, Wiesbaden, 1968.

von Schroeder, L., *Mysterium und Mimus im Rigveda*, Leipzig, 1908.

Singh, S. D., *Ancient Indian Warfare with Special Reference to the Vedic Period*, Leiden, 1965.

Srinivasan, D., "The Myth of the Paṇis in the Rig Veda", *JAOS* 93 (1973) 44-57.

—— "Saṃdhyā : Myth and Ritual", *IIJ* 15.1 (1973), 161-178.

—— "The Religious Significance of Multiple Bodily Parts to

denote the Divine : Findings from the Rig Veda", *Asiatische Studien* XXIX (1975), 137-179.

—— "The Religious Significance of Divine Multiple Body Parts in the Atharva Veda", *Numen* (1979). xxv, fasc. 3.

Strauss, O., *Bṛhaspati im Veda*, Ph.D. diss., Kiel Univ., Leipzig, 1905.

Thieme, P., Der Fremdling im Ṛgveda (vol. 23, 2 in *Abhandlungen für die Kunde des Morgenlandes*), Leipzig, 1938.

—— "Brahman," *ZDMG*, 102 (1952), 91-129.

—— "Agastya und Lopāmudrā," *ZDMG*, 113 (1963), 69-79,

Thomas, E. J., *Vedic Hymns* in *Wisdom of the East*, London, 1923.

Turner, R. L., *A Comparative Dictionary of the Indo-Aryan Languages*, London, 1962-66.

Vājasaneyi Sanhitā, ed. A. Weber, Berlin, London, 1852.

Velankar, H. D., "Similes in the Atharvaveda," *Journal of the Asiatic Society of Bombay*, N. S. Vol. 38 (1963).

Venkatasubbiah, A., "The Act of Truth in the Ṛgveda", *Journ. of Oriental Research* 14 (1940), 133-165; 210-236; 274-285.

—— "On Indra's Winning of Cows and Waters", *ZDMG* 115 (1965), 120-133.

Viśva-Bandhu Śāstrī, *Vaidika-Padānukrama-Koṣaḥ*, Vol. I (Saṁhitās) in 6 parts; part 1 Lahore, 1942; parts 2-6 Hoshiarpur, 1955-1963.

Wackernagel, J., *Altindische Grammatik*, Band I, Band II_1, Göttingen, 1896-1905; Band III (by Debrunner, A., and Wackernagel, J.), Göttingen, 1929-1930.

Walde, A. and Pokorny, J., *Vergleichendes Wörterbuch der indogermanischen Sprachen*, 3 vols, Berlin, 1927-1932.

Whitney, W. D., *The Roots, Verb-Forms and Primary Derivatives of the Sanskrit Language*, Leipzig, 1885.

—— *Sanskrit Grammar*, Leipzig, Boston, 1891.

—— *Atharva-Veda Saṁhitā*, translated (vols. 7 and 8 in *HOS*), Cambridge, 1905.

INDEX OF RIGVEDIC PASSAGES CITED

Verse	*Page*
1·4·1	42, 43
1·4·2	80
1·6·5	112
1·7·3	101
1·8·8	47
1·10·7	18, 77
1·10·8	18
1·11·5	102
1·16·9	79
1·18·7	105
1·20·3	134
1·23·15	14, 43-44
1·25·16	55
1·28·9	63
1·29·1-7	79
1·30·19	134
1·31·12	16
1·32·2	53
1·32·9	49
1·32·11	83-84
1·32·12	84
1·33·1	13, 17-18
1·33·3	14, 15
1·33·10	13
1·33·12	21
1·33·15	130
1·37·5	49
1·38·2	45
1·38·8	45, 48
1·43·2	9, 16
1·43·6	9, 16, 35
1·51·3	111
1·52·5	87
1·53·2	141
1·53·4	80
1·53·5	78
1·61·10	83, 84
1·62·2	109, 110
1·62·3	97, 101, 108, 111, 112, 122, 126
1·62·4	97, 100, 102, 112
1·62·5	98, 109, 114, 126, 127
1·66·2	49
1·66·9	40-41
1·70·9	57
1·71·1	144
1·71·2	98, 100, 107, 110-111, 114, 121, 122
1·71·9	16
1·72·8	102
1·79·1	36
1·81·7	15
1·83·1	26, 71
1·83·4	97, 100, 116
1·84·15	136, 137
1·84·16	143
1·85·3	143
1·86·3	18
1·90·5	78
1·90·8	13, 17
1·91·13	44
1·91·22	67, 89
1·92·1	119, 122
1·92·2	119, 122
1·92·4	52, 119
1·92·7	78
1·92·12	128
1·93·2	79
1·93·4	100, 118, 122
1·93·12	56, 120
1·95·6	49
1·95·8	61
1·100·4	112
1·101·4	141
1·102·6	141
1·103·5	88
1·110·8	134
1·112·3	135
1·112·12	132
1·113·4-6	62
1·113·9	62
1·114·9	54
1·114·10	16
1·116·22	9, 134
1·117·20	134
1·118·2	16
1·118·8	134
1·119·6	135
1·120·9	13
1·121·2	88, 142
1·121·4	114
1·121·5	117
1·121·7	9, 102
1·121·9	9, 21
1·121·15	15
1·122·2	9, 52
1·122·7	76
1·124·5	144
1·124·10	99
1·124·11	49, 119, 121, 122
1·125·4	15
1·126·2	76
1·126·5	76

1·130·3	102
1·130·5	53-54
1·132·4	102, 111, 113
1·134·2	64
1·135·8	9, 56
1·137·3	50, 71-72, 81
1·146·3	146
1·151·1	15
1·151·4	19
1·151·8	9, 61, 62
1·153·3	146
1·153·4	71
1·154·6	131-132
1·158·2	138
1·161·3	134
1·161·7	134
1·163·7	139
1·163·8	73
1·164·3	137
1·164·7	86
1·164·9	144
1·164·17	144
1·164·26	72, 145
1·164·27	72, 144
1·164·28	144
1·164·40	145
1·164·41	145
1·168·2	48
1·173·3	142
1·173·8	9, 57
1·180·3	135, 136
1·180·5	59
1·181·8	13
1·186·4	72
1·186·7	54
1·187·11	56
1·190·1	105
1·190·4	105
1·191·4	13, 17, 38
2·1·3	105
2·2·2	37, 45
2·3·6	72
2·5·1	30
2·7·5	59
2·11·2	106
2·11·18	87
2·11·20	87, 97, 102
2·12·3	104
2·12·7	88
2·14·3	104
2·14·10	46
2·15·8	87, 97, 101, 102, 109, 114
2.17.1	102, 104, 109
2·19·3	10, 85-86
2·21·1	141
2·21·5	113
2·23·1	105
2·23·2	105
2·23·18	101, 102, 126, 127

2·23·19	105
2·24·3	97, 98, 101, 102, 114
2·24·4	126
2·24·9	105
2·24·14	96, 108-109
2·24·16	105
2·25·2	13
2·25·4	14, 26, 71
2·26·2	126
2·30·5	14
2·30·7	80
2·34·1	86
2·34·12	52
2·36·1	63
2·40·2	135, 136
3·1·12	108
3·1·23	56
3·5·11	56
3·6·4	146
3·6·11	56
3·7·2	145
3·7·11	56
3·15·7	56
3·17·3	107
3·22·5	56
3·23·5	56
3·30·10	9, 102, 109, 121, 123
3·30·14	13, 51, 119, 144
3·30·20	14
3·30·21	14, 27, 28-29-141
3·31·4	104, 119, 122
3·31·6	101
3·31·7	101
3·31·10	112
3·31·11	104, 113, 114, 118, 122
3·31·15	98
3·31·20	14
3·31·21	29-30
3·33·1	53
3·34·9	89
3·34·10	87
3·35·8	63, 64
3·36·5	75
3·39·4	110
3·39·5	112
3·44·5	97
3·45·3	48
3·50·3	14, 65
3·53·14	15
3·53·17	19
3·53·18	19
3·53·20	22
3·55·1	139
3·55·8	9, 56
3·55·16	131
3·58·1	62, 145, 146
3·58·4	51
3·60·2	134
4·1·6	47, 62
4·1·19	51

4·1·13 102, 107, 121, 122
4·1·15 101, 102, 113, 114
4·1·16 36, 136, 137, 144
4·3·9 9, 146
4·3·11 111, 121
4·3·12 126
4·5·3 139
4·5·9 144
4·5·10 139
4·5·12 95
4·7·9 80
4·13·2 14, 38
4·16·6 102, 113, 114, 127
4·16·8 102, 109, 114, 126, 127
4·17·11 95
4·19·7 87, 126
4·20·6 27
4·20·8 18
4·22·8 9, 22-23
4·22·10 141
4·23·9 115
4·23·10 146
4·24·10 74-75
4·25·7 99
4·27·5 50, 64
4·28·5 9, 116, 123
4·32·18 80
4·33·1 50
4·33·4 134
4·33·8 134
4·34·9 134
4·36·4 134
4·38·4 14, 26, 31, 32, 71
4·40·5 142
4·41·5 11, 54
4·41·8 54, 69
4·44·1 144
4·50·1, 4 100
4·50·5 56, 117, 120, 122
4·51·2 108
4·51·8 51
4·52·3 119, 144
4·52·5 51
4·57·1 9, 17
4·58·4 9, 123, 124, 145
5·1·1 52
5·1·3 61-62
5·3·2 61, 62, 73
5·3·3 136, 137
5·6·1 41
5·6·7 14, 30-31
5·14·4 89
5·20·4 13
5·27·1 9, 14, 19, 76
5·27·2 76
5·27·5 63
5·29·3 84, 85, 86
5·29·12 112
5·30·4 123, 126
5·30·7 10, 57
5·30·12 76
5·30·13 76
5·31·4 106
5·32·4 21
5·33·4 14, 24
5·33·10 76
5·34·5 18, 96
5·34·8 27
5·41·18 9, 59, 146
5·42·4 78
5·45·1 101
5·45·2 144
5·45·6 9, 114, 119, 121, 123
5·45·7 97, 112
5·45·8 97, 112, 126
5·47·4 10, 94, 107
5·52·16 146
5·53·7 52
5·53·16 14
5·55·5 131
5·56·3 9, 49
5·56·4 49
5·56·5 48
5·58·6 143
5·59·3 48
5·61·8 98
5·61·10 76
5·62·3 89
5·63·5 14, 38
5·69·2 130
5·79·5 62
5·79·7 78
5·80·3 49
5·83·8 16
6·6·5 14, 15, 32, 38
6·10·2 62
6·13·3 126
6·16·47 59
6·17·1 104, 118, 127
6·17·2 141
6·17·5 101, 104
6·17·6 102, 109, 122, 136
6·18·5 107
6·19·12 14, 26, 79
6·20·4 102
6·23·7 51
6·25·4 14, 26, 79
6.26.2 14
6.27.7 19
6.27.8 76, 78
6.28.1 13, 17
6.28.4 15, 32
6·28·6 13
6·28·7 16
6·28·8 36-37
6·31·1 26
6·32·2 101, 112
6·32·3 113
6·35·2 14, 28
6·35·5 50

6·39·2 101, 102, 104, 107, 113, 114, 122
6·39·5 79
6·40·2 63
6·41·1 42
6·43·3 104
6·44·22 100
6·44·24 135, 136
6·45·7 42, 43
6·45·21 79
6·45·22 9, 48
6·45·26 42, 141
6·46·2 9, 78
6·46·14 9, 23
6·47·14 63
6·47·24 74, 76, 78
6·47·26 9, 21-22
6·47·27 22
6·48·22 65
6·50·11 143
6·53·9 25
6·54·5 16
6·54·6 15
6·59·7 14
6·60·2 10, 88-89
6·62·7 135
6·63·8 13, 135
6·63·9 59, 76
6·64·3 49
6·65·1 62 2
6·65·5 111, 114, 11
6·66·8 14, 26, 79
6·67·11 20-21
6·72·4 135, 136
6·73·3 102
6·75·2 14
6·75·11 19-20, 22
7·2·6 72
7·6·3 99, 100, 102, 103
7·6·4 103
7·9·4 10
7·10·1 61
7·16·7 75
7·18·1 13, 15, 80
7·18·2 79
7·18·4 47
7·18·10 45
7·18·22 76
7·21·1 51
7·23·4 9, 53
7·27·1 96
7·32·16 15, 28
7·33·6 25, 37
7·35·12 16, 35
7·35·14 143
7·36·1 10, 122
7·41·3 13
7·44·3 9
7·54·2 13
7·56·17 16
7·68·8 135
7·74·3 65
7·75·1 62
7·75·7 108, 120, 121, 122, 137
7·76·6 144
7·77·2 144
7·78·3 6
7·79·2 107, 119, 122
7·80·2 6
7·81·2 108
7·87·4 137-138
7·90·4 126, 128
7·90·6 73, 95, 116
7·98·6 141
7·101·3 143
7·102·2 16
7·103·2 9, 46
7·103·10 13
7·104·10 16
8·1·2 48
8·1·10 47, 141
8·2·3 63, 66
8·2·6 57
8·3·19 132-133
8·4·8 61
8·4·18 13, 15
8·4·20 76
8·4·21 76, 116
8·5·20 9, 16, 35
8·5·26 14
8·5·37 76
8·6·47 76
8·9·19 46
8·14·3 9, 13, 47
8·14·7 102, 127
8·14·8 111
8·20·8 64, 143
8·20·19 14, 44
8·20·21 48
8·21·16 141
8·22·4 46
8·24·6 54
8·30·4 9, 17, 35
8·32·5 9, 27, 104, 123
8·32·25 135
8·34·14 28
8·36·5 141
8·41·1 16, 38
8·41·3 107
8·41·5 137
8·41·6 40
8·43·11 59
8·43·17 54
8·45·19 141
8·45·21 28
8·45·30 132
8·46·9 18
8·46·22 76
8·46·30 39
8·47·14 17

8·49·5 57
8·51·2 75
8·51·5 18
8·52·4 43
8·52·5 9, 79
8·61·6 141
8·63·3 111
8·64·2 98
8·65·3 43
8·68·13 9, 15
8·69·6 57, 117
8·69·9 24-25
8·70·6 13
8·71·5 26
8·72·12 71
8·74·10 142
8·75·7 14, 15, 31
8·78·1, 2 78, 116
8·81·3 48
8·82·5 63, 66
8·88·1 37
8·92·11 141
8·92·12 44, 54
8·92·25 79
8·94·1 146
8·96·5 84, 86, 106
8·96·17 133
8·97·2 78, 98
8·100·9 22
8·100·11 146
8·101·15 11, 146
8·101·16 11, 146
8·102·19 57
9·2·4 66
9·6·6 68
9·8·5 66
9·9·9 9, 79
9·10·3 64
9·11·3 9, 16, 35
9·11·7 9, 16, 35
9·12·2 9, 45, 49
9·14·3 63, 66
9·14·5 67
9·16·6 71
9·19·5 50, 68
9·22·7 102, 113
9·24·2 65
9·26·2 69, 70
9·31·5 71
9·32·3 64
9·32·5 69, 70
9·33·4 70
9·34·6 70
9·41·1 68
9·42·1 66
9·43·1 63, 66
9·45·3 63, 64
9·46·4 66
9·49·2 15
9·50·5 64
9·58·2 14
9·61·13 64
9·61·15 9, 16, 35
9·62·3 9, 16
9·62·5 63, 71
9·62·19 71
9·64·3 13, 18
9·64·13 70
9·65·17 79
9·65·25 63
9·66·6 65
9·66·12 9, 42
9·66·13 66
9·66·29 63
9·67·6 79
9·67·12 62
9·67·32 13
9·68·1 9, 46, 67, 120
9·68·9 61, 66
9·69·4 68, 70
9·70·1 138
9·70·7 63
9·71·4 71
9·71·5 139
9·71·7 68, 70
9·72·1 64
9·72·3 70
9·72·4 68, 142
9·72·6 70
9·74·3 143
9·74·7 50
9·74·8 50, 64, 76
9·77·1 53
9·77·4 70
9·78·1 70
9·78·4 142
9·79·4 63
9·80·2 69, 70
9·81·1 36, 71
9·82·3 63
9·84·3 68
9·84·5 71
9·85·5 64
9·86·12 71
9·86·23 111, 113
9·86·25 138
9·86·26 67
9·86·27 22, 66
9·86·47 64
9·87·3 137
9·87·7 14, 71
9·87·8 113
9·87·9 70
9·89·3 71
9·90·4 89
9·91·3 9, 51, 71
9·91·6 78
9·93·2 64, 69, 120
9·93·3 71
9·94·5 9, 79, 116

9·95·1 67
9·96·7 68, 71
9·96·8 70
9·96·14 70, 120
9·96·15 65
9·96·16 79
9·96·22 64
9·97·9 70
9·97·13 68, 70
9·97·22 68, 70
9·97·31 70
9·97·34 68, 70, 142
9·97·35 70
9·97·39 110
9·97·43 71
9·99·3 10, 81
9·101·8 70
9·101·11 63
9·103·2 64
9·104·4 65, 66
9·105·4 65
9·107·2 66
9·107·9 64-65, 142
9·107·18 66
9·107·22 64
9·107·26 51, 67
9·108·6 116, 126, 128
9·109·17 66
9·111·2 102, 107
9·112·3 13
10·4·2 40
10·5·7 81, 142
10·7·2 78
10·11·3 36
10·16·7 11, 73
10·25·1 44
10·25·5 116
10·27·20 9, 19
10·27·22 9, 20, 23
10·28·10 24, 25
10·28·11 25
10·30·10 15
10·31·4 64
10·31·6 11
10·31·10 80, 142
10·31·11 52
10·32·3 80
10·32·4 73
10·34·13 13
10·35·4 144
10·38·1 14
10·39·13 134
10·42·2 42
10·42·10 80
10·45·11 113
10·46·3 133-134
10·47·1 141
10·48·2 133
10·48·9 131
10·49·10 135
10·53·5 143
10·59·10 19
10·60·6 98
10·60·8 22
10·61·4 30, 119
10·61·10 112, 116
10·61·11 118, 122
10·61·26 120
10·62·2 87, 97
10·62·7 116
10·64·11 13
10·65·6 145
10·65·10 126
10·65·11 89
10·67·3 106-107, 114
10·67·4 107, 122
10·67·5 11, 98, 114
10·67·6 100, 101, 104, 112, 114, 117, 122
10·67·8 108, 122, 143
10·67·7 102, 122, 144
10·68·3 101
10·68·4 101
10·68·5 102
10·68·6 87, 97, 102, 108, 114
10·68·7 101, 108, 137
10·68·9 97, 98, 102, 114, 116
10·68·10 102
10·68·11 97, 101
10·68·12 79
10·73·9 135
10·75·4 53
10·76·7 81
10·79·6 13, 18-19, 38
10·80·5 16
10·85·10 19
10·85·11 14, 19
10·85·13 73
10·87·16 13, 16
10·87·17 16, 120
10·87·18 16
10·88·2 121
10·89·7 87
10·89·14 13
10·90·10 59
10·91·14 59
10·94·9 9, 63
10·95·6 9, 49
10·96·11 139
10·97·4 9, 78, 116
10·97·8 41
10·99·4 14, 15
10·100·10 44
10·100·12 78
10·101·9 11, 54
10·102·5, 7, 8, 9 130
10·103·6 141
10·106·10 26
10·106·11 16, 17, 35-36

10·107·1	74
10·107·7	74, 78, 116
10·108·1	90, 91, 92
10·108·2	91, 92-93
10·108·3	91, 93
10·108·4	93, 102
10·108·5	91, 93, 107, 126
10·108·6	94, 102, 114
10·108·7	73, 91, 95, 101, 116-117
10·108·8	91, 95
10·108·9	96, 100, 101, 114
10·108·10	96, 109
10·108·11	96-97, 102, 114, 115
10·111·3	142
10·116·4	9, 63
10·118·4	62
10·119·4	54
10·120·8	30, 107
10·127·8	54
10·133·7	11, 54
10·138·1	113, 126, 127
10·138·2	107
10·145·6	9, 45
10·146·3,4	41
10·149·4	45-46
10·155·5	60
10·156·2	14, 32
10·160·3	15
10·165·5	60
10·166·1	13
10·169·1	16
10·169·2	138
10·169·3	58
10·189·1	142

WORD INDEX

Agni 16, 30-32, 40-41, 142
aghnyā 8, 16, 70, 73, 130, 134, 135, 144, 145
Aṅgirases 109ff
√aj, ud 132
Aditi 5, 143, 146
adri 101
anaḍvah 19
ari 15
aruṇa 49
arka 114
avata 26
Aśvins 16, 134
Indra 5, 7, 14, 15, 21, 27-30, 47-48, 82ff; 103ff; 141
upaparcana 36-37
Uṣas 5, 16, 36, 51-52, 111, 118-122; 144-145
usrā 107, 120, 122, 144
usriyā 108, 120, 122, 128, 132, 136, 143, 144
ūrva 95-96, 127, 128
Ṛbhus' cow 134
gavāśir 5, 57
gātu 132
go
as dakṣiṇā and in dānastutis 75ff; dative use 35; epithet 141-146; etymology 8; figurative uses 8, 10, 51, 80; literal uses 9, 78ff, 134; locative uses 17, 26ff, 31; masculine 8, 9, 19, 81; as a metonymy 9-10; 19-24; 61-62; 63ff; as ox' 43-44, 60ff; summary of usages 1-11; 12-17, 56-58, 82-83, 89-91. Major contexts of *go* are listed in Contents.
gorjīka 51
goopaśā 25
gojā 142
gojāta 143
gojit 141, 142
gotra 28, 111
gotrabhid 141
godatra 141
godari 141
godā 141
godhā 24-25
godhāyas 144
gopati 141, 142, 143
gobandhu 143
gomat 142
gomātṛ 143
goṣuyudh 15
goṣṭha 17
dakṣiṇā 5-8; 111; 126; 128ff; the goddess Dakṣiṇā 144; 145; 146
Dadhikrā 31
Dasagvas 112
√dṛ, ā 28, 141
dhāman 29; 70
dhī; dhīti 54, 134, 145
dhenu 9, 46, 47, 49ff, 52-53; 54, 131, 134, 141, 142, 145, 146
Navagvas 112
√nah, sam 22
nīcīnabāra 26
paṇi, Paṇis 15, 31, 86, 89ff
payas 49, 50
Parjanya 16, 143
Pūṣan 15, 43
Pṛśni 5, 48, 143, 146
Pravargya 72
Bṛhaspati 105ff
brahman (neut.) 7, 105, 111
√bhid with vala and vṛtra 87
madhu 17, 36
Maruts 16, 48, 143
Mitra-Varuṇa 16
yaśas, yaśasvat 36
Rātrī 5, 52, 145
reṇukakāṭa 32
Rodasī 5, 49, 146
vacas 114
vajra 21, 22
Varuṇa 16
Vala 100ff;
vaśā 8, 19, 58ff
vahni 112
vāja 35
Vāta 16
Vāc 5, 145-146
Viṣṇu 131-132
Viśvedevas 17, 143
Viśvarūpa 133
√vṛ, apa 18
vraja 18, 27, 30-31; 102, 141
śam 16, 35
Śayu's cow 134
śukra 50
śuci 50, 51
śveta 50
saṃskṛtatra 32
sanutara 31
sudughā 9, 141
sūnṛtā 29, 30, 47, 120
√sṛj, ud 27
senā 32
Soma 5, 16, 113, 142
starī 9, 52, 53, 80, 87, 134, 135, 143
√sphur, anu 20
svarvat 28
havyasūd 57